Citizen Categories
in the Danish Welfare State

Citizen Categories in the Danish Welfare State

From the Founding Epoch to the Neoliberal Era

Edited by

Jesper Vestermark Køber
Niklas Olsen
Heidi Vad Jønsson

University Press of Southern Denmark 2021

© The authors and University Press of Southern Denmark 2021
University of Southern Denmark Studies in History and Social Sciences vol. 623
Printed by Tarm Bogtryk A/S
Cover by Dorthe Møller, Unisats Aps
Artwork by Inger Scharff

ISBN 978-87-408-3363-8

Citizen Categories in the Danish Welfare State is published with support from:
3F's Medie- og Kulturfond
Den Hielmstierne-Rosencroneske Stiftelse
Institut for Historie, Syddansk Universitet
Landsdommer V. Gieses Legat
Lilian og Dan Finks Fond

University Press of Southern Denmark
55 Campusvej
DK-5230 Odense M
www.universitypress.dk

Distribution in the United States and Canada:
Independent Publishers Group
www.ipgbook.com

Distribution in the United Kingdom:
Gazelle Books
www.gazellebookservices.co.uk

Table of Contents

Acknowledgements 7

Introduction 9
Jesper Vestermark Køber, Niklas Olsen and Heidi Vad Jønsson

The Consumer 23
From a Weak to a Sovereign Figure
Niklas Olsen

The Democrat 47
Three Democratic Citizens in the Early Social Democratic Welfare State
Jesper Vestermark Køber

The Worker 67
Mobilized by the New Left and the Ultra-Liberal Right to Challenge the Social Democratic Welfare State
Margit Bech Vilstrup

The Mentally Ill 89
From Insane to User of Psychiatry
Marie Meier

The Migrant 111
A New Legal, Social and Political Category
in Welfare State Policy and Debate
Heidi Vad Jønsson

The Patient 135
Citizen, Consumer and Partner in Health Governance
Anja Svejsgaard Pors, Kirstine Zinck Pedersen and Peter Kjær

The Entrepreneur 161
The Invention of a Pedagogical Ideal of Societal Behaviour
Clara Lyngholm K. Mortensen

The Unemployed 187
From Guilting to Shaming the Jobless in the Welfare State
Jon Helt Haarder and Mathies Græsborg Aarhus

Editors 207

Acknowledgements

This book is the outcome of a productive workshop in Odense in May December 2019. As editors, we would like to express our gratitude to the "Uses of Literature: The Social Dimensions of Literature Project" (granted by the Danish National Research Foundation DNRF127) and the research program for Political History at University of Southern Denmark for funding the workshop. We are also grateful to Jeppe Nevers, Casper Sylvest, Peter Simonsen, Aske Hennelund Nielsen, Beate Sløk-Andersen, Julian Lamberty and Silke Holmqvist, who provided useful feedback on chapter drafts and the overall framework at the workshop. Moreover, Niklas Olsen and Jesper Vestermark Køber would like to thank The Independent Research Fund Denmark (Project: "Key Actors: Peopling the Neoliberal Economy") and Riksbanken (Project: Neoliberalism in the Nordics) for generously funding their research for the book. Thank also to Jannick Schou Hansen for vital input in the early phases of the project.

Introduction

Jesper Vestermark Køber, Niklas Olsen & Heidi Vad Jønsson

Since the 1970s, the Danish welfare state has been criticized, dramatically reformed and even declared dead. Criticism of the welfare state has been a key aspect of Danish political debates for decades and has functioned as both a factor for and a response to policy reforms.[1] In other words, the welfare state is not a static model, but rather a type of state characterized by universalistic ambitions and the legitimacy of its normative foundations is constantly being contested and negotiated.[2]

This book approaches the question of the political legitimacy of the Danish welfare state from a new perspective. We argue that this process of legitimization is inextricably linked to particular ideas about the nature of its citizens, encompassed in what we call "citizen categories". Citizen categories are by no means exclusive to the Danish welfare state: ideas about the nature of citizenship are pillars of the political order. Such ideas not only provide directions for how individuals should relate to their fellow individuals, conduct their lives in and across diverse societal contexts or behave in society more generally. They are also important for legi-

---

1   Jørn Henrik Petersen, Klaus Petersen & Niels Finn Christiansen, eds., *Dansk Velfærdshistorie vol. 5* (Odense: Syddansk Universitetsforlag, 2013), 68-72.
2   Jørn Henrik Petersen, Klaus Petersen & Lis Holm Petersen, *13 værdier bag den danske velfærdsstat* (Odense: Syddansk Universitetsforlag, 2007).

timizing institutional change, justifying stable political orders and securing sustained electoral support from conflicting groups in society.

Hence, societies are bound up with ideal versions of their citizens, whose interests – both imagined and real – are continuously defended, protected, supported or portrayed as threats to be handled through more or less coercive means. Consequently, these ideas occupy a major role in contemporary politics, societal practices and public debates.

Arguably, it is impossible to govern and administer a society without a set of assumptions about its citizens. Yet these assumptions change through time, as all societies produce unique ideas about their citizens and use changing categories to label them. For example, absolutism was upheld and administered by attributing specific capabilities and functions to the king, the nobles, the peasants and the priesthood. In more recent times, socialism has been inextricably linked with the virtues and historical mission of the worker, whereas the National Socialist ambition to create a Thousand-Year Reich relied on a belief in the unity and shared mission of the Führer and the Germanic people. Today, these citizen categories largely belong to history. Yet present-day societies in Europe and beyond rely on a number of categories and social imaginaries to name and explain their undertakings. It is our contention that we can arrive at a better understanding of any society through a study of its citizen categories, that is, by studying them as vehicles of political legitimacy, stability and change. In the case of Denmark, the most significant citizen categories are intimately connected to the welfare state. In this volume, we explore the making and function of eight such categories in the Danish welfare state from the late nineteenth century until today: the worker, the consumer, the democrat, the mentally ill, the migrant, the patient, the unemployed and the entrepreneur.

These categories are familiar and few would disagree that they have been important in the development of the Danish welfare state. However, from a scholarly point of view the historical development and societal function of such categories remains unstudied and poorly understood. The chapters in this book seek to fill this lacuna.

Our theoretical premise is that citizen categories are rarely natural or neutral terms. Instead, they are discursively constructed notions that have acquired their meanings in specific historical contexts and reflect distinct normative and moral ideals. Over the course of history, the formation of these citizen categories has evolved in numerous ways. Moreover, each category has been assigned different, competing and potentially converging meanings and their importance has repeatedly been reevaluated in ongoing exchanges with scientific knowledge and political debate. Crucially, all citizen categories have been mobilized and used as political tools to legitimize, stabilize or challenge the social order of the welfare state. Not only politicians and parties, but also unions, interest groups, private corporations, scholars, civil servants, intellectuals and academics, have continually sought to legitimize political decision-making and institutional arrangements by referring to a range of different societal capabilities, interests and needs that these citizen categories are said to have. For example, large-scale labour market reforms have been launched to improve the existence of workers, marketization of the public sector has been introduced to satisfy the needs of consumers and educational reforms have been implemented to foster modern-day entrepreneurs. Hence, in different ways, each of these categories has been central to the development of the Danish welfare state.

By offering the first major study of citizen categories, their origins and alterations over time and their role in shaping welfare policies and institutions, this volume helps us bridge the gap between our understanding of the historical development of the welfare state and the present political situation. We argue that there is a strong link and interconnectedness between welfare institutions and those citizen categories that have been shaped by the welfare state as a model of society. In this respect, the welfare state is not only the historical context of the development of new citizen categories or the re-negotiation of old ones, it is also the analytical lens through which we explore citizen categories. Hence, in this perspective the welfare state is simultaneously an institutional framework (legislation), a model of society (based on different logics of solidarity) and an ideational context (composed of ideas and arguments for policy-makers, academics and debaters).[3]

---

3   This very broad defition of welfare states is based on Christopher Pierson & Francis Castles, *The Welfare State Reader* (Cambridge: Polity Press, 2006), 1-7.

The Danish Welfare State: Approaches and Chronologies

Research into the history of the Danish welfare state has grown tremendously since the turn of the millennium. In explaining the development and characteristics of a state with a high level of social and economic security and social services, political historians have traditionally portrayed various structural changes, political actors and institutions as causes and effects of the historical development of the welfare state.[4] However, in recent decades there has been an increasing focus on the role played by ideas and discourses in political debates, social institutions and cultural practices.[5] For examples, studies of widely disseminated and contested concepts such as "security" (tryghed), "near democracy" (nærdemokrati) and "the welfare state" (velfærdsstat) have served to map and interpret many of the ideological positions and struggles that have shaped the welfare state.[6]

This volume contributes to the ongoing trend in analyzing the ways in which social-political language shapes and creates certain ways of understanding, ordering and reforming the welfare state. In particular, we aim to shed new light on two aspects of the Danish welfare state. As announced at the outset, the first concerns the *legitimization* of its systems of governance. By viewing citizen categories as tools of legitimization and drivers of

---

4 See Svend Aage Hansen & Ingrid Henriksen, *Velfærdsstaten 1940-78. Dansk socialhistorie vol. 7* (København: Gyldendal, 1980); Gösta Esping-Andersen, *The Three Worlds of Welfare Capitalism* (Cambridge, 1990); Peter Baldwin, *The Politics of Social Solidarity. Class Bases of the European Welfare States, 1875-1975* (Cambridge, 1990); Klaus Petersen, *Legitimität und Krise. Die politische Geschichte des dänischen Wohlfahrtsstaates 1945-1973* (Berlin, 1998); Niels Finn Christiansen & Klaus Petersen, "Velfærd med vilje – men hvis?," in *Den danske velfærdsstats historie*, eds. Niels Ploug, Ingrid Henriksen & Niels Kærgaard (København: Socialforskningsinstituttet, 2004), 142-170; Jørn Henrik Petersen, Klaus Petersen & Niels Finn Christiansen, eds., *Dansk Velfærdshistorie vol. 1-6*, (Odense: Syddansk Universitetsforlag, 2010-2014)

5 Daniel Beland & Robert Henry Cox, eds., *Ideas and Politics in Social Science Research* (Oxford: Oxford University Press, 2011).

6 See Henrik Madsen, *For velfærdens skyld: En analyze af de danske debatter om velfærdsstat og medlemsskab af EF 1950-1972* (Ph.D. Thesis, Department of History, University of Southern Denmark, 2006); Michael Kuur Sørensen, "Den innovative ideolog i politisk historie: Mogens Glistrup som case," *Temp* 8 (2014): 115-129; Nynne-Cecilie Kelager Schmidt, *Tryghed: Begrebet, der sejrede ad helvede til… godt!* (Ph.D. Thesis, Department of History, University of Southern Denmark, 2017); Jesper Vestermark Køber, *Et spørgsmål om nærhed: Nærdemokratibegrebets historie i 1970'ernes Danmark* (Ph.D. Thesis, The Saxo-Institute, University of Copenhagen, 2017); Jørn Henrik Petersen & Klaus Petersen, "The concept of "Welfare State' in Danish Public and Political Debates," in *The Changing Meanings of the Welfare State: Histories of a Key Concept in the Nordic Countries*, ed. Nils Edling (New York: Berghahn Books, 2019), 137-178.

political stability, crisis and change, the volume seeks a new opening for engaging with the question of legitimacy in relation to the welfare state.

The second aspect concerns the *periodization* of the welfare state. While understanding the modern Danish welfare state as the product of a gradual development that has been taking place from the late nineteenth century to the present day,[7] we view its history as a three-phase process of genesis, a golden age and marketization. As for its genesis, although there is a good case for emphasizing the importance of Lutheranism and tracing the roots of the welfare state to pre-democratic Denmark, few scholars doubt that a significant development occurred in the period between 1892 and 1933.[8] More specifically, with the reform of the Poor Law system, the organization of philanthropy and the rise of charitable institutions in the larger cities, as well as the influence of social democracy in Danish municipalities, the path towards later welfare-state institutions and the principle of universalism emerged in this period.[9]

During the rest of the twentieth century, the social system underwent significant alterations. As part of the country's greatest economic and political settlement, as well as being an important stepping stone towards a social security system without the loss of rights, the Social Reform of 1933 gathered several social acts together in a single reform and increased the state's intervention in the economy. The second phase, the golden age, took off with the economic boom from the late 1950s to the early 1970s, when the welfare state expanded rapidly and introduced universal social rights, eradicated the socially degrading Poor Law system and created a boom in the social services, such as day care. In the early 1970s, at the end of the golden age, a new social reform introduced an ambitious social security system.

---

7   Niels Finn Christiansen & Klaus Petersen, "The Dynamics of Social Solidarity: The Danish Welfare State, 1900-2000," *Scandinavian Journal of History* 26, no. 3 (2001): 177-196.
8   Uffe Østergaard, "Lutheranismen og den universelle velfærdsstat," in *Velfærdsstat og kirke*, eds. Jens H. Schjørring & Jens Torkild Bak (København: Anis Forlag, 2005), 147-184; Tim Knudsen, "Tilblivelsen af den universalistiske velfærdsstat," in *Den nordiske protestantisme og velfærdsstaten*, ed. Tim Knudsen (Aarhus: Aarhus Universitetsforlag, 2000), 20-64; Jørn Henrik Petersen, Klaus Petersen & Niels Finn Christiansen, eds., *Frem mod socialstaten: Dansk Velfærdshistorie vol. 1* (Odense: Syddansk Universitetsforlag, 2010); Jørn Henrik Petersen, *Luther og konkurrencestaten* (Odense: Syddansk "Universitetsforlag, 2016).
9   Søren Kolstrup, *Velfærdsstatens rødder. Fra kommunesocialisme til folkepension* (København: SFAH, 1996); Karen Lützen, *Byen tæmmes. Kernefamilie, sociale reformer og velgørenhed i 1800-tallets København* (København: Hans Reitzels Forlag, 1998).

The climax of the golden age was also a moment of crisis in the Danish welfare state, as the international oil crisis, rising taxes and growing unemployment hit Denmark. These developments gave birth to new types of social criticism, as political debaters on both left and right questioned the very legitimacy of the welfare state. Some of these debaters also presented ideas for marketizing the public sector as a cure for what was perceived as a crisis in the ever-expanding, inefficient and undemocratic welfare state.[10] While the conservative-liberal government of the 1980s elaborated on these visions in various ways, the third phase, marketization, only took off in the 1990s. The Social Democratic Party was central to this phase, as it introduced market-oriented reform processes within the welfare state by implementing New Public Management principles in parts of the public sector. This included, among other things, new budgetary models, steering policies, calculation and methods of documentation; new leadership, employment policies and wage systems; new initiatives to de-bureaucratize government by standardizing administrative procedures; new methods of evaluation using consumer feedback; new public/private partnerships and collaborations; and, finally, privatizations of state-owned companies, such as the national airport and the national telecommunications company. Other reforms focused on incentives heralding a new activation line in Danish social policy as a way to decrease the level of unemployment, for example, by reducing the maximum number of years that an individual could receive unemployment benefits and requiring them to participate in programmes in order to receive benefits.[11]

We equate the phase of marketization with the neoliberal age, understanding neoliberalism here as the extension of market mechanisms to all spheres of social life, fostered and enforced by the state and other political institutions. Covering the period from the founding epoch to the neoliberal era, we aim to show how each period has been "peopled" and sustained, by a particular cast of citizen categories and how transformations from one phase to another have involved negotiating these categories.

Until now, only few scholars have understood the transformation of the welfare state by connecting reforms in the public sector with the legit-

---

10 Niklas Olsen, *The Sovereign Consumer: A New Intellectual History of Neoliberalism* (Cham: Palgrave Macmillan, 2019), 185-226.
11 Jørn Henrik Petersen, *Pligt & ret – Ret & pligt* (Odense: Syddansk Universitetsforlag, 2014).

imization of certain key figures. Famously in the Danish context, Ove K. Pedersen's book *Konkurrencestaten* from 2011 argues that a new understanding of the human being, the "opportunistic personality" concerned with maximizing its own benefits on many levels, emerged during the so-called shift from welfare state to competition state.[12] However, Pedersen provides little empirical evidence for this claim. Moreover, by focusing solely on the opportunistic personality, he overlooks the many different citizen categories that actually inform our neoliberal age.[13] On the one hand, this era has seen the birth and dissemination of new identity formations, such as the innovative and value-creating entrepreneur. On the other hand, already existing categories, such as the consumer and the patient, have been reconfigured into personas who, it is now said, could contribute to creating a better society if only they would be allowed to act freely on the market or in marketized institutions.

The aim here is not to replace existing periodizations of the welfare state, but to nuance, qualify and enrich our knowledge of its different phases – and of how these phases emerged, changed and ended – by approaching it through a focus on its citizen categories. The individual chapters come together in a narrative countering a common assumption of a hegemony of "Social Democratic thought" to be found in Danish society and politics. Moreover, as indicated above, the book gives a much more detailed and complex account of the emergence of the "competition state" in Denmark than other available analyses. As historical prisms, the categories vividly illustrate the dramatic changes of the Danish political climate in the period and the important adjustments of the social contract, which the widespread and unceasing use of the term "welfare state" conceals and allows for careful documentation of other dominant discourses and sources for policy-making. As such, the volume seeks to offer a new analytical approach to and understanding of the welfare state and its historical development.

---

12   Ove K. Pedersen, *Konkurrencestaten* (København: Hans Reitzels Forlag, 2011), 190-191.
13   The same criticism applies to Michel Foucault's influential analysis of how neoliberal society compels us to transform ourselves into "entrepreneurs of the self" engaged in self-interested conduct as personal investment. In contrast to Foucault's focus on a single persona, we want to show that neoliberal society is peopled by a multiplicity of key actors endowed with different characteristics. See Michel Foucault, *The Birth of Biopolitics: Lectures at the College de France*, 1978–1979, ed., Michel Senellart, gen. ed. Francois Ewald and Alessandro Fontana, trans. by Graham Burchell (Basingstoke: Palgrave Macmillan, 2008 [2004]), 230.

Citizen Category: Definition and Approach

How, more exactly, do we define our key analytical object – the citizen category? The vast amount of literature on citizenship is generally concerned with the rights and obligations of each individual towards the community. We adhere to a broad definition of the citizen, taking citizen categories to designate *person categories or identity constructions that are produced and articulated as a means of making sense of, justifying and legitimizing societal organization and change*. We thus view citizen categories as discursive or ideational constructs that feature as part of wider political ideologies.[14] Any particular ideology can have multiple key political actors, each with their own normative contents and meanings. Being interested in the relationship between such categories and the development of the welfare state, we focus particularly on those categories that have been constructed by political decision-makers, policy-makers, political parties and other agents involved in the welfare state. For the sake of linguistic style, the chapters in the volume rarely employ the term "citizen category" but refer mainly to terms like "figure" or "actor" in speaking about the specific identity construction at issue.

The eight case studies included in this volume are dedicated to understanding specific citizen categories, using a variety of methodological approaches and sources, focusing on different historical periods and targeting distinct socio-political areas. To be sure, the range of categories chosen here is not exhaustive. The advanced welfare state obviously houses a number of other actors additional to those included here, such as the manager, the teacher, the pensioner, the child, the soldier etc. While the worker, the consumer, the democrat, the mentally ill, the migrant, the patient, the unemployed and the entrepreneur only represent a selection of available cases, they have all been indispensable to the welfare state. Some

---

14 To be sure, other scholars, especially in the field of sociology, have outlined theoretical frameworks and empirical analyses of citizen categories that resemble ours. For examples from the Danish context, see first of all Gitte Sommer Harrits & Marie Østergaard Møller, "Categories and categorization: towards a comprehensive sociological framework," I *Distinktion: Scandinavian Journal of Social Theory*, 12, no. 2, (2011) 229-247; David Budtz Petersen, Finn Collin & Frederik Stjernfelt, eds., *Kampen om mennesket: forskellige menneskebilleder og deres grænsestrid* (København: Hans Reitzel, 2018); Pia Ringø & Maria Appel Nissen & Mia Arp Fallov, eds., *Menneskesyn i socialt arbejde: om udviklingen af det produktive menneske* (København: Akademisk Forlag, 2018). Still, as noted above, this volume is the first major study of citizen categories in the history of the Danish welfare.

of them have functioned as role models for successful individual lives and social prosperity generally, such as the entrepreneur. Others have represented dangers, obstacles or challenges to the welfare state and prompted corrections of behaviour. The unemployed is a case in point here.

Along with the German conceptual historian Reinhart Koselleck, we analyze citizen categories as both "indicators" and "factors" of societal change. That is, we view them as linguistic constructions that at one and the same time register and effect change, the latter being the case when they are mobilized in various ways to meet the ends of the political actors using them.[15] Against this background, the methodological framework in each case draws on three heuristic questions: (1) which meanings, identities and capabilities have been attributed to the citizen categories; (2) how, in what contexts and by whom were the citizen category assigned its meaning, identity and capability? And (3) what roles have the key actors played in attempts to shape, uphold and transform the social order?

These eight chapters are ordered pragmatically with a focus on chronology. The main aim in ordering the cases has thus been to illustrate how each phase of the welfare state has been "peopled" and how this "peopling" has changed over time.

The consumer only arrived in Danish political language in the mid-1940s. However, as the contribution by Niklas Olsen shows, since then it has been omnipresent in the Danish welfare state and courted by its political parties and interest groups. Olsen focuses on two ideal types of consumer, both of which have been mobilized to shape and legitimize important social visions in the history of the Danish welfare state, namely the "weak" consumer and the "sovereign" consumer. The first type was associated with the idea that, in order to create a free, just and equal society, consumers had to be protected from market forces by the state, this being the key to the Social Democratic welfare-state project in the postwar era. The second type is associated conversely with the argument that, if consumers were going to be allowed to create economic efficiency and political democracy, they had to be protected from the state by market forces. This ideal was formulated

---

15 Reinhart Koselleck and Michaela Richter, "Introduction and Prefaces to the 'Geschichtliche Grundbegriffe'", *Contributions to the History of Concepts* 6, no. 1 (2011): 1-37.

by the liberal party, Venstre, as part of its critique of the welfare state in the 1970s and was mobilized in government programmes to reform the public sector in the 1980s. Moreover, it reappeared on the Social Democratic agenda in the 1990s, where, in the context of globalization, the party became more market-friendly and carried out many of the public-sector reforms that Venstre had been demanding since the 1970s.

The democrat became an important figure in the years following the Second World War by expanding the Social Democratic understanding of democracy as a way of life. In his contribution, Jesper Vestermark Køber shows how the conceptualization of the democratic citizen went hand in hand with a reformulation of the Social Democratic concept of democracy in constructing their visions of the welfare state in the postwar years. The focus is on three societal debators who all contributed to reformulating the Social Democratic concept of democracy, the theologian Hal Koch, the Social Democratic politician Julius Bomholt and the author and critic Poul Henningsen. While Koch, Bomholt and Henningsen all argued for the necessity to create and foster democratic citizens characterized by societal engagement, their approaches differed. Koch focused on democracy as a continual process that demanded civic education and a commitment to dialogue in all human relations. Bomholt's idea of the democratic citizen functioned as a common denominator for the notion of the so-called "spiritual welfare state" (*den åndelige velfærdsstat*). Finally, Poul Henningsen outlined an idealized notion of the democratic citizen as an autonomous individual. In spite of these differences, they all contributed to shaping and reinforcing the influential Social Democratic vocabulary on democracy in postwar Denmark.

The worker was a core concept in the Social Democrats" anti-capitalist production discourse from the 1870s to the 1930s. However, as the party gradually shifted its focus from the fight against capitalism to social reform in the 1950s and stopped using "the worker" as the key concept for unity and action, other political parties and societal movements mobilized and reinterpreted this citizen category. In her contribution, Margit Bech Vilstrup explores how on the one hand the so-called "new left" and on the other hand Mogens Glistrup and his newly established ultra-liberal party,

Fremskridtspartiet (the Progress Party) outlined alternative interpretations of the worker in the 1960s and 1970s. Both interpretations reduced the "worker" to an individual who performs productive or physical labour. But whereas representatives of the new left defined their "worker" in classical Marxist terms as opposed to the capitalist or the employer, Glistrup's "worker" became associated with the employer in a positive way through the concept of "the working class." More specifically, he contrasted this class with the big new groups of bureaucrats and other public employees that he named "the ruling class." These ideational developments introduced a period of change when, after the postwar era's political decline, there was a fracturing, rearticulation and reideologization of "the worker" in society generally.

The mentally ill, as Marie Meier shows in her article, have been part of the societal discourse in the Danish welfare state from the last decades of the nineteenth century until today. However, the category of "the mentally ill" has undergone several transformations in this period. Using fiction as an analytical entry to probing historically situated encounters between the mentally ill citizen and the authorities of the welfare state, Meier concentrates on tracing three time-specific configurations of this citizen category in the context of the developing Danish welfare state: "the insane", "the patient" and "the user of psychiatry". The idea of the mentally ill as "insane" was characteristic of the period at the threshold of the twentieth century and connoted a conception of *insanity* as a personal characteristic, as behaviour that needs to be tamed or morally disciplined. The idea of the mentally ill as "patients" was characteristic of the so-called "golden age" of the welfare state and connoted an idea of "the patient" as a suffering subject who needs professional care and protection within welfare-state institutions. Finally, the idea of the mentally ill as "a user of psychiatry" has characterized our increasingly commercialized and marketized society from the 1990s onwards, in which individuals are addressed as customers in an administrative machinery that offers hardly any possibility for a long-term stay, personal contact or protection of the individual.

The migrant is a highly contested figure in current social policy debates and has challenged the very notion of what a "citizen" is, in legal and political terms. In her contribution, Heidi Vad Jønsson explores how the migrant has been reconfigured over three phases. In the years of welfare state expansion, this category was tightly linked to labour-market issues under the label "guest worker". It was also ascribed a dual meaning as either a passive labourer with a high degree of commodification or an active worker whose membership of a union was crucial to avoid the consequences of commodification (wage pressure) and to enable guest workers to become active (but temporary) members of society. This dual meaning of the migrant was challenged in the 1970s and 1980s, when immigration became a heated and highly emotional political issue. In this period, characterized by economic recession and the increasing immigration of asylum-seekers, the migrant was ascribed meaning as a legal category pertaining to international law and to the Danish Aliens Act. In addition, the migrant became a politically contested figure with opposing meanings both between and within political parties. Fuzzy and multiple layers of meanings were accumulated as the migrant became a political target group in the third phase of categorization, when a new welfare policy was introduced in 1998, which came to shape the debate over social policy and integration. This became an important benchmark for the continuous conflict over migrants in the twenty-first century.

The patient has been enacted as one of the particular rationalities of governance in the welfare state in both national policy-making and hospitals. In their contribution, Peter Kjær, Kirstine Zinck Pedersen and Anja Pors examine how the patient and associated rationalities of governance have been reconfigured and mobilized in the Danish healthcare system from the 1970s onwards in the context of particular historical and organizational ideals. The patient in this period was central to two key healthcare policy debates: the debate on the effectiveness of healthcare and the control of public expenditure on the one hand and the debate on the quality of healthcare and service optimization on the other. In these debates, two new patient figures were formulated: the socio-economically responsible citizen and the empowered consumer. The first figure was expected to accept ultimate responsibility for his or her own health and a necessity to act accordingly, as well as to alter expectations of healthcare services in order to accept the limits of the system's capacity. The second figure was expected to develop individual preferences towards healthcare services and to actively express these preferences by demanding and choosing services as a consumer in a market. This was in line with the internationally growing spread of so-called New Public Management, which gained ground in the Danish welfare state in the 1990s.

The unemployed have been central to the welfare state ever since its foundational period. In their article, analyzing representations of the unemployed and their encounters with unemployment offices in Danish literature, Mathies Græsborg Aarhus and Jon Helt Haarder shed light on the changing conceptions of this citizen category since the 1970s. Most importantly, whereas the unemployed were earlier governed by feelings of guilt and of violating an implied social contract, unemployment has increasingly been tied to feelings of shame and of the whole self as a failure. These changes in attitude towards the unemployed correspond to recent changes in the institutions and "ethos" of the welfare state, where hierarchies built on cultural capital have been accompanied by new norms of entrepreneurship and marketability as the central currency in the cultural hierarchy of the welfare state. This has created new losers who fail to live up to these norms because they do not possess the necessary cultural (and affective) resources. Today, those who are uncultured are those who fail to display a repertoire of marketable affective dispositions and competencies. In other words, losers are those who fail to sell themselves. At the bottom of the welfare state's social and cultural hierarchy, we find "the unemployed" or those excluded from paid labour.

The entrepreneur has become one of the most prominent citizen cagegories in the neoliberal era. In her contribution, Clara Lyngholm K. Mortensen approaches this citizen category by focusing on how it has been promoted politically through the introduction of entrepreneurship into the Danish educational system and thus become a pedagogical ideal of societal behaviour in the welfare state more generally. Three developments have conditioned the making of this citizen ideal. First, academic disciplines, in particular economic theory and business management and transnational organizations such as the World Bank, the Organization for Economic Co-operation and Development (OECD) and the European Commission

(EU-Commission) have introduced the new educational—cum-political concept of entrepreneurship to Denmark. Second, alongside Danish think tanks and consulting companies, these transnational organizations have exerted pressure on the Danish government, helping to put entrepreneurship on to the education policy agenda. Third, entrepreneurship has been implemented and disseminated in the Danish education system because the concept encapsulates and promotes a citizen ideal that meets the Danish competition state's emphasis on growth – namely the entrepreneur.

The Consumer

From a Weak to a Sovereign Figure

Niklas Olsen

The consumer is omnipresent in the Danish welfare state and is courted by it. The Danish population are addressed as consumers not only in the market, but also in the public sector and in cultural life. Striving to make Danish society as consumer-friendly as possible, all the major political parties claim to pursue policies that benefit and protect the interests of Danes as consumers. But where does the idea of the citizen as a consumer come from? What role has this idea played in the history of the Danish welfare state?

As we shall see, politicians in Denmark have claimed to be pursuing consumer-friendly policies ever since 1945. However, Danes have been addressed as consumers in many different ways and the pursuit of consumer-friendly policies has served numerous political agendas from 1945 until today.

The focus in this paper is on two ideal types of consumer, both of which have been mobilized to shape and legitimize important social visions in the history of the Danish welfare state. The first ideal type is the "weak" consumer, which is associated with the idea that, to create a free, just and equal society, consumers had to be protected from market forces by the state and this notion was key to the Social Democratic welfare-state project in the postwar era. The second ideal type is the "sovereign" consumer, associated conversely with the argument that, if consumers were going to be allowed to create economic efficiencies and political democracy, they had to be protected from the state by market forces. This ideal was formulated by the liberal party Venstre as part of its critique of the welfare state in the 1970s and was mobilized in government programs aimed at public-sector reforms in the 1980s. The "sovereign" consumer, so this chapter argues, reappeared as part of the Social Democratic agenda in the 1990s, where the party turned more market-friendly and carried out many of the public-sector reforms that Venstre had been demanding since the 1970s. To reform the Danish economy for the era of global competition, the Social Democratic Party privatized some parts of the public sector and marketized others with reference to a citizen category that resembled but also added layers to the "sovereign" consumer whom liberal politicians had invented twenty years earlier.

Both "weak" and "sovereign" consumers were constructed in different contexts and by different political actors who were wrestling with changing social challenges. In response, these actors ascribed diverse capabilities, including different degrees of sovereignty and rationality, to the figure of the consumer and held a variety of views concerning the appropriate role of the state in a consumer-driven economy. Using the consumer as an analytical prism, this article therefore adopts a fresh angle to probe how the social and economic order of the Danish welfare state has been shaped and reshaped by shifting visions of state institutions, markets and individuals, as well as of the desired relations between them. These changing visions mirror international developments in many ways but, as we shall see, the transformation from the "weak" to the "sovereign" consumer in Denmark had certain unique features.[1]

---

[1] This chapter draws on sections of Niklas Olsen, *The Sovereign Consumer: A New Intellectual History of Neoliberalism* (Cham: Palgrave Macmillan, 2019). I would like to thank my fellow editors for useful comments on this version.

The Emergence of the Consumer as a Socio-Political Figure

To speak of human beings as consumers is, in fact, a quite new practice. As Frank Trentmann has demonstrated, the consumer was virtually absent from social discourse in most countries until around 1800. Even in the context of what are today understood as acts of consumerism, few defined themselves or others as consumers or referred to the concept in social debates.[2]

This situation changed during the nineteenth century when the consumer began to be referred to as an individual with legal and personal rights, for example, when citizens mobilized in the pursuit of collective interests related to consumption (e.g. the provision of utilities such as water, gas and coal). In many countries in the late nineteenth century, such as Great Britain, this development linked the consumer to a model of citizenship that embraced ideals of accountability, representation and protection and that saw citizens uniting in organizations such as consumer defense leagues. Moreover, in a growing number of social contexts, consumers were equated with the general public.[3]

The late nineteenth century also saw the beginning of a broad intellectual search for and debate over the consumer, led by public intellectuals, reformers and academics, who began to ponder what characterized consumers and their behaviour, including how modern society could be reformed in ways that protected and enhanced consumer interests. For example, reformist economists such as J.A. Hobson in Britain, Simon Patten in the US and Charles Gide in France made efforts to theorize and politicize consumer needs within larger debates over the social, political and economic organization of society.[4] Similarly, at the turn of the twentieth century, governments and civil-society institutions increasingly attempted to construct and instrumentalize consumer ideals in the pursuit of larger, national economic and political goals. For example, in Sweden, the cooperative movement launched a large-scale educational campaign that viewed

---

2 Frank Trentmann, "The Modern Genealogy of the Consumer: Meanings, Identities and Political Synapses," in *Consuming Cultures, Global Perspectives: Historical Trajectories, Transnational Exchanges*, eds. Frank Trentmann and John Brewer (Oxford: Berg, 2006), 19-69; and Frank Trentmann, *Empire of Things: How We Became a World of Consumers, from the Fifteenth Century to the Twenty-First* (New York: Harper Collins, 2016).
3 Trentmann, "The Modern Genealogy," 26–37.
4 Trentmann, "The Modern Genealogy," 29 and Trentmann, *Empire of Things*, 155–156.

Swedish women as rational consumers whose correct and disciplined consumption at home (which involved paying with cash and not by credit) would raise the moral and economic status of the population and make government intervention in the economy superfluous.⁵ At this point, civil society and commerce in Great Britain successfully created the new identity of the morally aware and civic-minded consumer in order to legitimize the agenda of an open global economy.⁶

Consumer politics and rhetoric were increased in scale and given a more state-focused dimension during the First World War when governments called on consumers to act in accordance with and in support of the regulated economies of the various national political communities. However, inflation and shortages also led to consumer boycotts and demands for representation in politics. For example, this was the case in Germany, where the state and civil society debated intensely how consumers could contribute to a more productive nation that would permit greater levels of public spending.⁷

In the interwar period, the figure of the consumer was irrevocably pushed to the centre of public and political discourse around the world. In this process, previously separate discourses of the consumer within, for example, social politics and economic thought were joined to debates over issues like the nature of human behaviour, citizenship, the dynamics of economic growth and modes of social organization. This created a more universal category of the consumer, a figure now imbued with a plurality of social practices and virtues and elevated into a key actor in modern society.⁸ Moreover, in many countries, consumers organized themselves on a hitherto unprecedented scale. For example, the United States saw the creation of the world's first consumer protection agency, Consumers Research Inc., in 1929.⁹ More generally, from the interwar period onwards, it became impossible for political actors in many countries to communicate any vision of society without including the role of consumers and consumption

---

5   Peder Alex, *Den rationella konsumenten: KF som folkuppfostrare 1899–1939* (Stockholm: Brutus Östlings bokf Symposion, 1994).
6   Frank Trentmann, *Free Trade Nation: Commerce, Consumption and Civil Society in Modern Britain* (Oxford: Oxford University Press, 2008).
7   Trentmann, "The Modern Genealogy," 43 and Trentmann, *Empire of Things*, 274–276.
8   Trentmann, "The Modern Genealogy," 43–53.
9   Lawrence Glickmann, *Buying Power: A History of Consumer Activism in America* (Chicago: The University of Chicago Press, 2009), 189–218.

in matters economic and political. In this context and in response to the turmoil of the time, governments sought to legitimize new social orders with reference to new consumer ideals that varied with national traditions and contexts.

For example, in the United States, the citizen consumer was launched by New Deal reformers as an ideal that would secure the rights of individual consumers in the face of unsafe products, unfair pricing and misleading advertising. The citizen consumer invoked a vision of the new American democracy as based on the popular mobilization of consumers in cooperatives and movements, with consumers also represented in federal advisory boards and agencies and supported by a state-regulated welfare economy.[10] In Germany, similarly, the realization that in order to consolidate support for the regime Germans must be provided with the products they desired, the National Socialists collaborated with consumer researchers, businesses and advertising agencies to construct a community-oriented and racist consumer who bought German products and thereby reinforced the dictatorship and its policies.[11] In Russia, communist efforts in the 1920s to create a proletarian individual prepared to sacrifice personal comfort for the socialist good were replaced in the 1930s by attempts to bring into existence a new type of consumer who could participate in a state-driven politics of productivity and drive communism as a new and materially superior civilization.[12]

In Denmark, the emergence of consumer identities and activism is usually traced back to the founding of a co-operative society in Thisted in 1867, the rules of which were based on those of the famous Rochdale Society in Britain. In 1896, the resulting co-operative chain of shops (originally called *arbejderforening* or "workers", "co-operative"), but soon renamed *brugsforening* or "user co-operative chain", were gathered into the Fællesforeningen for Danmarks Brugsforeninger (the Danish Central User Co-Operative).[13] Initially a rural phenomenon, user co-operatives gradually

---

10 Lizabeth Cohen, *A Consumers' Republic: The Politics of Mass Consumption in Postwar America* (New York: Random House, 2003).
11 Pamela E. Sweet, *Selling under the Swastika: Advertising and Commercial Culture in Nazi Germany* (Palo Alto, CA: Stanford University Press, 2013).
12 Trentmann, *Empire of Things*, 292-296.
13 Kristoffer Jensen, ed., *Brugsen – en anderledes forretning? 1866-2016 Dansk brugsbevægelse fra Pastor Sonne til COOP* (København: Samvirke, 2016), 26-73; Mary Hilson, "The Nordic Consumer Co-operative Movements in International Perspective, 1890-1939," in *Nordic Associations in a European Perspective*, eds. Risto Alapuro and Henrik Stenius (Baden-Baden: Nomos, 2010), 215-240.

took hold in the cities, in particular after 1908 when it became an official policy of the workers' movement, after the Social Democratic Party had abandoned its opposition to the initiative.

Soon afterwards, other consumption-related organizations emerged. The most important was De danske husmoderforeninger (The Danish Housewives' Association), founded in 1920 to gather together all the newly established local housewives' organizations. Developing into the largest such association in Denmark, De danske husmoderforeninger worked for the recognition of women's domestic work and supported and educated women in housework. In 1935, Statens Husholdningsråd (the Danish Government Home Economics Council) was founded to advices housewives on how to improve the nutritional, hygienic, economic and technical aspects of household management.[14] By this time, Fællesforeningen for Danmarks Brugsforeninger had expanded massively, having been extended to the cities. Moreover, the association began to sell its products by using the techniques of modern advertising and informing about and coordinating its activities through a members' magazine.[15]

These initiatives formed the basis of important institutional developments in Danish consumer politics in the postwar period. However, in contrast to other countries, consumer languages and policies were limited in Denmark until 1945. For example, Denmark had not experienced any broad intellectual search for or debate on over the category of the consumer, no political party had communicated its social visions with a focus on the role of consumers and consumption and no comprehensive mobilization of the population as consumers by the state had taken place. Moreover, there was an absence of advocacy groups pursuing "pure" consumer interests and referring to themselves through the category of the consumer. Instead, the above-mentioned groups aimed to further the interests of the peasant, the worker or the housewife. While these groups were occasionally referred to as consumers, this category was generally used in separate spheres and given narrow meanings, for example, in discussions within Statens Husholdningsråd, where the work of the housewife remained the central issue, not consumption in any broader sense. A universal category of con-

---

14 T. Janus Andersen, *Forbrugerpolitik og forbrugerorganization i Skandinavien* (København: Samfundslitteratur, 1980), 77-100.
15 Jensen, *Brugsen – en anderledes forretning?*, 63-73.

sumer, one that could be used to communicate broader social visions, was only established after 1945.

The Weak Consumer

As in other Scandinavian countries, Social Democratic parties heavily influenced the politicization of the consumer in postwar Denmark. In collaboration with interest groups and experts, they framed consumption as a public matter and supported the creation of new practices and legislation that aimed to promote consumer interests.[16] These initiatives relied on the idea of consumers as weak beings, whose basic social, political and economic rights, including rights to free choice, fair prices and accurate information on the market, had to be protected by the regulatory powers of the state.

The new focus on consumption in Denmark's Social Democratic Party was first expressed in *Fremtidens Danmark* (The Future of Denmark), the famous program of August 1945 in which the party addressed the issue of Denmark's economic and political future after the Nazi occupation. The program aimed to replace what it called the defective and crisis-ridden system of "liberal capitalism" with a system that called for a redistribution of income to finance an expansion of the social sector, permanent state control of imports and extensive "socialization", that is, the nationalization of crucial parts of Denmark's industrial and financial sectors. A focus on consumption was central to the program, which initiated a new practice of addressing the Social Democratic electorate as consumers, mentioning this word a total of 22 times, often interchangeably with "worker" so that the two words denote one and the same person. For example, the program argued that state-supported consumption was necessary to prevent economic crisis, boost production and ensure efficiency. It also aimed to give consumers influence over the management of production and to further their political and economic interests through representation in state agencies and various measures of market regulation to ensure fair

---

16 For a Scandinavian perspective on these developments, see Iselin Theien, "Shopping for the 'People's Home': Consumer Planning in Norway and Sweden after the Second World War," in *The Expert Consumer: Associations and Professionals in Consumer Society*, eds. Alain Chatriot, Marie-Emmanuelle Chessel and Matthew Hilton (Aldershot: Ashgate, 2006), 137-150.

competition and cheaper goods. The aim was a social order in which the "freedom to establish private monopolies and to exploit consumers and workers would disappear" in favour of "free choice in consumption."[17]

Clearly, *Fremtidens Danmark* was concerned to portray the consumer as an individual with the capacity to guarantee economic efficiency *and* democratic institutions in postwar Denmark. However, the consumer was also depicted as a vulnerable being in need of government protection from and regulation of a malfunctioning, monopolistic and exploitative market if its social capacities were to be unleashed. This conception of the individual as a weak consumer in need of protection became important to the Social Democrats' welfare-state agenda.

The regulatory framework for economic politics that informed this agenda encouraged the application of a wide range of networks and interest groups seeking representation in matters related to consumption and consumers, which became increasingly prominent in the party's political rhetoric at the expense of its support for the workers.[18] The most important independent consumer association was Danske Husmødres Forbrugerråd (Danish Housewives' Consumer Council), founded in 1947 as the first state-supported organization in Scandinavia specifically devoted to consumer affairs. Gathering together the various Danish housewives' associations and expanding in the 1960s to include trade unions, cooperative societies, civil servants and individual consumers, Danske Husmødres Forbrugerråd was successful in creating coalitions with industry and had a number of different roles. For example, it participated in government agencies and commissions and negotiated with industry and trade groups to develop codes of practice, quality marking, contract terms, invoice formats, commercial rules and fee structures. It undertook price surveys, represented consumer interests to the government, ran twelve consumer information sites around the country and aided consumers with their complaints. In 1963, because its work no longer only concerned housewives, but the Danish population at large, the association changed its name to Forbrugerrådet (The Consumer Council). Moreover, in 1964, it launched

---

17 Socialdemokratiet, *Fremtidens Danmark* (1945), 12.
18 On the disappearance of the worker from the Social Democratic vocabulary in this period, see Margit Bech Vilstrup, *Kampen om arbejderne: Arbejderbegrebets politiske historie 1750-2019* (Selskabet for Arbejderhistorie: København, 2019), 191-240.

the magazine *Tænk* (Think), which published comparative product tests and discussed consumption-related issues.[19]

Danske Husmødres Forbrugerråd was a close ally of the Social Democratic Party and contributed to the politicization of the consumer that took place in Denmark after 1945. Lis Groes, who was chair of Danske Husmødres Forbrugerråd from 1949 to 1953 and Social Democratic Minister of Trade from 1953 to 1957, personified the close ties between the two organizations and was a key player in the consumer politics they jointly pursued in the 1950s.[20] When, upon taking over the post as chair of Danske Husmødres Forbrugerråd in 1955, Viola Nørløv stated that "consumers are and remain the weak link in today's society", she was echoing the basic premise of the consumer politics that Groes had pursued on behalf of the organization since the late 1940s.[21] Accordingly, like the Social Democratic Party, Danske Husmødres Forbrugerråd sought to take measures to protect and enhance the economic and political well-being of consumers. These measures ranged from countering the individual consumer's lack of wisdom through education and product testing to advocating government protection of the consumer from a flawed market, in particular from advertising that was deemed capable of manipulating consumers into buying things they neither wanted nor needed.

However, in the 1960s, due to disagreements, the alliance between Forbrugerrådet and the Social Democratic Party ended, as Forbrugerrådet intensified its campaign for further government regulation of economic issues related to consumption, in particular advertising. Alongside its criticism of these issues, it began to argue that unrestrained advertising activities would result in a consumer culture that undermined the democratic basis of modern society.[22] These arguments were developed, among other places, in *Tænk*, whose prolific and polemical editor, Poul Henningsen,

---

19 Gunnar Trumbull, *Strength in Numbers: The Political Power of Weak Interests* (Cambridge, MA.: Harvard University Press, 2012), 43.
20 Morten Bendix Andersen, "Kampen om forbrugersamfundet: Lis Groes og debatten om reklame i Danmark 1945–1965," *Arbejderhistorie* 2 (2011): 46–67; Karen Møller, *Lis Groes: En kvinde i sin tid* (København: Gyldendal, 2000). Groes returned to a chair of Danske Husmødres Forbrugerråd in the period 1958-1964.
21 Lis Groes, ed., *Forbruger: elsket, ombejlet – svigtet? En debatbog om forbrugeren i det moderne samfund* (Albertslund: Det danske forlag, 1972), 103.
22 Bendix Andersen, "Kampen om forbrugersamfundet," 54–60.

drew inspiration from the writings of international critics, such as John Kenneth Galbraith and Vance Packard, which were translated into Danish in the 1960s.[23] Sounding an alarm over postwar consumption culture and politics in their books *The Hidden Persuaders* (1957) and *The Affluent Society* (1958), Galbraith and Packard both argued that certain actors in the market (consumer research and advertising) were attempting to manipulate consumer desires and needs.[24] In a review of Packard's book, Henningsen labeled the techniques of modern advertising "some of the most shocking a democracy can face" and described "the modern depth psychology that, like a worm, drills out people's brains, steals their will and makes them blindly obedient to the salesman." According to Henningsen, "The methods are exactly the same as those used in brainwashing."[25]

Although prominent Danish Social Democrats were influenced by Galbraith's writings, the party had already adopted a more positive attitude towards material welfare and individual consumption when it began to pursue economic growth and technological innovation rather than regulation in the 1950s.[26] This change was in keeping with the demand for the liberalization of the Danish economy that had been raised both internationally, with the implementation of OEEC programs and the Marshall Plan and nationally by other political parties and the business community.[27] In this process, the Social Democratic Party adjusted its productivity policies to satisfy the public demand for mass consumption and increasingly addressed the electorate as consumers instead of workers.[28]

Social Democratic politics nevertheless remained rooted in the notion of consumers as vulnerable beings whose rights to free choice, fair prices and accurate information on the market had to be protected by

---

23   Hans Hertel, *PH – en biografi* (København: Gyldendal, 2012), 351–354; Anne Borup, "PH og Tænk: Forbrugeroplysning og reklamekritik," *Poul Henningsen – dengang og nu*, ed. Hans Hertel (København: Gyldendal, 2009), 292–300; Bendix Andersen, "Kampen om forbrugersamfundet," 54–56.
24   Daniel Horowitz, *Vance Packard and American Social Criticism* (Chapel Hill: The University of North Carolina Press 1994) and *The Anxieties of Affluence: Critiques of American Consumer Culture, 1939–1979* (Amherst: University of Massachusetts Press, 2004).
25   Bendix Andersen, "Kampen om forbrugersamfundet," 56.
26   Niels Ole Finnemann, *I broderskabets aand, den socialdemokratiske arbejderbevægelses idéhistorie 1871–1977* (København: Gyldendal, 1985), 280–347.
27   Thorsten Borring Olesen and Poul Villaume, *I blokopdelingens tegn, 1945–1972* (København: Gyldendal, 2005), 126–143.
28   Sissel Bjerrum Fossat, *Den artige lille pige med iskagen: Marshall-plan, produktivitet og amerikanisering* (Odense: University Press of Southern Denmark, 2015), 221–222.

means of state institutions. Most Danish political parties came to share this vision in the 1960s when, like the Social Democrats, they began to address the electorate as consumers, prioritize the issue of how to protect consumer interests in their agendas and argue for the necessity of a state-directed framework for consumer policy. "Consumer politics is a part of a modern social politics," the liberal Venstre Party stated in its new 1970 party program, which highlighted advertising, food control and pollution among the areas of consumer protection.[29] As such, the party became part of a consensus in Danish politics according to which state action was needed to ensure free, fair and healthy consumption.

In the early 1970s, at the height of the expansion of the welfare state, the Danish government took a new step by launching a program of direct administrative involvement in consumer policy. The program was the result of the establishment of a Consumer Commission (in 1969) that was to offer proposals for new initiatives in this area. As a result of the Commission's work, two new institutions addressing consumer politics were established in 1975. Forbrugerombudsmanden (the Consumer Ombudsman) was to ensure that private companies complied with consumer protection and marketing rules (the work conducted by the Commission also led to the passing of new marketing legislation in 1974), while Forbrugerklagenævnet (the Consumer Complaints Board) was tasked with considering consumer complaints related to goods and services purchased from traders.

Next to these institutions, the Danish Government Home Economics Council, created already in 1935 within the Ministry of Industry, conducted consumer test results and tracked technical consumer issues. Food safety and labeling was managed by the Ministry for the Environment. The 1973 Food Act gave the Ministry broad powers to regulate food content and labeling, restrict or block sales and limit pesticide use. The placing of food safety within the Ministry for the Environment forged a link between consumer and environmental policy and was a response to demands that environmental organizations had been voicing since the late 1960s.[30]

---

29 Groes, *Forbruger*, 285.
30 Trumbull, *Strength in Numbers*, 44-45; Jensen, *Brugsen*, 230-234.

Responding to the increased attention given to consumption across the political spectrum, all these institutions mirrored the idea of consumers as vulnerable beings in need of protection from the market. This idea also informed the first text to appear in Denmark devoted to the notion of consumer sovereignty, that is, the idea that consumer preferences determine the production of goods and services in the market. Written by the economist Jørn Henrik Petersen, it was published in the Social Democratic journal *Ny Politik* (New Politics) in 1972.[31] In this piece, tellingly titled "Bedrag at forbrugerne styrer produktionen?" ("Deceit that consumers control production?"), with reference to the efforts made by advertising and businesses to create artificial demand, Petersen argued that the lack of consumer sovereignty should be answered by state-driven consumer policies. Nonetheless, ideas of consumer sovereignty, the sovereign consumer, were currently gaining ground in Denmark.

The Sovereign Consumer

The idea of the sovereign consumer entered Danish political debates in the early 1970s, when the international oil crisis, rising taxes and growing unemployment hit Denmark. These developments gave birth to widespread discussion of the crisis in the welfare state, as politicians and intellectuals from across the political spectrum challenged its fundamental values and very legitimacy. As summarized in volume 5 of *Dansk velfærdshistorie* (Danish Welfare History):

> A whole range of issues were increasingly questioned: the tax burden, the expansion of the welfare system, the number of public servants, equality as a political aim, the efficiency of the public sector, the deficiencies and negative side-effects of the welfare state, the standardization of its services, the lack of control mechanisms, the bureaucracy and the lack of regard for individual preferences.[32]

---

31   Jørn Henrik Petersen, "Bedrag at forbrugerne styrer produktionen?," *Ny Politik* 2 (1972): 10–18.
32   Jørn Henrik Petersen, Klaus Petersen and Niels Finn Christiansen, eds., *Velfærdsstaten i tidehverv. Dansk Velfærdshistorie, vol. 5, 1973–1993* (Odense: University Press of Southern Denmark, 2013), 83.

As shown in this quotation, criticism of the welfare state and its growing public sector was economic *and* political in nature. According to its critics, the welfare state was ineffective and expensive, as well as repressive and undemocratic because it subjected its citizens to a system that was particularly beneficial to its rulers, namely the public servants and that made them dependent on it. In other words, people were allegedly being repressed and exploited by the system.

Criticism of the welfare state in Danish political debates was spurred first of all by Mogens Glistrup, who rose to fame as a lawyer, tax protester and founder of the populist party Fremskridtspartiet in the early 1970s and by the economist and Marxist Jørgen Dich, who authored the most intensely debated book of the era, *Den herskende klasse* (The Ruling Class) from 1973, which portrayed the welfare state as the political project of the ruling class of public employees.[33]

In this context, a new generation of politicians in the Venstre Party introduced the idea of the sovereign consumer into political debates in Denmark in order to address the contemporary crisis of the welfare state, as well as renew the ideological foundations of their party and respond to the demands for emancipation from and criticisms of authoritarian state structures that had been launched by leftist movements since the 1960s and had gained traction in social debates.

Key members of this generation included Bertel Haarder, Henning Christophersen, Uffe Ellemann-Jensen, Peter Brixtofte and Anders Fogh Rasmussen, all academics with social science backgrounds who authored a veritable flood of books and articles on liberal ideology and politics in the 1970s. The importance of these entrepreneurial ideologists can hardly be overstated. They all became members of parliament for Venstre, as well as prolific and powerful ministers. Moreover, Christophersen, Ellemann-Jensen and Fogh Rasmussen became chairs of Venstre and Fogh Rasmussen was a very influential Prime Minister from 2001 to 2009.

Locating the main source of the crisis in the welfare state in its ever-growing, ineffective and undemocratic public sector, these liberals did not aim to abolish the public sector but to reduce its size and change its content. Breaking with long-standing traditions in Venstre of treating the state

---

33 Jørgen S. Dich, *Den herskende klasse* (København: Gyldendal, 1973).

and the market as separate and antagonistic to one another, they aimed to introduce market-like competition mechanisms into public administration and service provision. In doing so, they launched new ideas concerning the decentralization of and free choice in the public sector. Moreover, they argued that turning citizens into sovereign consumers by subjecting the functions of the public sector to their demands would turn the Danish welfare state into a more efficient and democratic society.

Henning Christophersen's 1972 book *En udfordring for de liberale* (A Challenge for the Liberals) spearheaded the ideological transformations within Venstre.[34] In his book, Christophersen argued that, while the state had become Denmark's largest business enterprise, it differed from all other enterprises in that its incomes and sales were guaranteed and exempt from all the dynamics that characterized the free market, including free demand, competition and the price mechanism. In other words, it lacked a way of measuring the efficiency and quality of its services. The result was an inefficient and expensive system, with a concentration of power in the public sector that was escaping political control, as bureaucrats and interest groups ran the administrative apparatus. To regain control of the public sector and limit its expenses, expansion and power, Christophersen envisaged:

> (...) another way to organize public production. A method which is not a copy of the private market, but provides the same inbuilt regulation of quality, costs and accordingly prices that is found on the private market. In short, a system that secures a reasonable degree of free consumer choice for every individual, an efficient use of the resources the public sector can dispose of and growing public productivity.[35]

According to Christophersen, by letting citizens as consumers decide for what purposes public-sector funding should be used, the system would be exposed to competition mechanisms and forced to produce new, better and cheaper goods. He wrote: "The voter is seemingly the perfect consumer. He requests only the best and is willing to pay the price for it. New

---

34 Henning Christophersen, *En udfordring for de liberale* (Holte: Forlaget Liberal, 1972).
35 Christophersen, *En udfordring for de liberale*, 22.

products or better versions of old goods are received with great interest and placed on the shopping list."[36] Clearly, Christophersen expected free consumer choice to result not only in a more effective, productive and innovative order, but also in a more democratic system that responded to individual needs and desires.[37]

Similarly, Bertel Haarder repeatedly complained that the public sector forced consumers to accept its products, thereby enforcing what in a 1973 book he labeled "state collectivism and waste production". He wrote: "The public subsidies, decision-making systems, hiring procedures etc. seem to be more influenced by public-sector concerns than concerns about the interests of the consumer, who would be better off – and save money – *if they were allowed to decide more by themselves*.[38] Aiming to marketize the public sector by subjecting it to consumer sovereignty, in his 1974 book *Institutionernes tyranni* (The Tyranny of Institutions), Haarder explained: "The important thing is to *liberalize* the public as well as the private sector (…). Similar to the private sector, the public sector must be subjected to the demands of the consumer, so that needs and expenses are kept in check." [39]

More generally, Christophersen, Haarder and their fellow Venstre politicians wanted to reform the public sector by approaching its service institutions and agencies through the lens of what is today known as New Public Management. In their writings, they sketched out an ambition to make the public service more business-like and to improve its efficiency by implementing quasi-market production structures that focused on consumer services, de-centralized delivery models and cultivated both co-operation and competition with private companies, while at the same time introducing individual incentives to employees and assessing performance through audits, benchmarks and evaluations.

Two new features characterized the consumer ideal that Venstre placed at the centre of its reform ambitions. First, this ideal no longer conceptualized consumers as vulnerable and susceptible beings, but as

---

36   Christophersen, *En udfordring for de liberale*, 20.
37   Christophersen, *En udfordring for de liberale*, 16-27.
38   Bertel Haarder, *Statskollektivisme og spildproduktion: om årsagerne til overforbruget, skatteplyndringen, institutionernes tyranni og det tiltagende misbrug af vores ressourcer* (København: Bramsen & Hjort, 1973), 67, emphasis in original text.
39   Bertel Haarder, *Institutionernes tyranni* (København: Bramsen & Hjort, 1974), emphasis in original text.

strong, independent and ultimately sovereign individuals. Second, it no longer aimed to protect consumers from market mechanisms *through* state powers but to protect them *from* state powers through market mechanisms that involved subjecting the public sector to the competition-enhancing dynamics of consumer demand. Accordingly, the consumer was depicted as a saviour who could solve the crisis of the welfare state and who ought to be placed at the centre of a new, more efficient and more democratic way of organizing society.

In line with the current *Zeitgeist*, Venstre's liberal reform program co-opted progressive social visions of "local democracy," "participation," "well-being," "free choice," and "decentralization" that had been launched by the left since the mid-1960s.[40] The program also bore similarities to ideas formulated by neoliberal ideologists such as Milton Friedman, who had proposed to let consumers make the American public sector more efficient and democratic by subjecting its services to consumer demand. Likewise, the liberal program outlined by the Venstre politicians was in tune with the neoclassical paradigm, which became dominant in the discipline of economics during the 1960s. This paradigm elevated consumer sovereignty to the only norm according to which social well-being could be measured, reworked the ideal of traditional political democracy by interpreting it through market metaphors and questioned the role of the state as a collective decision-maker and social planner.[41] However, none of the Venstre politicians referred to current trends in economics and Bertel Haarder was alone in citing scholars such as Milton Friedman. As such, Venstre's ideal of the sovereign consumer was apparently developed largely within a Danish political context.

These ideals arguably had roots in ongoing discussions about what Danish economists had already identified in the 1950s as deep-rooted challenges and problems in the ideational foundations and institutional dynamics behind the system.[42] As we have seen, in the early 1970s, in the

---

40 Jesper Vestermark Køber, *Et spørgsmål om nærhed: nærdemokratibegrebets historie i 1970ernes Danmark* (Ph.D. Thesis, University of Copenhagen, 2017).
41 Olsen, *The Sovereign Consumer*, 141-181.
42 See first of all Jørn Henrik Petersen, Klaus Petersen and Niels Finn Christiansen, eds., *Dansk velfærdshistorie. Vol. 3: 1933–1956: Velfærdsstaten i støbeskeen* (Odense: University Press of Southern Denmark, 2012), 117–151 and Jørn Henrik Petersen, Klaus Petersen and Niels Finn Christiansen, eds., *Dansk velfærdshistorie. Vol. 4: 1956–1973: Velfærdsstatens storhedstid* (Odense: University Press of Southern

context of the crisis of the welfare state, these debates morphed into direct criticisms of the public sector and were coupled with demands from debaters from across the political spectrum for individual representation and choice in social processes. It was in this context that Venstre politicians picked up and recast the increasingly popular figure of the sovereign consumer with the purpose of transforming the welfare state in a more liberal direction.

While the new generation of liberals effectively kickstarted Venstre's transformation from an agrarian party into a modern party with a broad electoral appeal, their visions were initially central to both social debates and practical politics. They offered only one of many (mostly more leftist) answers to the crisis of the Danish welfare state that were voiced during the 1970s, an answer that was certainly not the most prominent. However, the long-term significance of these ideas for the push from the welfare state to the so-called competition state can hardly be overstated.

To begin with, these ideas about reform of the public sector were turned into concrete policy options in the early 1980s, when the Venstre politicians mentioned above served as influential ministers in a government headed by Poul Schlüter's Conservative Party. Particularly important was the first of a series of so-called modernization programs that Henning Christophersen introduced as Minister of Finance in 1983.[43] As part of the attempt to reduce the state budget deficit and create a new society that promoted individual responsibility and reduced guardianship, the key objective of the program was to change the relationship between the individual and the state through a set of reforms to make the public sector less bureaucratic and more productive, effective and responsive to individual demands and desires.[44] The program's ideas of implementing self-regulating, decentralized mechanisms and competition systems with a strong focus on free consumer choice echoed many of the concrete proposals that Venstre politicians had been putting forward since the early 1970s.

The program was met with criticism both within and outside the government, due to its critical attitude toward the welfare state. However,

---

Denmark, 2012), 145–162.
[43] Finansministeriet, *Redegørelse til Folketinget om regeringens program for modernisering af den statslige administration* (1983).
[44] Niels Ejersbo and Carsten Greve, *Moderniseringen af den offentlige sektor* (København: Akademisk forlag, 2014), 34–36; Petersen, Petersen and Christiansen, *Velfærdsstaten i tidehverv*, 115–116.

Schlüter's governments launched six additional modernization programs during the next decade, where ideas regarding public-sector reforms, based on the ideal of the sovereign consumer, were widely disseminated and broadly accepted in Danish politics. When Schlüter's government was forced to resign in January 1993, following an investigation into how the Minister of Justice, the Conservative Erik Ninn-Hansen, had decided to impose delays on the family reunification of Tamil refugees, the Social Democratic Party had come to share many of its visions for public-sector reform. The latter's own ideas thus also hinged on the idea of the "sovereign" consumer, albeit with various added discursive layers being to the figure.

The Social Democratic Party and the Sovereign Consumer

In the late 1970s and early 1980s, the Social Democratic Party had denounced the reform agendas launched by its opponents and held onto the ideas that had guided its politics in previous decades. However, during the 1980s, the party gradually came to share some of the ideological visions of its opponents, including reforming the public sector by marketizing its functions. This was, for example, seen in the new working program for the period 1990-1995, which the Social Democratic Party presented in 1989. Among other things, the program stated that "decentralization and increased freedom to choose had to be the guiding principle. Responsibility and the economy have to be outsourced to the users and employers in the individual public institutions."[45]

As soon as the party came back into power in 1993, it elaborated on this aim, for example, in the report *Nyt syn på den offentlige sektor* (New Perspective on the Public Sector), issued by the Ministry of Finance in 1993.[46] The report was not identical to the modernization programs that had appeared under Poul Schlüter. For example, it referred to "renewal" rather than "modernization," toned down the rhetoric of free choice, and argued to a significant extent for the need to balance the pursuit of efficiency in relation to other policy concerns, such as social equality. However, as with earlier modern-

---

45 Socialdemokratiet, *Gang i 90'erne: Socialdemokratiets bud på en samlet indsats 1990–1995* (1989).
46 Finansministeriet, *Nyt syn på den offentlige sektor* (1993).

ization programs, *Nyt syn på den offentlige sektor* encouraged a number of competition-enhancing initiatives to make the public sector more efficient and user-friendly. These included increased public–private collaboration, institutional decentralization, new employment policies, user involvement and instruments to steer, control and measure performance.[47]

This reform agenda became a defining feature of Social Democratic ideology, which, in the 1990s, was shaped by the challenge of globalization. This was seen in the 1994 book *Sans og Samling* (Sense and Unity), written by the influential Minister of Finance, Mogens Lykketoft, which anticipated the debate over "the competition state" in Denmark. With reference to remarks made by the then American Secretary of labour, Robert Reich, on the rise of a new globalized economy, Lykketoft argued that the increased international competition between nations required a new type of welfare state. According to Lykketoft, the aim was a competitive and efficient "welfare society" in which "every individual had the right to develop and realize her-/himself – where we must get rid of repression, exploitation and unemployment."[48] Nonetheless, he emphasized the need to ensure a good life for the lower strata of the population.

In the book *Velfærd i vanskeligheder* (Welfare in Troubles), also published in 1994, a group of younger Social Democrats argued more plainly for reform of the public sector by adopting a pro-market perspective.[49] According to the authors, to create a society characterized by autonomy, solidarity and participation and to regain control of what they described as an ever-growing welfare state that had been captured by special interest groups, the public sector had to be decentralized, marketized and, to some extent, also privatized. This included creating a system of consumer choice for the services covered by the state, for example in relation to schools and hospitals. "The political challenges to autonomy," the authors wrote, "concerns ensuring further *self-determination*, *participation* and *freedom of choice* for the individual citizen."[50]

---

47 Ejersbo and Greve, *Moderniseringen af den offentlige sektor*, 46–52.
48 Mogens Lykketoft, *Sans og Samling: En socialdemokratisk krønike* (København: Samleren, 1994), 26. See Jørn Henrik Petersen, Klaus Petersen and Niels Finn Christiansen, eds., *Hvor glider vi hen? Dansk velfærdshistorie, vol. 6, 1993–2014* . (Odense: University Press of Southern Denmark, 2014), 99–101.
49 Jacob Christensen, Peter Mogensen and Eskil Thuesen, *Velfærd i vanskeligheder, Socialdemokratiet mellem autonomi og autoritet* (København: Fremad, 1994).
50 Christensen, Mogensen and Thuesen, *Velfærd i vanskeligheder*, 70.

Two years later, a Social Democratic group called Hilden & the Hackers published a policy agenda that echoed more closely the modernization rhetoric pursued by the former government. "We must develop the welfare system," the group declared, "by placing the citizens at its centre."[51] This would involve streamlining through marketization, outsourcing and the decentralization of both functions and authority. *Velfærd i vanskeligheder* and the agenda launched by Hilden & the Hackers inspired strong debates over the Social Democrats' vision of reform, especially with respect to the role of privatization in these visions, causing Prime Minister Poul Nyrup Rasmussen to declare that extensive privatization was not on his agenda.[52] The idea of changing the public sector by marketizing its services and functions had nevertheless become integral to Social Democratic ideology, along with the rhetoric of free choice. Indeed, creating greater choice in the public sector and thus ensuring a society characterized by freedom was consistently portrayed as a key ambition in Social Democratic reform agendas.[53]

The consumer figure that emerged as part of the new Social Democratic agenda differed from the figure of the "weak" consumer that the party had embraced in the postwar era. It was characterized by a much stronger belief in the capacity of people to achieve autonomy and freedom by making individual choices regarding the market or in market-like settings and to adopt a more critical attitude towards the idea that welfare-state institutions always worked to protect and enhance the interests of its population in all aspects of their lives. As such, it resembled the "sovereign" consumer that Venstre politicians had put forward in the 1970s.

It also resembled the figure of the so-called "political"cconsumer that was widely disseminated in Danish public debates in the mid-1990s. This consumer figure did not have the welfare state as its point of departure, but reflected a new political culture focused on the new market structures brought about by globalization. These new structures were nevertheless perceived as having consequences for the organization of the welfare state and its public sector. The emergence of the "political" consumer was therefore an important context for the dissemination and traction of the Social Democratic "sovereign" consumer in the 1990s.

51   Cited from Petersen, Petersen and Christiansen, *Hvor glider vi hen?*, 105.
52   Petersen, Petersen and Christiansen, *Hvor glider vi hen?*, 105–108.
53   Ejersbo and Greve, *Moderniseringen af den offentlige sektor*, 46–58.

The ideal of the "political" consumer was widely disseminated in relation to the coverage of the so-called Brent Spar conflict of June 1995 by Denmark's mass media.[54] According to many commentators, Danish consumers were creating a new form of political activism by boycotting Shell due to its plans to dump an oil storage tanker into the sea. Like earlier constructions of political consumers, such as the interwar American citizen consumer, this figure drew on the idea of turning shopping into a political statement. It relied on the conception of a consumer who expressed her or his opinions about, for example, politics, environmental issues and ethics through the acquisition of products and goods on the market. This consumer, so it was assumed, not only pursued individual demands and desires but also contributed to the making of a better society and a better world by making appropriate decisions when buying on the market.

Yet the notions of political consumer and citizen consumer differed by virtue of their more market-friendly and state-critical subtexts. Steen Svendsen from the consultancy bureau Institut for Fremtidsforskning (Institute for Future Research), who introduced the political consumer idea in Denmark, explained the distinct ways in which this ideal related to the state and the market by referring to three contexts that he deemed vital for its advent.[55] First, economic prosperity allowed the expression of post-material political concerns and demands which were transformed into concrete political demands. Second, due to deep-seated social changes, individuals had lost their belief in the ability of the authorities, such as politicians and governments, to build the good society and wanted to play a much greater part in this effort. Third, increasing internationalization had created a global market over which nation states were losing influence and control, whereas individuals had become capable of shaping this new global order by shopping politically on the market. Indeed, according to Svendsen, the global market offered a much greater potential for individual social participation than traditional politics as practiced within and through the political institutions associated with the nation state.

The Social Democrats' consumer discourse was not identical to that outlined by Svendsen. Most importantly, the Social Democratic Party was

---

54 Mads P. Sørensen, *Den politiske forbruger, i det liberale samfund* (København: Hans Reitzel, 2004), 9–56; Hans Rask Jensen, "Staging political consumption: a discourse analysis of the Brent Spar conflict as recast by the Danish mass media," *Journal of Retailing and Consumer Services* 10 (2003): 71–80.
55 Steen Svendsen, "Den politiske forbruger," *Politiken*, June 24, 1995.

not silent in the same way regarding ideas concerning social, political and cultural rights or economic redistribution. Moreover, in the 1990s the party reintroduced the themes of participatory, local and economic democracy that had been central to its agenda in the 1970s. As witnessed in the working program *Frit og Fælles* (Free and Common) from 2000, consumer protection also remained a central theme in Social Democratic politics and was revitalized in the discussions relating to European integration. However, consumer protection was increasingly seen as a matter of ensuring an enhanced level of product information to assist consumers in making the right choices on the market rather than of thoroughly regulating the market. Moreover, it was now viewed as something that the market was capable of doing and interested in securing by itself, rather than as something that needed comprehensive enforcement by the state. "It is', the program *Frit og Fælles* stated, "an outdated idea that consumer interests are in conflict with the interests of business."[56]

More generally, during the 1990s, the Social Democratic Party came to share the idea that there were limits to what the state could do for citizens as consumers and that market forces and mechanisms were better at satisfying individuals' rights to choose in politics and their ability to participate in the shaping of their own lives and contemporary society more generally. In this context, the Social Democratic figure of the consumer came to resemble Venstre's sovereign consumer to such a degree that the two figures became increasingly difficult to separate. In this process, the Social Democratic Party abandoned its traditional values in many areas. For example, it now held that unemployment was linked to the individual, her or his lack of a work ethic, or other personal shortcomings, rather than to structural causes.[57] Moreover, it no longer viewed employment as an individual right, but as a duty imposed on the individual by society. These changes testify to the extensive ideological convergence that took place between the Social Democratic Party and Venstre.

However, in contrast to Venstre, the Social Democratic Party aimed to transform the state into a positive social force and to re-enchant the public sector by modeling it in the mirror of the market and by portraying the

---

56 Socialdemokratier, *Fri og fælles* (2000).
57 Jørn Henrik Petersen, *Pligt og ret – ret og pligt, refleksioner over den socialdemokratiske idéarv* (Odense: University Press of Southern Denmark, 2014).

citizen as its customer and captain. This positive shaping of the state and of its relations with its citizens was a key difference between the party's reform agenda and its liberal origins. The same was true of the globalization discourse that accompanied the Social Democratic reform program, which mirrored the third-way globalization agendas voiced by center-left parties led by Tony Blair and Bill Clinton in the Great Britain and the United States, who also pursued the ambition of liberating the consumer from the authoritative powers of the state through the mechanisms of the market. Tellingly, the sociologist Anthony Giddens, the chief theoretician of Labour's third-way agenda in the Great Britain, declared that "consumer choice is real choice" and argued that in the global era the market was far better equipped to accommodate individual self-making and self-fashioning than the state.[58] This belief came to be widely shared among centre-left parties across the western world in the 1990s.

In Denmark, the practical implementation of reforms began in the 1990s, when the Social Democratic Party applied New Public Management principles in parts of the public sector.[59] This included new budget models, steering policies, calculation and documentation methods; new leadership and employment policies and wage systems; new initiatives to de-bureaucratize the public sector by standardizing administrative procedures; new methods of evaluation using consumer feedback; new public–private partnerships and collaborations; and, finally, privatizations of state-owned companies, such as the national airport and the national telecommunications company.[60]

The reform agenda continued when Anders Fogh Rasmussen succeeded Poul Nyrup Rasmussen as prime minister in 2001. Emphasizing free consumer choice as a key element of the modern public sector, his government introduced among other changes the right to free choice of hospitals, which extended to the ability to choose a private hospital. Since

---

58 "An Interview with Anthony Giddens," *Journal of Consumer Culture* 3, no. 3 (2003): 387–399.
59 Jørn Henrik Petersen, "Marketization and Free Choice in the Provision of Social Services: Normative Shifts 1982–2008: Social Democratic Lip Service as a Response to Problems of Legitimacy," in *Beyond Welfare State Models: Transnational Perspectives on Social Policy*, eds. Klaus Petersen and Pauli Kettunen (Cheltenham: Edward Elgar Publishing, 2011), 170–198; Christoffer Green-Pedersen, "New Public Management Reforms of the Danish and Swedish Welfare States: The Role of Different Social Democratic Responses," *Governance* 15, no. 2 (2002): 271–294.
60 Ejersbo and Greve, *Moderniseringen af den offentlige sektor*, 101–234.

then, changing governments have continued their effort to reform the Danish public sector using New Public Management techniques.

Epilogue

Since the 1970s, the "weak" consumer and the "sovereign" consumer have co-existed and informed the Danish welfare state in their different ways. However, in recent decades, ideas of the "sovereign" consumer have in many respects overshadowed those of the "weak" consumer. The ideal of the "sovereign" consumer has only recently been subjected to substantial criticism, as scholars and welfare-state professionals, such as doctors and nurses, have identified problems inherent in the attempt to govern in the name of this figure, that is, in the framing of the "sovereign" consumer as a motive and tool for public-sector reforms. Inquiries and statements thus confirm what Christopher Hood and Ruth Dixon concluded in their recent evaluation of three decades of reform and change in British central government, namely that the attempt to turn the citizen into a consumer of public goods has increased neither economic efficiency nor political democracy.[61] Instead, it has led to a system in which political decision-making power remains centralized in the ministries; new, expensive and time-consuming bureaucratic procedures have been introduced to conduct consumer assessments, internal evaluations and reports; consumers have very few, largely unattractive products to choose between due to incessant cuts and reductions in the public sector; and the administration has little capacity to help weaker consumers navigate in the "choice" system.[62]

However, no real alternative to the ideal of the market-focused consumer has emerged to replace it, whether in the present or the near future. The notion of the green consumer, connoting the idea that consumers could be the driving force behind positive environmental change, is one possible alternative. But only time will tell whether this idea will triumph and perhaps end the habits of (over)consumption that the market-friendly consumer ideal has also helped legitimize in recent decades.

---

61 Christopher Hood and Ruth Dixon, *A Government That Worked Better and Cost Less? Evaluating Three Decades of Reform and Change in UK Central Government* (Oxford: Oxford University Press, 2015).
62 Niklas Olsen, "Velfærdsstatens krise og neoliberalismens indtog i Danmark i 1970erne," *Slagmark* 74 (2016): 138.

The Democrat

Three Democratic Citizens in the Early Social Democratic Welfare State

Jesper Vestermark Køber

In 1943, as the momentum of the German army evaporated on the battlefields, the Danish architect, cultural critic and left-wing public intellectual Poul Henningsen, known as PH, commenced a series of lectures on the resilience of democracy and society after the war. In neutral Sweden and surrounded by other Nordic authors and intellectuals who had fled the German occupation of their home countries, this influential critic warned his contemporaries about the threats from National Socialism after the war: "During the war, we fought it with its own means. Soon, this will not be the case. Soon, we will have to fight it by becoming democrats – true democrats."[1]

PH's speech was an early comment in the debate on whether there should be a legal purge after the war, but it was also a foretaste of his most consistent contribution to the postwar discussion on democracy: his ar-

---

1 Poul Henningsen, "Nazismens blomstring efter krigen," In *Kulturkritik III 1943-56*, eds. Carl Erik Bay and Olav Harsløf (København: Rhodos, 1973), 11-18.

gument for the development of democratic citizens. National Socialism was not a specifically German ideology, he argued, but a nationalist, militaristic, sadistic and intolerant way of thinking that would spread and gain strength unless Danish society produced free, emancipated individuals.[2] PH thus assumed that the survival and development of democracy depended less on parliamentary culture, free and fair elections and economic reforms than on creating a specific mentality in a society inhabited by democratic human beings.[3]

PH was only one of many debaters who proposed solutions for Denmark's future.[4] However, the idea of developing a stronger democratic spirit resonated well among Danish politicians and intellectuals who were worried about the fragilities of democracy after the war.[5] As this chapter argues, especially among Social Democrats and intellectuals affiliated with the party, "the democratic citizen" was one of their integral ideas on how to bolster Danish democracy and create the conditions for the good society they were seeking to create.

This chapter describes the making and characteristics of "the democratic citizen" in the immediate postwar debates on democracy and in the welfare state's formulation phase in the 1950s.[6] It does so by exploring three visions of the democratic citizen outlined respectively by Hal Koch, Julius Bomholt and PH, who all influenced the debate over the Social Democratic concept of democracy from a position within or close to the Party. Bomholt was an influential Social Democratic politician and contributor to several books on Social Democratic ideology. Koch was a highly regarded public intellectual and theologian whose affiliation with the party grew stronger in the postwar years, especially after his wife Bodil Koch had become a Social Democratic Member of Parliament in 1947 and was appointed Minister

---

2 Poul Henningsen, "Hvad Nazisme er," in *Vi er selv historie*, ed. Henrik Stangerup (København: Thaning & Appels forlag, 1963), 104.
3 Hans Hertel, *PH – En biografi* (København: Gyldendal, 2012).
4 Lasse Horne Kjældgaard, "Fremtidens Danmark: Tre faser i dansk fiktionsprosa om velfærdsstaten, 1950-1980," *Kritik*, 191 (April 2009): 31-42.
5 On the fragility of democracy, see Johanna Rainio-Niemi and Martin Conway eds., *Journal of Modern European History*, 17, no. 4 (October 2019).
6 On the welfare state's formulation phase, see Jørn Henrik Petersen, Niels Finn Christiansen and Klaus Petersen, "Det socialpolitiske idelandsskab," In *Velfærdsstaten i støbeskeen*, eds. Jørn Henrik Petersen, Klaus Petersen, Niels Finn Christiansen (Odense: Syddansk Universitetsforlag, *Dansk Velfærdshistorie, vol. 3*, 2013), 117ff.

for Ecclesiastical Affairs in 1950.[7] PH was more of an outsider who never became a member of the Social Democratic Party, but from the 1920s up until his death in 1967, he was a significant left-leaning critic of cultural and political debates in Denmark. In the 1950s he strengthened his relationship with the Social Democratic Party and became a columnist for the newspaper *Social-Demokraten*. He also took part in Social Democratic reading groups and held lectures with prominent party members, politicians and intellectuals such as the future prime minister Jens Otto Krag, as well as with Bodil and Hal Koch.[8]

In focusing on these three intellectuals, the chapter revisits the origins of the alleged fusion between leading intellectuals from the Folk High School milieu, cultural radicals and Social Democrats that was the subject of newspaper editor and cultural critic Henning Fonsmark's influential and highly acclaimed *Historien om den danske utopi* (*The Story of the Danish Utopia*) of 1990.[9] In this book, Fonsmark illuminates certain similarities between leading intellectuals such as Koch, PH and Bomholt and criticizes their reformulation of the concept of democracy and the construction of the Danish welfare state for being totalitarian. According to Fonsmark, this dominant intellectual force in postwar Denmark demoted the principles of representative democracy and promoted a novel concept of welfare democracy that distrusted the citizen and relied on the idea that it was only through education and cultural regimentation that the citizen could become "worthy of handling the voter's task."[10] Through a comprehensive analysis of the previous 45 years of cultural and political debate, Fonsmark heavily criticized the political consensus over the principles of the welfare state and the "utopian" desire to create democratic citizens through the school system, social science and a number of cultural policies.

Rather than criticizing the welfare state form of democracy, this chapter examines three concepts of the democratic citizen as a response

---

7   See Birgitte Possing, *Uden omsvøb: Portræt af Bodil Koch* (København: Gyldendal, 2007).
8   Klaus Petersen, "Fra opstand i Budapest til kulturpolitik i Tivoli," *Arbejderhistorie*, vol. 4 (1999): 88; Klaus Petersen, *Socialdemokratisk Samfund: De loyales ungdomsoprør* (København: SFAH, 2001), 10-11; Klaus Petersen, "Kold krig og velfærdsstatens kulturpolitik," In: *Der truer os i tiden: Velfærds- og koldkrigstænkning i 1950'ernes danske kulturdebat*, eds. Nils Gunder Hansen and Rasmus Mariager (Odense: Syddansk Universitetsforlag, 2013), 91. Hertel, *PH*, 355-356.
9   Henning Fonsmark, *Historien om den danske utopi* (København: Gyldendal, 1990).
10 Ibid., 188.

to the problematic legacy of democracy in postwar Europe and as part of the internal Social Democratic debate on democracy as a progressive idea for a future socialist society. In doing so, the chapter stresses that these three visions of "the democratic citizen" formed part of the ideological reformulation of Social Democracy that took place as the party moved away from previous ideas of socialism and egalitarianism in the postwar period.

Overall, Koch, Bomholt and PH argued for the necessity to create "the democratic citizen" and shared the belief that each individual was obliged to participate in society for a true democracy to flourish. Moreover, the chapter shows that they did so from different perspectives on and adopting different approaches to the Social Democratic idea of democracy as a progressive concept. As a theologian, Hal Koch formulated his vision of the democratic citizen by arguing that being a democrat was a continual process that demanded civic education and a commitment to dialogue in all human relations. Bomholt understood the trope of the democratic citizen as a way of expressing Danish values, which he used as a common denominator for the contemporary ideas of a "spiritual" welfare state and a cultural democracy. Finally, PH regarded the democratic citizen as an autonomous individual freed from the constraints of the consumer society and he sought to strengthen democracy through cultural practices and democratic education. In sum, these thinkers contributed to and expanded Social Democratic ideas of democracy, thereby stressing that democracy was a political system as well as a way of life.

The Postwar Democratic Settlement

Democracy became a key concept in the reconfiguration of war-torn Western Europe, as political parties, intellectuals and lawmakers across the region embraced democratic rule and debated the principles of democracy.[11] The question they all asked was how to secure democracy in the wake of the catastrophe that a great number of European democracies had suffered in

---

11   Martin Conway and Volker Depkat, "Towards a European History of the Discourse of Democracy: Discussing Democracy in Western Europe, 1945-60," In *Europeanization in the Twentieth Century*, eds. Martin Conway and Kiran Klaus Patel (London: The Palgrave Macmillan Transnational History Series, Palgrave Macmillan, 2010), 132-156; Pepijn Corduwener, *The Problem of Democracy in Europe* (London: Routledge, 2016).

the interwar period. The Weimar Republic stood out as a particularly grim democratic experiment, plagued as it had been by political violence and anti-democratic forces. Consequently, faced with the ambivalent legacy of democracy, in 1945 politicians and intellectuals across Western Europe agreed on the necessity of learning from the negative experiences of the recent past if democracy was to succeed in the present.[12] In response, however and to guard against the dangers of unlimited popular sovereignty, which many regarded as having been one of the greatest challenges to democracy between the wars, several Western European countries installed strong executive offices, constitutional courts and bicameralism in an attempt to establish a type of democracy that constrained the people from participating too much in politics.[13]

Denmark, like the rest of Scandinavia, stands out as a remarkable exception from this postwar trend.[14] Unlike other European countries, it had not experienced the overthrow of Parliament or any other breakdown of political institutions between the wars. At every election in the crisis-ridden 1930s, a significant majority of the Danish people expressed trust in the parliamentary system by backing the established political parties. Moreover, the evolution of the Danish postwar constitution diverged from that in other Western European countries. When amending the constitution in 1953, Denmark did not set up a constitutional court, nor did Danish politicians express a particular distrust of popular sovereignty. Instead, the 1953 constitution abolished the bicameral system and replaced the upper chamber with referenda if a third of Parliament so decides, if less than five-sixths of Parliament hands over sovereignty to a foreign jurisdiction, if the constitution is changed or if a majority in Parliament votes to change the voting age. As Jeppe Nevers and Jesper Lundsby Skov argue, this particu-

---

12 Martin Conway, "Democracy in Western Europe after 1945," In *Democracy in Modern Europe: A Conceptual History*, eds. Jussi Kurunmäki, Jeppe Nevers, Henk te Velde (New York: Berghahn Books, 2018), 235.
13 Jan-Werner Müller, *Contesting Democracy: Political Ideas in Twentieth-Century Europe* (New Haven and London: Yale University Press, 2011), 147-150.
14 Jeppe Nevers, "Democracy and European Integration: A Transnational History of the Danish Debate." In *Democracy in Modern Europe: A Conceptual History*, eds. Jussi Kurunmäki, Jeppe Nevers, Henk te Velde (New York: Berghahn Books, 2018), 283; Johan Strang, "Scandinavian Legal Realism and Human Rights: Axel Hägerström, Alf Ross and the Persistent Attack on Natural Law," *Nordic Journal of Human Rights*, vol. 36, no. 3 (2018): 203.

lar Danish model of postwar European democracy rested on a romantic understanding of a unity between the Danish people and democracy that had been shaped by both the agrarian movement and the Social Democrats from the nineteenth century.[15]

However, the intellectual debates on democracy within the Danish Social Democratic party reflect a more complex story. Since its formation in the late nineteenth century, the party has considered itself the vanguard of democracy. In the period of limited suffrage in the late nineteenth and early twentieth centuries, the party argued vigorously for the extension of the franchise, as it hoped to fulfill its political ambitions by achieving a parliamentary majority based on the working class.[16] However, just like Social Democrats in other European countries, its definition of democracy was not restricted to political or parliamentary democracy: it also had the aim of creating social and material equality and of dismantling the class society.[17] Most notably, the party distinguished between political democracy that gave everyone equal political rights and social and economic democracy that provided equal opportunities for everyone to enjoy public goods. When the party formed its first government in the 1920s, Social Democrats presented parliamentary democracy as a means to democratize society further in a way that would bring about a social and economic democracy. Consequently, the Social Democratic understanding of democracy came to be connected with the idea of progress and with idealized visions of a future egalitarian Danish society.[18]

In the process of becoming the major political party, the Social Democratic Party replaced socialism with democracy as its key ideological concept.[19] During the first half of the twentieth century, it transformed itself from a class-based, socialist party into a "people's party" emphasizing the

---

15 Jeppe Nevers and Jesper Lundsby Skov, "The Folkish Heritage in Nordic democracy: Examples from Denmark and Norway," *Journal of Modern European History*, vol. 17, no. 4 (2019): 432–447.
16 Claus Bryld, *Den demokratiske socialismes gennembrudsår* (København: SFAH, 1992).
17 Joris Gijsenbergh, "The Semantics of 'Democracy' in Social Democratic Parties: Netherlands, Germany and Sweden, 1917-1939," *Archiv für Sozialgeschichte*, vol. 53, (2013): 147-174; Anna Friiberg, *Demokrati bortom politiken: En begreppshistorisk analys av demokratibegreppet inom Sveriges socialdemokratiska arbetareparti 1919–1939* (Stockholm: Atlas, 2013).
18 Jeppe Nevers, *Fra skældsord til slagord* (Odense: Syddansk Universitetsforlag, 2011).
19 Jeppe Nevers, "Reformism and Nordic Democracy," in *Rhetorics of Nordic Democracy*, eds. Jussi Kurunmäki and Johan Strang (Helsinki: Finnish Literature Society, 2010), 177.

connection between the social, the national and democracy.[20] Important in this context was the party's 1934 manifesto, *Danmark for folket* (*Denmark for the people*), which downplayed the distinction between the working class and the bourgeoisie and sought to include society's different classes in a single political project.[21] The transformation culminated in the party winning 46% of the votes in the 1935 election for the second chamber, Folketinget. The Social Democratic ambition was to carry out social reforms while maintaining a stable political order that was parliamentary and democratic. The Social Democratic strategy thus helped keep fascists and communists away from political influence by connecting democracy to the supposed essence of the Danish character.[22]

Although the transition to the postwar era was characterized by continuity, the postwar Danish political debate focused as much on the dangers of modern democracy as did debates elsewhere.[23] Following the Second World War, politicians, writers, priests, lawyers and other academics initiated substantial discussion of how democracy should fight its enemies in order to survive and remain stable.[24] As in the interwar period, debaters also voiced concerns for democracy's fragility by expressing anxieties about the masses and their capacity to rule, as well as about the consequences of centralized planning for individual freedom.[25] Most participants in the debate argued for some sort of social and economic democracy. The resistance movement and the Communist Party in particular, which prospered in the summer of 1945, argued vigorously for the democratization of many

---

20   Ove Korsgaard, "The Danish Way to Establish the Nation in the Hearts of the People," In: *National Identity and the Varieties of Capitalism. The Danish Experience*, eds. John L. Campbell, John A. Hall and Ove K. Pedersen (Québec: McGill-Queen's University Press, 2006), 150-151.
21   Socialdemokratiet, *Danmark for folket: For Arbejde, Brød og Frihed* (1934); Bo Lidegaard, *En fortælling om Danmark i det 20. århundrede* (København: Gyldendal, 2011), 135-138.
22   Niels Kayser Nielsen, "Demokrati og kulturel nationalisme i Norden i mellemkrigstiden: en realpolitisk højredrejning," *Historisk Tidskrift* (Sweden), vol. 124, no. 4 (2004): 581-603.
23   Volker Depkat, "Discussing democracy," In *Transatlantic Democracy in the 20th Century: Transfer and Transformation*, ed. Paul Nolte (Berlin: Walter de Gruyter, 2016), 117-13.
24   Esther Oluffa Pedersen, *Fremkaldte kulturrum: diskussioner om demokrati og diktatur, humanisme, ansvar og videnskab i tiden omkring anden verdenskrig* (København: Hans Reitzels Forlag, 2019); Niels Kayser Nielsen and Søren Hein Rasmussen, eds., *Strid om demokratiet: Artikler fra en dansk debat 1945-46* (Aarhus: Aarhus Universitetsforlag, 2003).
25   Johan Strang, "The other Europe? Scandinavian intellectuals and fragility of democracy in the wake of World War II," *Journal of Modern History*, vol. 17, no. 4, (2019), 14.

social spheres such as the school system, culture and the military.[26] The Social Democratic Party reacted with a party program called *Fremtidens Danmark* (*The Future of Denmark*), issued a few months after liberation in 1945.[27] The program argued among other things for the completion of democracy through economic and industrial democratization in the form of business councils. Through *The Future of Denmark* and other political programs, which promoted this vision of economic and industrial democracy, the Social Democratic Party maintained its dual notion of democracy as both a parliamentary system and a progressive move towards achieving economic equality and social justice.[28]

The Social Democratic proposals for the further democratization of Danish society coexisted with a concern about whether the people actually had the proper democratic attitudes. In line with this, *The Future of Denmark* emphasized the importance of the individual's commitment to democracy: "In the long run, a democratic system can only function if citizens are aware of their responsibility and duty."[29] Following this line of thought, democracy in Social Democratic ideology was a matter not so much of continued progress, but of continued struggle. In an article entitled "Democracy and the future" ("Folkestyret og fremtiden"), published in the edited volume "Folkestyrets Problemer" ("Problems of Democracy") from 1946, the Social Democratic Folk High-School teacher Frode Kristensen argued that democracy could only survive through constant struggle and by placing the democratic citizen at the centre of society:

---

26 See Frit Danmarks Bibliotekargruppe, *Bibliotekernes krav til bibliotekerne* (1945), Knud Jarmsted, ed., *Demokratiets Dagblad: Et nyt instrument i demokratiets tjeneste* (København: Ejnar Munksgaards Forlag, 1946); Palle Roslyng Jensen, "En demokratisk og folkelig hær," In *Fra mellemkrigstid til efterkrigstid: Festskrift til Hans Kirchhoff og Henrik S. Nissen på 65-årsdagen oktober 1998*, eds. Henrik Dethlefsen and Henrik Lundbak (København: Museum Tusculanum, 1998), 629-670.

27 Socialdemokratiet, *Fremtidens Danmark* (1945); Åge Hoffmann, "Fremtidens Danmark: En analyze af Socialdemokratiets efterkrigsprogram, dets tilblivelse indhold og formål," *Årbog for arbejderbevægelsens historie* (København: SFAH, 1993), 245-281; Niels Wium Olesen: "Fremtidens Danmark: tilbage på plads," *Arbejderhistorie*, vol. 1 (1995), 35-50; Niels Wium Olesen, "Jens Otto Krag og 'Fremtidens Danmark'," *Historie*, Jyske samlinger, Ny Række Vol. 19, no.1 (1991), 46-72.

28 Henry Grünbaum, *Industrielt demokrati* (København: Arbejdernes Oplysningsforbund, 1946); Jens Otto Krag, "Socialisering og økonomisk demokrati," In *Vejen til Demokrati og Socialisme: En Redegørelse om Fremtidens Økonomiske og Politiske Problemer* (København: Arbejdernes Oplysningsforbund, 1946), 9-17; Niels Dalgaard, *Ved demokratiets grænse: Demokratisering af arbejdslivet i Danmark 1919-1994* (København: SFAH, 1995).

29 Socialdemokratiet, *Fremtidens Danmark*.

> The future is (…) shrouded in darkness. Democracy won't last forever, although the ideologies of dictatorship have suffered a defeat at the moment. Democracy is (…) not a certain set of rules about suffrage, representation and parliament, about the legislative, judicial and executive power, it is primarily a question of mindset, upbringing and each citizen's culture.[30]

The profound concern for the creation and preservation of the proper democratic spirit in society was also the subject of political interventions made by the three debaters Hal Koch, Julius Bomholt and Poul Henningsen in the postwar era. They framed their contributions to the debate over democracy as solutions to the question of how enhanced democracy could lead to greater progress and harmony.

Hal Koch and Democracy as a Way of Life

In his 1945 book *Hvad er demokrati? (What is democracy?)*, Hal Koch, a professor of church history, unfolded one of the most widely read discussions on the dilemmas facing modern democracy and democratic citizenship in the postwar era.[31] Koch's main contribution to the debate on democracy was his definition of democracy as a way of life and a dialogue.[32] According to Koch, democracy could not be established merely by building strong political institutions and supporting parliamentary democracy. In his opinion, it was just as important to create a distinct democratic spirit that committed each individual to engage in dialogue and respect divergent opinions. Following this argument, every new generation would have to relearn to be democratic through an education in humanism and democracy that would immunize it against immaturity and mass mentality.[33] In other words, it was necessary to create generations of democratic citizens.

---

30 Frode Kristensen, "Folkestyret og Fremtiden," In: *Folkestyrets Problemer*, eds. Oluf Bertolt, Chr. Christiansen and Frode Kristensen (København: Forlaget Fremad, 1946), 200.
31 Hal Koch, *Hvad er demokrati?* (København: Gyldendalske Boghandel, 1945).
32 See Uffe Jakobsen, "Inventions and developments of democracy: The approach of conceptual history," *European Political Science*, 9, no. 3, (2010): 321-322.
33 Koch: *Hvad er demokrati?*, 47.

Hal Koch's idea of the "democratic citizen" grew out of his wartime experiences and reflected his background as a theologian. During the German occupation, as *Dansk Ungdomssamvirke (Chair of the Danish Youth Asscociation)* set up in 1940, he aimed to politicize young Danes and turn them into democrats.[34] Contrary to the original intention of forming an apolitical association that sought to unite the people on the basis of common Danish values and responsibility for the country, Koch rejected nationalist approaches to educating young people as this would, he argued, make it difficult to distinguish the Danish Youth Association from the National Socialist youth organizations. Therefore, he emphasized the political, the interpersonal, the democratic community and democratic citizenship as features that should unite the country against totalitarian threats.[35] In this regard, he stressed that creating a community was possible only if its democratic citizens were active and aware of their obligations.

Koch's vision of the democratic citizen rested on a moral, Christian commitment to the fellow man. In the midst of the war, Koch consequently appealed to each citizen's responsibility and commitment to the community.[36] In his 1942 book *Dagen og vejen (The Day and the Road)*, he argued that the German occupation had created a situation in which each Dane would have to understand his commitment to his fellow human beings.[37] According to Koch, democracy obviously demanded great things from each citizen. He thus emphasized the need for civil society to constantly awaken the people and to educate them as democratic citizens. Consequently, he stated, "a human is not something you are but something you become."[38] The survival of democracy was in Koch's account all about civic education and active community life.[39] The notion of democratic citizenship and the need to educate people as democrats, which became the underlying philosophy of Koch's approach to democracy, thus rested on the idea that becoming a democrat was a continual process to be practiced in all human relations between family members, neighbours, countrymen and nations.[40]

---

34 Jes Fabricius Møller, *Hal Koch: En biografi* (København: Gads Forlag, 2009), 99-112.
35 Korsgaard, "The Danish Way," 152.
36 Ove Korsgaard, "Hal Koch: En republikaner i grundtvigiansk klædedragt." In *Poetisk demokrati: Om personlig dannelse og samfundsdannelse*, ed. Ove Korsgaard (København: Gads Forlag, 2001), 63-82.
37 Hal Koch: *Dagen og Vejen* (København: Westermann, 1942).
38 Ibid., 27.
39 Ibid., 42.
40 Koch: *Hvad er demokrati?*, 12.

This particular concept of democracy, which emanated from his Lutheran background, differed from the progressive, future-oriented, socialist vision of democracy that was often associated with Social Democracy. In his arguments about democracy as a dialogue and a way of life, he implied that democracy was an ongoing process more than an end goal. In fact, he rejected the idea that human progress as such was possible.[41] Nevertheless, by declaring that democracy was a way of thinking more than a political system, he stressed the everlasting need for public education.

After the war, Koch continued his work to maintain the spirit of cohesion and community, which, he argued, many people had felt during the war. As head of the government commission tasked with examining the economic, social and cultural conditions of young people in Denmark (Ungdomskommissionen), he oversaw the writing of fourteen reports in which he stressed that Danish society had to educate its young people to become democratic citizens.[42] Likewise, when he became the first principal of Krogerup Folk High School in 1946, he proclaimed the ambition to form Denmark's future citizens in the mirror of democracy. At the school's inauguration in 1946, Koch declared that the greatest danger to democracy was people retreating to become private citizens interested only in their own jobs, businesses, houses, families and convenience and not in society in general.[43]

Together with his wife Bodil, Koch was one of the most important intellectuals behind the bond that was created between theologians and Social Democracy in the postwar period.[44] In 1943, Koch publicly declared himself to be a Social Democrat and announced his agreement with the Social Democratic idea of social security as a means to secure democracy.[45] Several years later, his political standpoints and arguments in favour of economic democracy and greater equality earned him a reputation as the ideological founding father of Denmark's welfare state, or as the Danish

---

41 Tine Reeh, *Kristendom, historie, demokrati: Hal Koch 1932-1945* (København: Museum Tusculanum, 2011), 654.
42 Jes Fabricius Møller, "Hal Koch, de politiske partier og ungdomskommissionen," *Historisk Tidsskrift*, 116, no. 2 (2016): 370-398.
43 Hal Koch. "Ved Krogerup Højskoles Indvielse," *Højskolebladet*, 49, (1946), 574.
44 Jørn Henrik Petersen, *Luther og konkurrencestaten* (Odense: Syddansk Universitetsforlag, 2016), 237.
45 Hal Koch, "Opgørets time," *Lederbladet*, 3, (1943): 357-362. Fonsmark, *Historien*, 54.

equivalent to T.H. Marshall and his ideas of social citizenship.[46] Although this influence has been exaggerated, he merged the idea of the democrat as an ideal citizen with the Social Democratic idea of the welfare state.

Julius Bomholt and Democracy as the Essence of Being Danish

In the 1950s, the Social Democratic Party officially moved away from the socialist and Marxist doctrines that had hitherto characterized it by formulating new ideological aims for the creation of a better society. With the mechanization of the agricultural sector and growing urbanization, Danish society was changing rapidly. In this context, the Social Democratic Party sought to plan the future with Keynesian ideas of facilitating economic growth and increased state planning. The Social Democratic transformation came at a moment when workers were beginning to abandon institutions of the labour movement.[47] In the early 1950s, the welfare state became a unifying term connoting the Social Democrats' political ambitions.[48]

The party's pursuit of the welfare state was correlated with its frequent use of the term *mennesket* ("the human being"). In numerous books dedicated to explaining the party's political visions, high-placed young Social Democrats thus positioned the human being as a pivotal figure in modern society. This was, for example, the case with books like *Mennesket i centrum* (Putting the human being at the Centre) from 1953, *Tidehverv og samfundsorden* (Epoch and social order) from 1954 and *Mennesket i nutidens samfund* (The human being in contemporary society) from 1959.[49] Finally, the new 1961 party program *Vejen Frem* (The way forward) declared "the liberation of the human being" to be the party's overall ambition.[50] The focus

---

46 T.H. Marshall, *Citizenship and Social Class* (Cambridge: Cambridge University Press, 1950); Fonsmark, *Historien*; Ove Korsgaard, *Kampen om folket* (København: Gyldendal, 2004).
47 Svend Aage Andersen, *Arbejderkultur i velfærdssamfundet* (København: SFAH, 1997).
48 Jørn Henrik Petersen and Klaus Petersen, "The Concept of "Welfare State". In Danish Public and Political Debates," In *The Changing Meanings of the Welfare State: Histories of a Key Concept in the Nordic Countries*, ed. Nils Edling (New York: Berghahn Books, 2019), 137-178.
49 Julius Bomholt, ed., *Mennesket i Centrum* (København: Forlaget Fremad, 1953); Jens Otto Krag, ed., *Tidehverv og samfundsorden: En socialistisk orientering* (København: Forlaget Fremad, 1954); Bent Pihl, ed., *Mennesket i nutidens samfund* (København: AOF, 1959).
50 Socialdemokratiet, *Vejen Frem: Socialdemokratiets principprogram, vedtaget på den 28. kongres, juni 1961* (1961), 1.

on the human being indicated a shift from the traditional Social Democratic praise for the working life that saw people as workers, farmers, merchants etc., to placing greater value on the individual.[51]

In this process, ideas of "the democratic citizen" became part of the Social Democratic historical narrative that sought to establish a balance between the past achievements of the party and its expectations for the future. On the one hand, the party's ideological transformation downplayed the more idealized connotations of democracy in favour of a stronger focus on the existing parliamentary system.[52] On the other hand, Social Democrats emphasized "the democratic citizen" as an ideal of the Danish approach to democracy that could explain the historical development of Danish democracy and at the same time present an ideal for the future society.

More than anyone, the Social Democratic politician Julius Bomholt promoted the democratic citizen and contributed to the formulation of the Social Democratic concept of democracy that presented both a romantic interpretation of the symbiosis between the people and democracy and a connection between democracy and the emerging welfare state. Bomholt had established himself as a Social Democratic intellectual in the 1930s and became Minister of Education and Culture in the postwar years. He had a background as a theologian and shared views on democracy and humanism with Hal Koch.[53] As Speaker of Parliament, Bomholt delivered a speech at the celebration of the centenary of the Danish constitution in 1949. He paid tribute to what he spoke of as the historical transformation of democracy from "a form of government" that provided an opportunity for development to "a way of life". Throughout the past hundred years, he argued, the Danish people had grown, matured and established rule by the people.[54] It is no coincidence that he frequently used the vernacular term *folkestyre* ("rule by the people") instead of *demokrati* ("democracy"), as this term carried a different connotation from "democracy", stressing the strong association between the ordinary Danish people and the political

---

51 Niels Ole Finnemann, *I broderskabets aand: Den socialdemokratiske arbejderbevægelses idéhistorie 1871-1977* (København: Gyldendal, 1985), 308.
52 Karin Hansen and Lars Torpe: "Demokratiet i Danmark: Socialdemokratisk set," *Årbog for arbejderbevægelsens historie*, vol. 13 (1983): 121-162.
53 Pedersen, *Fremkaldte kulturrum,* 272.
54 Julius Bomholt, "Referat af tale ved grundlovsjubilæet," In *Grundlovsjubilæet den 5. juni 1949. Taler m.v.* (Rigsdagens Bureau, 1949), 16.

system, as well as the sharing of beliefs between rulers and ruled.[55] At the same time, Bomholt argued that the Danes had maintained their support of parliamentary democracy and resisted totalitarian threats during the German occupation because of their democratic spirit, caused by the successful integration of the peasants and workers into the country's parliamentary democracy.[56] In this line of thought, "the democratic citizen" in fact became equivalent to "the Dane".

In another speech on the same day, Bomholt emphasized the connection he saw between a well-functioning democracy and the duties of each citizen. Moreover, like Hal Koch, he stressed the importance of the commitment of each individual to the community:

> When it comes to the rights of freedom, the responsibilities are great. Every citizen is met with a demand for active citizenship in order to be Danish in the full sense of the word … One cannot grasp the essence of democracy if one has no understanding of the unity that ties the pieces together. It takes citizenship education in one or more of the many democratic institutions to translate knowledge into action.[57]

The connections between Danish mentality, democracy and active citizenship formed the core of Bomholt's vision of "the democratic citizen". However, according to Bomholt, the events of recent history implied that democracy might not have been entirely achieved. The rise of the totalitarian threat had shown that social problems could cause the death of democracy. Thus, to Bombolt the idea of "the democratic citizen" also expressed the political aim of liberating and creating social rights for each citizen, coupled with the desire to create a new type of human being. In his chapter "Aktiv humanisme" ("Active Humanism"), from *Mennesket i centrum*, to which he contributed no less than five articles, Bomholt identified what he called a "divided and disharmonious capitalistic society that tears individuals apart and burdens the most gifted individuals with a sense of

---

55 Nevers and Skov, "The folkish", 432.
56 Bomholt, "Referat," 17.
57 Julius Bomholt, "Referat af tale ved grundlovsjubilæet", In *Grundlovsjubilæet den 5. juni 1949. Taler m.v.* (Rigsdagens Bureau, 1949), 41.

insecurity and loneliness."[58] Furthermore, he argued that the "longing for community" was one of the deepest trends of the time," one that could no longer be satisfied in a specialized society.[59] As a counter to the industrialized society of his time, Bomholt promoted a type of humanism that differed from the understanding of the independent, self-expressing individual. In this new democratic humanism, he argued, "the idea of citizenship adds the strongest contribution."[60]

In essence, this liberated human being was a democratic citizen and the driver of continued democratic progress. In his article "Kulturelt demokrati" ("Cultural Democracy") in *Mennesket i centrum*, Bomholt described how the vision of creating a democratic citizen made the individual's relationship to democracy more important than social class.[61] According to Bomholt, traditional notions of class society had become antiquated, as a rising middle class and a growing number of functionaries had emerged. Essentially, Bomholt's vision of the democratic citizen aimed to liberate man from his identity as a worker in order to give him an identity as a free individual.

Bomholt's view of the democratic citizen contributed to the intense debate on the welfare state that took place in the latter part of the 1950s. Conservatives and liberals criticized what they portrayed as *formynderstaten* ("the guardian state"), which presented a threat to individual freedom and the shaping of responsible citizens.[62] One of the responses to this criticism from those supporting the welfare state was to frame the welfare state as a means rather than an aim. In this process, the democratic citizen became a particularly important figure in turning the welfare state into a tool for creating the conditions for each individual's personal existence, as the writer Villy Sørensen famously defined the welfare state.[63] Sørensen's

---

58 Julius Bomholt, "Aktiv humanisme," in *Mennesket i Centrum*, ed. Julius Bomholt (København: Forlaget Fremad, 1953), 28.
59 Ibid., 27.
60 Ibid., 30.
61 Julius Bomholt, "Kulturelt demokrati," in *Mennesket i Centrum*, ed. Julius Bomholt (København: Forlaget Fremad, 1953), 17.
62 Poul Møller, "Svaret til velfærdsstaten," in *Til alle mænds tarv* (København: Nyt Nordisk Forlag, 1956), 83-103. Petersen and Petersen, "The Concept".
63 Villy Sørensen, "Velfærdsstaten og den suspenderede personlighed." In *Ståsteder søges*, eds. Karl Bjarnhof and Johannes Smith (København: Det danske forlag, 1956), 77-88; Lasse Horne Kjældgaard, *Meningen med velfærdsstaten: Da litteraturen tog ordet – og politikerne lyttede* (København: Gyldendal,

argument was that, since the social system did not solve the problem of individual alienation in modern society, it was important to create a spiritual welfare state on top of the social welfare state. Sharing Sørensen's idea of the importance of immaterial values, Bomholt regarded cultural and educational policy as important tools in creating the democratic citizen in the 1950s.

In his contribution to *Mennesket i nutidens samfund* (Man in contemporary society) from 1959, in which he dealt with culture and education, Bomholt urged society to "educate every new generation to democracy and expand the existing, imperfect democracy into a consistent democracy."[64] In his analysis of the "consistent democracy," Bomholt added to the Social Democratic concept of democracy by presenting cultural democracy as the key to the future and as more important than social or economic democracy. Only by giving people opportunities to use their leisure time for cultural purposes would democracy make sense to the people and turn them into true democrats, he argued.[65]

Strengthening the democratic spirit was also an important part of the many reforms of the cultural life that Bomholt and his successors in the Ministry of Cultural Affairs issued after its establishment in 1961. During the subsequent years, the Ministry introduced reforms to almost every part of cultural life through the Theater Act of 1963, the renewal of the Public Library Act in 1964, the creation of the Danish Arts Foundation and the renewal of the General Education Act in 1968.

PH and the Democratic Citizen as the Completion of Democracy

PH's ideas about the democratic citizen resembled but also distanced themselves from those of Koch and Bomholt. As an influential part of the left-wing intelligentsia, it was difficult for Social Democrats to avoid the opinions that PH expressed on democracy and the welfare state. His numerous articles and features arguing that the continued democratization of society involved the formation of democratic citizens echoed both Koch's

---

2018).
64 Julius Bomholt, "Velfærdsstaten som kulturmiljø," In: *Mennesket i nutidens samfund*, ed. Bent Pihl (København: AOF, 1959), 15.
65 Ibid., 22-24.

and Bomholt's focuses on democratic education and each individual's role as a participant in society. However, his views accentuated the individual more than the community. In his entire postwar oeuvre, PH emphasized the education of the democratic citizen and individual self-realization as his main concerns regarding modern society.[66] Furthermore, he often criticized the equation between being a Dane and being a democrat.

He nonetheless shared the socialist understanding of democracy as a future-oriented project in the making and in the 1930s, sought to reconcile socialism, cultural radicalism and particular forms of political art. He considered appreciation of art to be a political tool for creating the proper mental conditions for a new democratic society. In this process, PH established himself as one of the Social Democratic government's most steadfast critics, most notably in his 1933 booklet *What about Culture?* (Hva" mæ kulturen?), in which he condemned the Social Democrats for their lack of a cultural policy that could counter the threats from National Socialist ideology. To accentuate his argument, PH placed a collage of Hitler growing out of the Social Democratic Danish Prime Minister Thorvald Stauning's head on the back cover.[67]

While exiled in Sweden in 1943-1945, PH became more aware of the danger to individual liberties from communism and turned to the idea of democracy as a parliamentary system with unlimited freedom of speech.[68] As discussions over the postwar legal order heated up in the summer of 1945, PH opposed the demands made by the resistance movement for a thorough legal purge. He regarded absolute freedom of speech as one of the most important aspects of democracy and he opposed the Communists, who demanded a cleansing of the state apparatus and restrictions on freedom of speech.[69] Consequently, his postwar concept of democracy was characterized by a strong commitment to individualism and humanism, which made it possible for him to subscribe to the Social Democratic vision of democracy. Overall, his postwar conception of the democratic citizen

---

66 Niels Peter Skou, *Fra samfundsopbygning til personlighedsdannelse: Demokratiske kulturbilleder hos Poul Henningsen 1021-1955* (Ph.D. thesis, University of Southern Denmark, 2010), 221-222.
67 Poul Henningsen, *Hva' mæ kulturen?* (København: Mondes forlag, 1933).
68 Hertel, *PH*.
69 Morten Thing, *Kommunismens kultur: DKP og de intellektuelle 1918-1960* (København: Tiderne Skifter, 1993).

presented a new goal for the completion of democracy and distanced him from his former Communist and Soviet-obedient allies.

After the war, PH portrayed democracy as an unfinished journey to be completed and he argued that creating the democratic citizen should be society's ultimate aim in completing the historic struggle for democracy. While culture and art remained an important element in his ideas about the completion of democracy, he accentuated the education of the individual and equated democracy with the individual's emancipation. In an article entitled "Det moderne menneske" ("The Modern Human Being") from 1949, PH summed up what he saw as the aim of the entirety of human progress as follows: "In politics and in cultural life, the aim is the same: the free human being that to the greatest extent possible masters his own destiny and determines his own life and wealth of experience: *democracy*."[70]

Whereas Bomholt's ideas of the democratic citizen as an active citizen and an essential part of being a Dane was aligned with Social Democratic conceptions of democracy, PH developed his vision of the democratic citizen in opposition to this view. In a 1945 feature article entitled "Democracy and Youth" in the Social Democratic newspaper *Social-Demokraten,* PH attacked the current equation between being a Dane and being a democrat: "For the time being, the word democracy means neither more nor less than a good Dane and that causes confusion. (…) It is no surprise that the young have been presented with the view that you are either a democrat or a traitor to your country, but that is completely wrong."[71] Instead, PH argued that the possibility of democracy depended on freedom of speech that extended to criticism of both patriotism and the popular resistance movement. In a review of Hal Koch and Alf Ross's book *Nordisk demokrati* (*Nordic Democracy*), he criticized its glorification of Nordic democracy and argued that democracy ought to be developed further: "There are so many who believe that the aim has been achieved and that we live in the best of all worlds. The book should from first to last have been characterized by a desire to explain that democracy is not something that exists but that we can only hope to approach its ideals by constant, awakened criticism." [72] In PH's view, the democratic cit-

---

70 Poul Henningsen, "Det moderne menneske," In *Vor tids opfindelser og fremskridt inden for teknik og videnskab,* ed. Olaf Becker (København: Georg Andersens Forlag, 1949), section 10, 14.
71 Poul Henningsen, "Demokratiet og ungdommen," In *Vi er selv historie,* ed. Henrik Stangerup (København: Thaning & Appels forlag, 1963), 107.
72 Poul Henningsen, "Bogen om Nordisk Demokrati," *Information,* April 27, 1949.

izen could only shape the coming democracy if it took part in the constant criticism of society.

As a columnist for *Social-Demokraten* and a contributor to the Social Democratic debate of the 1950s, PH sought to take part in the formation of the idea of the spiritual welfare state that corresponded with the Social Democratic interest in cultural policy.[73] PH considered his affiliation with the Social Democrats to be natural and he described it as a result of the Social Democrats' newly discovered interest in modern educational thinking.[74] Inspired by educational reformers, PH believed in modern pedagogy as a means to emancipate the individual and envisaged a form of education that focused on creating human beings with free and independent minds. In a lecture from 1948, he stated that only modern education could save democracy.[75] Later, in a 1955 feature article in *Social-Demokraten* entitled *I årtiers narredans* ("Decades of Fooling Dance"), he argued that the continued expansion of democracy was impossible without the education of the individual: "The pivotal point if democracy is to succeed is education that enables the individual to choose on the basis of his own convictions."[76]

The alliance between PH and the Social Democrats was only brief and he often expressed dissatisfaction with Social Democratic pragmatism. PH persistently focused on the ambition to maintain democracy as a progressive concept that would only be completed with the emancipation of the individual. From the late 1950s, PH's determination to create democratic citizens was influenced by a growing concern for the fragility of democracy and the threats posed by the consumer society in the age of mass consumption. In line with the critically acclaimed writers Erich Fromm, Vance Packard, John K. Galbraith and David Riesman, he feared conformity and in 1961 claimed that democracy was in even greater danger than in Hitler's time.[77] However, PH's idea of the democratic citizen coincided with the overall project of the postwar Social Democrats: to bolster parliamenta-

---

73   See Poul Henningsen, "Den åndelige Velfærdsstat," In *Hug og Parade: Tolv Indlæg om Velfærdsstaten og Kulturen*, eds. Frederik Nielsen and Ole Hyltoft (København: Forlaget Fremad, 1960). Hertel, *PH*, 350ff.
74   Hertel, *PH*, 340ff.
75   Poul Henningsen, "Stalinismens klippegrund," In *Kulturkritik*, vol. III 1943-1956, eds. Carl Erik Bay and Olav Harsløf (København: Rhodos, 1973), 163.
76   Poul Henningsen, "I årtiernes narredans," In *Kulturkritik*, vol. III 1943-1956, eds. Carl Erik Bay and Olav Harsløf (København: Rhodos, 1973), 213.
77   Hertel, PH, 377.

ry democracy with a strong democratic mentality in every citizen and a strong emphasis on cultural policy.

Epilogue

The overall aim of democratic education and the constant challenge to improve true democrats still resonates in democratic rhetoric in early twenty-first century Denmark.[78] Especially Hal Koch's notion of democracy as a way of life has prevailed in the public debate over democracy, as seen, for example, in the fact that the government included his conception of democracy in its official Danish Democracy Canon in 2007.[79]

However, new political views on the citizen that have diverged from the ideal of the democratic citizen can be seen in the various transformations of the public sector during the last thirty years.[80] In particular, the revival of liberal and conservative criticism of the welfare state that emerged in the 1970s and gained strength in the 1990s attacked the Social Democratic ideals of democracy and their understanding of democratic education.[81] In this decade, following the argument of Ove K. Pedersen, "the democratic citizen" of the welfare-state era differed from the later neoliberal ideal of the citizen as an "opportunist" or "soldier" that has emerged in the competition state.[82] Changes in the principles underlying social and unemployment benefits and the political focus on preventing the abuse of the welfare system rather than a commitment to its continued expansion, is perhaps a sign of the emergence and centrality of a new type of ideal citizen that is distinct from the democratic citizen of the postwar years.[83]

---

78 See Michael Böss, "Democracy as Dialogue and Partnership: The Democratic Philosphy of Hal Koch in the light of Democratic "Deficit' and "Decay'," In *Developing Democracies: Democracy, Democratization and Development*, eds. Michael Böss, Jørgen Møller and Svend Erik-Skaaning (Aarhus: Aarhus Universitetsforlag, 2013), 155-175.
79 Udvalget til udarbejdelse af en demokratikanon, *Demokratikanon* (København: Udvalget til udarbejdelse af en demokratikanon og Undervisningsministeriet, 2007), 72-73.
80 Lars Torpe, "Medborgeridentiteten er presset," In *Konkurrencestaten og dens kritikere*, ed. Søren Kaj Andersen (København: Djøf Forlag, 2017), 347-362.
81 Niklas Olsen, *The Sovereign Consumer: A New Intellectual History of Neoliberalism* (Palgrave Macmillan, 2018). Bertel Haarder, *Den bløde kynisme* (København: Gyldendal, 1997).
82 Ove K. Pedersen, *Konkurrencestaten* (København: Hans Reitzels Forlag, 2011).
83 Jørn Henrik Petersen, *Pligt &ret – Ret & pligt. Refleksioner over den socialdemokratiske idéarv* (Odense: Syddansk Universitetsforlag, 2014).

The Worker

Mobilized by the New Left and the Ultra-Liberal Right to Challenge the Social Democratic Welfare State

Margit Bech Vilstrup

The Danish Social Democratic Party was established in the 1870s. The party provided an identity, a political goal, a voice as well as hope for a better life in the future for the new group of wage earners that emerged as a result of the nineteenth century industrialization and urbanization. Central to the socialistic project was the need to rally voters and professional activists around the concept of "the worker" – that is to say, the idea of the worker as an assetless male wage worker within the supply chain of production, who was organized in a labour union and who was class conscious and visualized himself as being adversarial to the employers. From the end of the 1870s, the growing workers' movement gave rise to the worker as a leading dominant force in its fight for social reforms. According to Social Democratic ideology, following the mantra "Work is the source of all value and the profits of work should, therefore, accrue to the worker," the future was to be created by and for the worker.[1]

---

1   *Program og Love for det Socialdemokratiske Arbejderparti*, 1876.

In this way, the worker became a core concept in the Social Democratic anti-capitalist production discourse from the 1870s to the 1930s. But as the party gradually shifted its focus from the production sphere and the fight against capitalism to a social reform policy in the heyday of the welfare state from the 1950s and on, the party stopped using "the worker" as the key concept for unity and action. Meanwhile, the fight for the worker continued outside of the Social Democratic Party.

Subsequent to the 1960s, there was a new openness for alternative interpretations of the worker as a key figure in Danish society. The so-called "new left", which became the label for the different non-communist left wing movements, which emerged around the youth and student movements, revitalized the Marxist class theory by reintroducing concepts like "class struggle" and the "working class". By ascribing a revolutionary force to the worker, the new left encouraged new groups to join the fight against the suppression of capitalism. Especially large contingents of the party Venstresocialisterne (The Left Wing Socialists, VS) wrote long analyses about the need for an "awakening" of the "working class" (understood as wage workers employed in manual production), so that it could assume its proper role in the fight for a socialist society. Within certain segments of VS, this resulted in a radicalization and militarization of the concept of the worker, which had not previously dominated the Danish political debate.

Parallel to this – and in response to this leftist radicalization – Mogens Glistrup and his newly established ultra-liberal party, Fremskridtspartiet (The Progress Party), gained success by establishing a strong discourse for workers in a clash with the growing welfare state. Glistrup portrayed "the worker" as a figure that, in contrast to "the ruling class" of the public employee bureaucrats of the welfare state, represented the productive segment of the population with their specific values, such as diligence and initiative.

A common feature of the two positions – the socialistic one and that of The Progress Party – was that the "worker" was reduced to an individual who performs productive or physical labour. But whereas VS defined their "worker" in classical Marxist terms as being in contrast to the capitalist or the employer, Glistrup's "worker" became associated in a positive way with the employer through the concept of "the working class." He descibed/defined "the working class" in contrast to the large groups of bureaucrats and other public employees to which re refferes as "the ruling class."

This chapter describes the genesis and characteristics of the two new worker discourses. The purpose is to provide a new perspective on the period 1965-1990, in which a number of political concepts and figures were re-articulated, re-ideologized and mobilized to challenge and reshape the traditional Social Democratic welfare state.[2]

The Social Democratic Worker in the Time of the Welfare State

"The worker" has been a core concept in political struggles ever since the end of the eighteenth century when it appeared as a reference to a social group with political, revolutionary and transformational potential. In the final decades of the nineteenth century, "the worker" became increasingly synonymous with "the socialistic worker" as described above.[3]

The basis for this development was the new large group of wage workers emerging in the manual labour and manufacturing industries with the breakthrough of industrialization in Denmark and which the Danish contingent of the Internationale tried to organize from its start in 1871. The period between the mid-1890s to the First World War was characterized by a strong expansion of industrialized production, continuous mechanization and new faith in development and change. The expanding workers" movement gave "the worker" a central role at the time as being a crucial and decisive participant in the creation of the future society and socialists in Denmark as in all of Europe applauded the "historic role" of the workers and the proletariat.[4]

The vocabulary surrounding the concept of "the worker" was enormous. Not only in the upper echelons dealing with the policy making and organization of the Social Democratic movement, but also with reference to the more domestic relations at home and the question of what it meant to be a human being. "worker" became both a common concept internally in the movement and a political tenet that was meant to externally

---

2   The following analysis is based on Margit Bech Vilstrup, *Kampen om arbejderne* (København: SFAH, 2019).
3   Niels Finn Christiansen, "Arbejderbegrebet i historisk lys – en skitse," *Arbejderhistorie*, no. 2 (2012): 1-13.
4   *Program for Socialdemokratiet i Danmark*, 1913.

demonstrate the Social Democrats' power over blue collar wage earner labourers.⁵

In the party newspaper *Social-Demokraten* (The Social Democrat), which in the 1920s and 1930s had grown to become one of the nations' biggest daily newspapers with circulation totals between 45,000-50,000 newspapers, one could read about everything from "the workers' Theatre" to "the workers' Folk High School" and the "workers' Ball-Playing Union," as well as find ads for "the workers' Co-op Shoe Factory" or "the workers' Common Bakery." One could find a new home in "the workers' Cooperative Housing Association" – a life-insurance in "the workers' Life Insurance Program" and end the life in a coffin from "the workers' Coffin Makers."⁶ Social Democratic ideologists published books about "workers' culture," "workers' Parties" and "workers' Poetry" associated with "workers' democracy."⁷ The party's cultural trailblazer, Julius Bomholt, wrote about "the workers' street," "the workers' homes," "children of workers," "worker youth," and "working people." He emphasized that one could perceive the world from a "worker's perspective" and he referred to "the industrial worker's life".⁸

This fundamental conception of the socialistic worker peaked during the 1920s and 1930s as the Social Democrats grew increasingly powerful. At the same time, however, they shifted their focus from being a "worker's party" to being a "people's party." This was established by, among other things, the publication of the party manifesto *Danmark for folket* (Denmark for the People) from 1934.

It was a change that escalated after the Second World War. The development of the industrialized society led to a new business structure, a shift in gender roles, the emergence of a welfare state, an increase in the basic

---

5 In this article I will refer to the wage earners in manual production as "blue collar workers". I do this to make a destinction between the political uses of the concept or idea of "the worker" and speaking in more general terms of what would in Danish statistical definitions be directly translated into "skilled and unskilled wage workers". I choose here the more common british term "blue collar worker" to underline the relation to wage workers in manual production. For a definition on "blue collar workers" see https://www.encyclopedia.com/social-sciences/applied-and-social-sciences-magazines/blue-collar-and-white-collar (accessed October 19, 2020).
6 *Social-Demokraten* September 19, 1926, *Social-Demokraten* April 6, 1930 and May 1 1938.
7 See Julius Bomholt, *Arbejderkultur* (København: Forlaget Fremad, 1932) and Christian Christiansen, *Arbejderfester: Haandbog for Foreninger* (København: Forlaget Fremad, 1932).
8 Julius Bomholt, "Kulturpolitik," in *Danmark for Folket: En Materialesamling til Brug i Oplysningsarbejdet* (Købehavn: AOF, 1936), 99-107.

standard of living and a new mass culture. These factors all contributed to a change in perspective for the Social Democratic Party, which completely stopped articulating "the workers'" culture" as an independent counter culture. Instead, the Social Democrats attempted to consolidate themselves as a broad people's party and within the ideological language, which developed over the coming decades, the historically and politically loaded concept of "the worker" was no longer considered a central political figure, but was replaced by new categories like "wage worker" and "employede" or broader notions of what it meant to be "human" or "the people". The worker did not disappear from the language but changed to a different status, from an ideological to a statistical category in which it was transformed into a more passive, neutral word. "The worker" became a functionary description for those working in manual production and no longer denoted the core of the social class that was to lead the way to the socialistic society.

There was not only talk of a new kind of rhetoric – but also a new ideology in which the former class-based policy of the Social Democrats was in a broad sense replaced by a social humanism that formed the basis for the welfare state. For the great, old workers' party, it was, from the 1950s on, no longer a question of the historic role of the working class in the encounter with capitalism. Workers, farmers, fishermen, carpenters, entrepreneurs were now joined together in their shared humanity. The anchoring in the production sphere, which had been inherited from Karl Marx, had been replaced by an existential, identity-related commonality based on notions of nation, democracy and society.[9] In 1952, the notion of the "worker" was for the first time not mentioned at all in a Social Democratic political program or manifesto. Now the Social Democrats appealed definitively to "the population", to "the human being" or to "the citizen" when democratic socialism was to be put into effect.[10]

The transformations in the Social Democrats' self-perception as a worker's party coincided, as mentioned before, with the great transformation of social and economic structures in the Danish society subsequent

---

9   Socialdemokratiet, *Fremtidens Danmark* (1945); Socialdemokratiet, *Vejen til fremskridt* (Arbejdsprogram, 1953); Socialdemokratiet, *Vejen Frem* (Principprogram, 1961). See also Niels Ole Finnemann, *I broderskabets aand. Den socialdemokratiske arbejderbevægelses idéhistorie 1871-1977* (København: Gyldendal, 1985), 308.
10 See Socialdemokratiet, *Frihed, arbejde og tryghed*, (Arbejdsprogram, 1952).

to the Second World War. The new middle classes of white-collar workers and small self-employed came to play a more dominant societal role concurrently with the growth of the public sector and the development of the industrial society. From 1950-1970 the number of employees within administration and public service rose from 190,000 to 475,000 (from 9.8 percent to 20.5 percent).[11]

The transition from an industrialized society in which the majority of the people were employed in primary and secondary occupations to a service society in which services in the tertiary sector became the largest occupational group naturally left its mark on a party like that of the Social Democrats whose wish was to be all-encompassing.

"The workers" were in Social Democratic language no longer first and foremost actors in the class struggle – they had now entered into a collaboration with the "labour market's" other participants in order to secure productivity. And where the semantic field, which characterized the political line of the Social Democrats in the decades around the year 1900, was based on words like revolution, fight, class, etc., from the 1950s on it changed into words like "administration", "planning" and "education" and was connected to expressions such as "the individual's personal development", "increased welfare", "full employment," "practical consumer policy" and "freer competition." Within these frameworks, it was possible to refer to "the workers" political role – namely as a figure contributing to the increase in productivity which was to ensure the welfare state that was in the pipeline.

The rhetorical shift on the part of the Social Democrats from "worker" to "people" to "human" reflected an ideological change within the party that demonstrated a fundamental re-orientation of the consciousness in large segments of society due to improved welfare where the basic struggle no longer revolved around fighting poverty and scarce resources, but rather having a right to enjoy the fruits of an expanding economy.[12]

At the same time, new political players emerged to take over the concept of "the workers" from the Social Democrats. This included, among others, the party Venstre (The Liberal Party), which from the end of the 1950s

11   Svend Aage Hansen and Ingrid Henriksen, *Dansk Socialhistorie 7: Velfærdsstaten 1940-1978* (København: Gyldendal, 1980), 121.
12   Finnemann, *I broderskabets aand*.

very actively sought to organize blue collar workers and the urban voters in general as the party's previous core voters in the countryside diminished.[13] But whereas the The Liberal Party's interest was transient, the "new left" and The Progress Party came to play a crucial role in the reactualization of "the worker" as a political figure in the 1970s.

The Worker of the New Left

The new left covered various left-wing oriented movements, groups and parties, which, all across Europe and the US during the late 1950s, positioned themselves to the left of the Social Democrats, yet at the same time were independent of the Moscow-oriented communist parties. Toward the end of the 1960s, parts of their movement became more radicalized because of the circumstances of American warfare in Vietnam. It was this young postwar generation that took the lead in challenging established society.

The development of the welfare state and the general increase in income had opened the gates for a liberation of youth, which was now demanding more personal freedom and the abolishment of family-oriented and patriarchal control.[14] New areas of social and private life were being politicized. "Hippies", "squatters" and "Marxist students" combined in new political groupings and popular movements, working against the nuclear bomb, the Vietnam War and capitalism and for experimental family structures, anti-militarism and euphoriants.

Many of these left-wing groups managed to integrate the concept of "the worker" as a central element in their political rhetoric. But there were also great divisions. Allied with Marxist-Leninist inspired scholars, traditional industry workers often found themselves in opposition to flower children and hippies, who did not consider the working class to possess any great revolutionary potential.[15] To some, "the workers'"were the only

---

13 See Vilstrup *Kampen om*, 212-230.
14 Morten Bendix Andersen & Niklas Olsen, eds., *1968: dengang og nu* (København: Museum Tusculanum Press, 2004). Steven L. B. Jensen & Thomas Ekman Jørgensen, *1968 – og det der fulgte – Studenteroprørets forudsætninger og konsekvenser* (København: Gyldendal, 2008).
15 Jens Otto Madsen & Per Askholm Madsen, *Fra sandkasse til kadreparti? VS' dannelse og udvikling 1967-73* (København: VS-Forlaget, 1980). Albert Jensen, "Venstresocialisterne (VS)," *Leksikon for 21. århundrede*, accessed July 20, 2017, https://www.leksikon.org/art.php?n=2742.

true bearers of the socialistic revolution and the only ones who could carry it through. To others, the so-called "bourgeoisified workers' were not radical enough.

Especially the party Venstresocialisterne (VS), which was established in 1967 after they broke away from Socialistisk Folkeparti (The Socialist People's Party, SF), came to be a driving force in the rearticulation of "the worker" as a central political figure. The party consisted of a broad range of former members of SF, left-wing Social Democrats, anarchists, Troskyists, Maoists, undogmatic socialists, flower children, independents, people from the anti-nuclear movement, the peace movement and the anti-imperial movements and the party was split in a number of factions which were constantly in intense battle with one another.[16]

The dispute over who "the workers" were and what role they were to play in the fight against capitalism can be seen in the very diverse programmatic platform produced by VS that reflected which faction assumed power at the party's often chaotic national conferences and in its governing body. In VS's party program from 1969, the "wage worker" (*lønarbejder*) was listed as a central figure. It was understood in the traditional Marxist sense as being part of the wage-worker class (*lønarbejderklasse*), who was "forced" to sell its manpower to "capitalism." "Force," "incapacitation," "exploitation," "powerlessness" and "alienation" became the discursive frame for the wage worker.[17] The wage-worker class included both blue and white collar workers and any attempt to exclude the salaried employees from the class was referred to as a "false distinction". According to the 1969 agenda, "Salaried employees (*funktionærer*) are also wage slaves who are subject to the same powerlessness and insecurity as manual labourers."[18]

When VS in its manifesto from 1969 portrayed the various wage – worker groups as a united front, this was justified as part of the "proletarianization", which the party thought was taking place in all areas of society. According to VS, the large increase in the number of service employees meant that not everyone could expect to be employed in managerial positions "on the side of those in power." Instead, the salaried employees would become "highly educated specialized wage slaves." An increasing amount

16 Jensen, "Venstresocialisterne (VS)."
17 *Programskrift for Venstresocialisterne*, 1969 (Principprogram vedtaget på 2. kongres 2.-4. maj 1969).
18 *Programskrift for Venstresocialisterne*.

of university students would also come to "discover their shared interest with manual labourers." The goal for VS was to create a sense of solidarity between these groups of wage workers and to "work on encouraging them to rise up against capitalism." For "the only power that can manage to push capitalism back are the exploited workers themselves."[19] Through a political activism that stemmed from below (at the work place, in political movements and through consumerism), the goal was to make wage workers aware of their power and ultimately organize themselves in a collective fight against capitalism. It was "the close combat" at the work places and in education that was to "open the wage workers' eyes to the great fight against capitalistic suppression," it said in the manifesto. And with the requirement of "activity from below", VS considered the old labour union associated with Landsorganizationen i Danmark (LO) (Danish Confederation of Trade Unions) to be an outdated and anti-revolutionary structure.

The manifesto from 1969 should be seen as a compromise – an attempt to create some sense of direction in the young but already disjointed party.[20] The factions within VS were expressed more clearly in the manifesto agreed on at the party's fourth congress in December 1971, and it was also reflected in a radically new interpretation of "the worker" as a key figure. The proposal for the manifesto had been prepared by the so-called Leninist faction, which won the majority of votes at the congress. An important innovation in relation to the agenda from 1969 was in the class analysis in which the faction, whose point of departure had been classical Marxism and Leninism, broke away from the notion of a "broad wage-worker class." In the new manifesto, the efforts supporting a socialistic revolution were given priority and it was a much narrower "working class" that was to lead this battle. The working class was defined in relation to the capitalist class, the petit-bourgeousie/small manufacturers, office and commerce workers, the technicians, as well as the government's so-called ideological and social servants, also known as the "system's repairers."[21] More specifically, the "working class" was seen mostly as "industrial and transportation workers", who, due to the "the suppression by the ruling [capitalistic]

19   *Programskrift for Venstresocialisterne.*
20   Madsen & Madsen, *Fra sandkasse*, 158.
21   *Venstresocialisternes program,* adopted on the Fourth Congress December 12, 1971. Reprinted in *VS-bulletin,* special issue, March 4, 1972.

classes' had had "a number of particularly brutal experiences", wich distinguished them from, for example, technicians, service employees and academic scholars. And which made them "less susceptible to the pacifist, bourgeoisie democratic ideology."[22]

According to the Leninist faction, the fact that it was "industrial and transportation workers", who had historically played a leading role in the wage workers' battle, was due neither to poverty nor hard work itself. Instead, the crucial factor had been the specific conditions for fighting and organizing which their position in the capitalistic production process had led to. For one thing, the concentration of capital in the big cities resulted in a group of industrial workers with equal living conditions and shared experiences there. This created the foundation for solidarity and raising political awareness among workers. For another, their "collective and disciplined form of work" created a certain ability for collective action and organization as being the "only way" in which one could defend one's interests. According to VS, the form of work in itself contributed to a removal of competition between industrial and transportation workers and instead incited them to fight as a class with a strong sense of class consciousness. To this narrowly defined group, the following applied: "It is able as the only class to act as a strong, leading and unifying force that has as its historic mission the abolition of the conditions of its own exploitation and thereby eliminate the last remaining class society."[23]

With this manifesto, in line with early socialistic thinking, VS attempted to reinstate the "worker" as the driving force behind the making of the future. Inspired by the Marxist theories regarding the collapse of capitalism, the "working class" (here in the narrow definition with reference to the industrial and transportation workers) was assigned the "historical task" of being in the front line in the fight for a socialistic, classless society. At the same time, a number of wage workers were marginalized from "the working class." This included, among others, the office and commerce employees and technical staff, which were compared with "the productive workers" and which, according to VS, were less inclined to acknowledge and act on the specific form of exploitation to which they were subjugated.

---

22   *Venstresocialisternes program, 1971.*
23   Ibid.

They were ranked together with the remaining service employees in an "intermediate stratum between the working class and the capitalist class."[24]

At the VS congress in December 1972, the party dispersed into atoms as several factions left it – including the Leninist faction. All that was left was the faction "Group 1" which came to lead the party forward and, during the congress of 1972, a manifesto was agreed upon that referred back to the manifesto of 1969. The broad concept of the wage worker was once again given centre stage and there was no mention of the delimitation of the various groups of wage workers or armed rebellions.[25]

But VS remained divided as to the question of whether they should pursue a pacifistic or an armed revolutionary strategy and what the role of the working class should be therein – and in the following years, there were several examples indicating the aim of "the development of a unified fighting militant working class" on the part of VS. That was, among other things, the case in the Workplace and Union Resolution which was agreed on at VS's eleventh congress in November 1980.[26] In this, the "working class's" leading role in "the transformation of society and the power struggle with the bourgeoisie" was once again emphasized.

Again, there was talk of the narrow working class consisting of wage workers in the industrial and transportation industries which, by way of its alleged "class consciousness" and "class solidarity", was to lead the way in the abolishment of "the societal power of capital and the bourgeoisie state apparatus."[27] Here, VS took up militant language, which had not been associated with the notion of the worker in Denmark since 1917-20, around the time of the Russian Revolution. Quotes like "the development of a unified militant working class" and "the armed clashes of the classes and the workers' revolutionary dictatorship" intimated a strong radicalization of the worker concept, which had up until now mostly taken place in syndicalist groups that had emerged from the far left in the years around the First World War.

---

24 Ibid.
25 *Program for Venstresocialisterne* (December 1972).
26 "VS Arbejdsplads- og Fagforeningsresolution", (vedtaget på 11. kongres november 1980), accessed July 20, 2017, https://www.leksikon.org/art.php?n=3740.
27 "VS Arbejdsplads- og Fagforeningsresolution."

The discussions with regard to both the demarcation of the working class and its role in the path toward socialism continued to be a central source of divisiveness. VS's overall goal was, basically for the entire period, a "mass organization of the Danish wage–worker class' through awareness and activism from below.[28] However, VS did not become a great success with the old working class of blue collar workers. Already after VS's first congress in 1968, large segments of the employees in manual production had left the party. While in the party's first temporary national committee, 50% consisted of wage workers with a vocational background, the percentage fell in the new national committee of 1968 to 20%. The many theoretical discussions that took place in VS quickly resulted in a loss of members from the traditional working class and the party's vocational policy was designated as practically catastrophic. The attempt to make LO a main enemy of the wage worker in a showdown deteriorated into the so-called "petrification" of the unions and "a misrepresentative system."[29]

At the same time, a rhetoric much more adverse to the blue collar workers was emerging in segments of VS's so-called "flower children."[30] Inspired by the German theorist Herbert Marcuse, the traditional working class consisting of skilled and unskilled workers in manual labour was perceived as having been bourgeoisified and integrated into the capitalist system. In the Danish journal *Kommunikation* (Communication), thoughts such as these had a breakthrough in the course of the spring and summer of 1968. Here, anarchists and "flower children" wrote about the "vegetating" and "authoritarian" working class, "souls of slaves" marked by political "apathy" and "the idolization of status symbols."[31] The articles led to big internal unrest in VS during the summer of 1968, resulting in two of the party's four members of the Danish parliament, i.e. the writer Kaj Moltke and the social worker Hanne Reintoft, along with a large segment of VS's traditional blue collar workers, leaving the party.[32]

---

28 See *Kongresvedtagelse om programarbejdet*, fra VS' 3. kongres. Reprinted in *VS/Bulletin*, no. 56 (November 24, 1970).
29 Erik Christensen, *Arbejderpartiernes faglige politik i 1970'erne* (København: Lindhardt og Ringhof, 1981).
30 Member of parliament from VS Kaj Moltke, in Madsen & Madsen, *Fra sandkasse*, 106.
31 Madsen & Madsen, *Fra sandkasse*, 105-106.
32 Ibid. 108-109.

Even though VS obtained the support of a number of skilled and unskilled workers in manual labour again at the end of the 1970s, when the party rent considerable support to strikers in several of the big labour conflicts of the time, the party remained both in its leadership and in general among party-members dominated by teachers, students and other so-called middle class groups.[33] In the parliamentary election of 1987, VS was voted out and never returned as an independent party. The party was worn out as a result of nearly 20 years of intense power struggles and the fact that the spirit of the times had changed – resulting in fewer labour market conflicts and a decline in left-wing movement activities in general.

VS's greatest success lay perhaps in the strong position, which the party gained in the great grassroots and left-wing movements in the 1970s and 1980s regarding issues such as international solidarity and the anti-nuclear bomb movement. From VS arose also a range of cultural initiatives aiming to create an "alternative culture" to the established so-called bourgeoisie culture. Even though the driving force behind this work – both on a theoretical and a practical level – continued to be carried out by scholars, university students and others from the middle class, the blue collar worker and the "working class" in the narrow sense (consisting of wage workers in manual labour) were the ideal and the ultimate unifying concepts.

The academic and cultural "tendency to cling" to "the worker" has been referred to as a kind of "alternative tourism."[34] It was the well-educated left wing that through its examination of Marx had learned that the working class had been the driving force of history and was now taking the lead in a leftist-radical worker-discourse. But even though fruitful collaboration could arise between the two groups in regard to political activities and the "wild strikes" of the time, the blue collar workers tended to distance themselves in organizational work from what they referred to as the "empty university talking and writing things to death."[35]

---

33 In 1971, 35 percent of the party members were students, 30 percent academics and other middle class groups, while only 16 percent came from the working class. Jensen, *Venstresocialisterne*. Madsen & Madsen, *Fra sandkasse*, 351-356 analyses VS' member and voter base.
34 See Erik Svendsen et al., *Dansk litteraturs historie vol. 5: 1960-2000* (København: Gyldendal, 2007), 319-320, and Benthe Østrup Madsen, *Du er ikke alene, kammerat: Seks uger af en lønarbejders liv* (København: Forlaget Tiden, 1982).
35 Written about the SK magazine *Skub* – "But it was expensive and quickly turned heavy and sincerely sad" … "Theory and nothing but theory. So died the magazine. And we workers were rarely heard

Even though the new radical left wing, that had emerged from the student protest of the spring of 1968, never became a serious success amongst voters, it could in the 1970s and in the beginning of the 1980s rally thousands of people to meetings, island camps and festivals all over the country.³⁶ Through this popular organization, "the new left" managed to maintain a strong socialistic worker discourse in the debates of the time.

'Workerism" and the idealization of the working class was so great that a number of students dropped out of university to take up unskilled work in order to become "proletarized" and thereby is members of the revolutionary class. And there can be no doubt that the many new left-wing groups and parties reinstated the socialistic "worker" on the agenda once again in the 1970s and 1980s after the concept had had a quiet political existence in the years after the Second World War. At the same time, VS's manifesto from 1971 represented some of Danish socialism's most detailed theoretical reflections on who "the working class" were and what particular role that class played in the developments toward a socialistic society.

The Worker Against the Elite

During the period of improved welfare in the 1960s, many blue collar workers had climbed up the social ladder. They could now afford material goods such as a house and a car and the collective identity and culture which had been strong due to the shared living conditions in the lower classes of society had been eradicated.³⁷ Large segments of the LO-organized workers (blue collar workers) no longer felt a natural affiliation with the Social Democrats and certainly not with the academic left wing surrounding VS. At the same time, the explosive growth of the welfare state throughout the 1960s and 1970s paved the way for a resistance to bureaucracy and expanded tax obligations.³⁸

---

so that all empty academic talkativeness and writing itch could be humanized" – Letter July 1981 by "worker" Gustav Christiansen. Printed in Anne Friis-Jensen, *Litteraturens afprofessionalisering* (Aarhus, Institut for Nordisk sprog og litteratur, 1982), 61.
36   See Olav Harsløf & Thomas Kruse, *Røde Mor* (København: Systime, 2004), 12.
37   See Torben Worre, *Dansk vælgeradfærd* (København: Akademisk forlag, 1987), 95-97.
38   For a more in-depth examiniation of the welfare state criticism see Klaus Petersen, Niels Finn Christiansen & Jørn Henrik Petersen, eds., *Dansk Velfærdshistorie IV: Velfærdsstatens storhedstid* (Odense: Syddansk Universitetsforlag, 2012), 147-162.

In the parliamentary election of December 1973, the Danish political system was shaken to its core. The "landslide election", as it was referred to, contributed to a radical change in Danish politics. The number of parties was doubled from 5 to 10. Forty-four % of the voters changed party and a third of the members of Parliament were replaced.[39] The landslide election's greatest victor was the ultra-liberal Progress Party's controversial and charismatic leader Mogens Glistrup, who was almost the sole face of the party in the first period. In 1971, he immediately gained national attention when he revealed on TV that he did not pay income tax and compared tax cheaters with railway saboteurs during the Nazi occupation. In the following years, he made a virtue of declaring his opposition to the state, bureaucracy and centralization and through his provocative and anarchistic style he became an icon for the showdown with the "system." The leader of The Progress Party took pride in the fact that the party (in his own words) was not "mossy" (*mosbegroede*), as opposed to the other "old parties" (*gammelpartier*), but pursued a politics for the "modern Dane" without considering historical traditions and alliances.[40] Through the election of 1973, the party obtained great success and became the second largest party in the Parliament with 28 mandates.

"The worker" came to play a central role in The Progress Party's communication in the 1970s and posed the first real challenge to what was referred to as, "The Social Democratic hegemony over the masses of the working class." [41] Glistrup's new party targeted the wage workers in manual labour, who to a much greater extent felt a sense of commonality with their employers at the workshop than with the employees and academic scholars working in the public sector. Many of the party's voters were blue collar workers. Voter surveys from the parliamentary elections of 1973 and 1975 revealed that during both elections, The Progress Party constituted the second largest "worker's party," only surpassed by the Social Democrats. Up to 20% of the traditional working class supported The Progress Party and approximately 35% of the party's voters were of wage workers in manual

---

39 See Peter Yding Brunbech, "Jordskredsvalget 1973", *Danmarkshistorien*, accessed August 11, 2017, http://danmarkshistorien.dk/leksikon-og-kilder/vis/materiale/jordskredsvalget-1973/.
40 Fremskridtspartiet, *Kildeskatten løber løbsk* (Fremskridtspartiet pamphlet, undated. Most likely autumn 1973) and Poul Møller, *De politiske partier* (Albertslund: Det danske forlag, 1974). 27-30.
41 Johannes Andersen, *Fremskridtsbevægelsen, arbejderklassen og venstrefløjen* (København: Forlaget Aurora, 1977), 33.

labour. The voters came first and foremost from the Social Democrats. It was the low-paid and unskilled workers and, even more worrisome to the Social Democrats, the younger voters, who were changing parties. Among the age groups of 20-35, The Progress Party was the preferred party for blue collar workers in the elections of 1973 and 1975.[42]

The concept of "the worker" became in The Progress Party's terminology associated with the party's rebellion against the welfare state represented by the so-called "ruling class" of public employees and academic scholars. In that sense, it very directly attempted to disconnect "the workers'"from all socialistic connotations: "The definition of a worker today has completely changed in relation to the definition that existed at the end of the last century in Engel's and Marx's time," wrote Kjeld Wamberg, one of the central party ideologists for The Progress Party. Even though, according to Wamberg, the parties of the left wing and the labour unions "desperately" tried to uphold "the illusion" that there continued to exist a class division between "the exploited, oppressed workers on the one side and the profit-seeking exploiters on the other," then it ought to be crystal clear to everyone that the real division in the population lay:

> between the productive part of the population and the swelling, barren, unproductive public administration in every segment, between the private job market we all have to live off and the rampant, to a large extent, expendable public sector, the ruling class, that wish to preside over everyone and everything.[43]

The attempt to dissolve the division between employer and employee was not new.[44] However, what was new was that, in the rhetoric of The

---

42 Ibid. 26.
43 Member of Parliament Kjeld Wamberg's article "Det klasseløse parti" from the magazine *Fremskridt* 21 (1976). A few months earlier, Mogens Glistrup almost identicaly wrote: "Socialists and petrified foremen have a hard time accepting Fremskridstpartiet as a worker's party. They behave as if they lived in the years of Karl Marx. Then, the deep divisions between the classes were between employers and workers. Now, society is torn between the productive making a useful product and the scroungers in the rulling class." *Fremskridt* 17 (1976), 4.
44 Fremskridtspartiet had an ambivalent view on the "workers" relation to the "employer". On one hand, Fremskridspartiet recognized the need for unions to balance the relation to the employer. On the other, the employer and worker allied against "the rulling class" of public servants and academics.

Progress Party, the "worker" was brought into a dichotomy between "the working class" consisting of employees together with employers and then the "ruling class of scholars ranging from administrative technocrats to the cultural elite and embracing a circle of know-alls in the remaining expendable social and educational apparatus."[45] It was The Progress Party's fight against what was perceived to be the Social Democratic state that became the driving force in their usage of the worker concept. "The workers" were "those who were productive" in private businesses.[46] They were people who yielded a piece of concrete craftsmanlike work – industrial workers, carpenters, fishermen, farmers, etc. They were the ones who produced products and services for which, according to The Progress Party, there was a "natural human need," a demarcation which was not further defined.

This "working class" was in opposition to "those who were unproductive" – the so-called vociferous theorists and anti-societal and work-reluctant service employees in the public sector with their "nonsensical organizing," "planned economical quackeries" and "barren administration work."[47] The opposition between the productive work and the "barren unproductive work" (a concept that was repeated in many of The Progress Party's writings) became central.[48] It was a showdown between "on the one hand those who work and have to make an effort to earn a living and on the other hand the ruling class who, without having to make any particular productive effort of their own, live high off the hog, picking the fruits of the working classes."[49]

Glistrup articulated the new thoughts harboured by many Danes after the abundant disbursement due to the welfare revolution of the 1960s. And his confrontation with the growing group of wage workers in the public sector struck at the heart of the simmering frustration among many a blue collar worker. Glistrup wrote: "There is a chasm that divides the good worker from the wealth of meaningless circulars and law enactments that

---

45 *Fremskridt* 17 (1976), 1.
46 The concept "The Productive" was used about sectors, companies and actors.
47 From the party platform "Det vil vi i Fremskridtspartiet", compilation of quotes from the partyplatform in 1974 and 1976.
48 See Fremskridtspartiet, *Kildeskatten*.
49 Socialdemokratiet, *Sådan vil Socialdemokratiet nedbryde Danmark* (Fremskridtspartiets faglige gruppe, 1977).

have emerged."⁵⁰ Although the "worker" had obtained both a house and a car and a safety net, some were struggling to find themselves in a continually growing public sector.

The success of The Progressive Party has been seen as an indication of an intensified dichotomy between the private, productive sector and the public, administrative and decision-making sector.⁵¹ In the early 1970s, there was increasing talk of a welfare crisis and Glistrup and The Progress Party would neither be the first nor only ones to voice their criticism of the growing public sector.⁵² More or less simultaneously with the founding of The Progress Party, the national economist and retired professor of social politics, Jørgen S. Dich, published the highly debated book *Den herskende klasse* (The Ruling Class) that criticized what he perceived to be the uncontrollable and self-perpetuating growth of the public sector in what at the time was a completely unheard of criticism of the welfare state from within the social democrats' own ranks.⁵³

Dich, too, wrote about a "new ruling class," namely in the form of "the service class" of academic scholars, bureaucrats, experts, pedagogues, school teachers and social workers, etc.⁵⁴ Dich criticized the lack of plans for how the growing welfare system was to be monitored and he wrote about how the increasing group of employees in the welfare sector had developed great special interests that, it appeared, were able to expand the workings and scope of the welfare sector and send its expenditure soaring to such an extent that Dich characterized it as social exploitation of the rest of the population, whose taxes were financing the public administration. "The politicians are so thriftless with the average man's money," as he wrote.⁵⁵ Dich did not care much for the Marxist student movement

---

50   *Brev til fhv. finansminister Poul Møller* July 31, 1973. Glistrup sents an article about Fremskridtspartiet to *De politiske partier* (KB-samling partiprogrammer).
51   Klaus Petersen, Niels Finn Christiansen and Jørn Henrik Petersen, eds., *Dansk Velfærdshistorie V: Velfærdsstaten i tidehverv* (Odense: Syddansk Universitetsforlag, 2013), 80.
52   For an analysis of the challenges facing the welfare stat in the 1970s, see Niklas Olsen, "Velfærdsstatens krise og neoliberalismens indtog i Danmark i 1970'erne," *Slagmark*, 74 (2016): 119-137.
53   Dich had already presented his arguments in the chronicle "The Rulling Class" in *Politiken* June 6, 1971. Dich regretted that his book was published immediately before the election where Fremskridtspartiet gained 28 mandates in the parliament. There was no alliance between the two critics of the welfare state. Petersen, Christiansen and Petersen, *Dansk Velfærdshistorie*, 82, note 10.
54   "In the later years and with almost revolutionary pace the service class have become the rulling class", in Jørgen S. Dich, *Den herskende klasse: En kritisk analyze af social udbytning og midlerne imod den* (København: Borgen, 1973), 108.
55   Dich, *Den herskende klasse*, 103.

either. To him, the university Marxists reflected precisely the unhealthy contempt that the middle classes had for the status of "physical labour."[56]

Just like The Progress Party, Dich's simplified theory on class struggle placed the focus on some of the challenges that arose through the rapid and intense growth of the middle classes and the public sector. He, too, utilized the concept of "the worker" as an indicator of the new division of the classes at the time – not between employer and employee but between "the average man" performing "physical labour" and the new elite of administrators and opinion makers who held academic degrees.

The Progress Party's success began to shrink at the end of the 1970s and their language lost its provocative and colourful appeal. Talk of the "ruling class" disappeared completely and in the party manifesto of 1978, the word "worker" was mentioned only once and in a very neutral tone.[57] Except from one time in 1989, the party's manifesto publications contained absolutely no mention of "the worker" which was replaced with "wage earner" or "work force" from the 1980s on. During the course of the 1980s, the party never rose above 10% of the votes in parliamentary elections and Mogens Glistrup's imprisonment for tax evasion caused a massive defection of voters from the party in the 1984 election. At the same time, the party had become split due to internal debates about the extent to which they should remain a protest party or enter a serious parliamentary collaboration with the other parties.

In 1995, the party's leader then Pia Kjærsgaard left The Progress Party and established Dansk Folkeparti (The Danish People's Party), which again made the "worker" a central figure during the end of the 1990s. The Danish People's Party drew attention to the non-academic wage workers and after just a few years the party abandoned its initial strong liberalistic line in favour of a more nationalistic welfare-political strategy. Already at the start of the 2000s, The Danish People's Party claimed the title as Denmark's "workers' party."[58] Just like The Progress Party and Dich, The Danish People's Party attempted to paint a picture of an "ever growing distance between the elite and the rest of the population" and they often spoke of a conflict between the "politically correct elite" of latte-drinking academics

---

56   Ibid. 100.
57   *Det vil Fremskridtspartiet. For den personlige frihed.* ("Party program" 1978).
58   *TV-Avisen* February 23, 2002. "Pia K: Vi er det store arbejderparti," *Politiken*, May 2, 2003.

in Copenhagen in contrast to an underrated population in the provinces consisting of "ordinary people."[59] The party added a new dimension to the debate in its attempt to portray a division between the big city and the provinces.[60] The rhetoric of The Danish People's Party of a growing dichotomy between "the average worker", who feels the threat of a globalized job market and an increasingly automated production and a well-fed upper class of value-relativistic scholars in the big cities can be seen once again in the so-called populistic parties all over the world. From Donald Trump in the US to UKIP in Great Britain and Front National in France, the concept of "the worker" is articulated in an attempt to create support for a more nationalist and anti-immigrant policy and a focus on the class divisions allegedly characterizing a knowledge-based society.

Conclusion

"The worker" was without question one of the core figures of the welfare state. It was the working class's demand for a more equitable distribution of the wealth of society which through the Social Democrat's democratic socialism resulted in the establishment of the welfare state. And the Social Democratic Party created, from 1871 and half a century on, a mass movement based on the concept of "the worker", which was frequently used to provide an identity and a direction for the large groups of wage workers pressured by the ever expanding industrial society.

But the Social Democratic Party gradually changed their traditional Marxist class-based societal analysis to a broad social humanism which matched the structural occupational changes of the nineteenth century and the party's great project – the welfare state. And with the desire to establish a universal welfare state, it also became clear that the concept of "the worker" was too narrow a category for the Social Democratic Party's comprehensive project. "The worker" in the communication of the Social Democratic Party was first replaced with "the people" and later with even

---

59 See Pia Kjærsgaard's speeches at Dansk Folkeparti's conventions in 2013 and 2014.
60 See "Pia K: Vi er det store arbejderparti," *Politiken*, May 2, 2003; Magnus Ulveman & Kasper Kildegaard, "Pia Kjærsgaard: Danmark er ved at knække over og kan ende som to folk," *Berlingske Tidende*, August 13, 2016.

more vague concepts like "human," "the population" or categories geared toward the job market like "wage worker" and "employees".

In a time, when the Social Democratic Party had abandoned the concept of "the worker" as a central political category, new parties rediscovered its potential. Both to the right and to the left of the Social Democratic Party new groups, as for example VS and The Progress Party, saw great mobilization opportunities in speaking to and about "the worker."

Culturally, politically and economically there was a difference between the old wage worker in industry and manufacturing and the new wage workers, when, for example, school teachers, pedagogues, social workers and scholars began to emerge in the public debate. And even though many of these groups, which also developed a kind of wage – worker mentality in the course of the 1970s, began to organize themselves in proper labour unions and supported the socialistic "workers' parties", the two wage – worker groups never merged into one.[61] VS's many challenges in terms of organizing "the workers" they so intensely spoke of and for is an example of how differently the old and the new wage workers envisioned the road forward.

To many, the new left's eternal theoretical discussions and struggles between factions was an indication of precisely the kind of academicization that Glistrup taunted. "the workers" wanted action to be taken – not theoretical clarification. Despite this there were many similarities between The Progress Party and the new countercultures on the left wing. They were both influenced by what Norwegian historian Jan Martin Iversen has called the anti-establishment fight against the establishment and what were perceived as self-satisfied rulers.[62] Both The Progress Party and large segments of VS wanted to see a development outside of traditional parliamentarism in a confrontation with the "interventionist" state.[63]

An examination of the concept of the worker contributes in this way to an understanding of the development of the welfare state. The working class shaped the welfare state – and the rapid expansion of the welfare state

---

61   See Flemming Mikkelsen, *Radikaliseringen af de offentligt ansatte i Danmark* (København: SFAH, 1994); Arthur Arnheim, "Akademikerkonflikten i 1969," *Historie* 4, no. 13 (1981): 285-328.
62   Jan Martin Iversen, *Fra Anders Lange til Carl I Hagen: 25 år med Fremskrittspartiet* (Oslo: Forlaget Millenium/N.W. Damm & Søn, 1998).
63   *Fremskridtsbevægelsen*, 54. See also Olsen, "Velfærdsstatens krise."

through the second half of the nineteenth century at the same time affected the possibilities for organization based on the concept "the worker" and the general societal role of both skilled and unskilled workers in manual labour.

The period from 1965-90 has been categorized as an epoch, a bridge and an "Age of Fracture." [64] Such designations are indeed very appropriate when summing up the concept of "the worker" during these years. It was a time of change where, after the postwar era's political decline, there was a fracturing, rearticulation and reideologization of "the worker" and the "working class" and then, particularly after the 1980s, a new development in which these concepts lost their momentum due to the postmodern and neoliberal tendencies of the time.

---

64   Daniel T. Rodgers, *Age of Fracture* (Cambridge, Belknap Press, 2011).

The Mentally Ill

From Insane to User of Psychiatry

Marie Meier

> "The *State* lays down, or moulds by its policies, the basic human relationships, the organization of help and security, the utilisation of resources, the giving or withholding of rights. There is no guardianship or detention in mental hospitals without State powers. Whatever the therapy, an arbitrary element is present which derives in the last resort from the authority and demands of the State."[1]

As Karl Jaspers points out in his *General Psychopathology* (1913), "the mentally ill" are inseparably bound to state formation and its embedded and ambivalent power dynamics of care and control. However, the state should not be conceived as a static, unified force. The "will" of the state, which Jaspers also refers to[2], develops according to ideological shifts, technical

---

1   Karl Jaspers, *General Psychopathology vol. II* (London: The Johns Hopkins University Press, 1997), 792. [*Allgemeine Psychopathologie* (Berlin Heidelberg: Springer Verlag, 1959)].
2   In the English edition *ein Wille* has been translated into "an arbitrary element", which – I would argue – does not fully capture how *ein Wille* can be conceived as a kind of "social totality": "Die

developments and broader socio-economic structures, out of which process new notions of "the mentally ill" emerge.³ Historically, conceptions of "the mentally ill" citizen have been affected by several factors: questions of security and finance, views on gender and heredity and medical interventions in the field of psychiatry. The sum of these factors has formed certain dominant imaginaries of "the mentally ill", which have intersected with different national political agendas, legislation and changing practices in public healthcare institutions.

One domain in which such imaginaries can be detected is fiction. In this chapter, I use literature as a cultural testimony to trace three time-specific configurations of "the mentally ill" in the context of the developing Danish welfare state. As an empirical source, literature allows a different entry into the history of "the mentally ill". In order to probe historically situated encounters between "the mentally ill" citizen and the state's authorities, I focus on and compare the novels *Professor Hieronimus* (Amalie Skram, 1895), *Ansigterne* (The Faces) (Tove Ditlevsen, 1968) and *HHV, FRSHWN* (Hanne Højgaard Viemose, 2019). By reading selected passages from these three works, I trace the broader transitions from "the insane" to "the patient" to the current "user of psychiatry" that have taken place from the 1890s until today. Moreover, drawing on Gilles Deleuze's notion of "societies of control", I suggest that the overall development exposed and indirectly problematized by these works can be seen to correlate with a broader social transformation and to new kinds of subjectification processes in the welfare state.⁴

Several scholars have examined how literary works relate to welfare state discussions and developments[5] and to issues of health, illness and

---

Staatsmacht begründet oder formt durch ihre Politik die menschlichen Grundbeziehungen, die Organization der Hilfe, der Sicherung, der Nutzbarmachung, gibt rechte und versagt solche. Ohne Staatsmacht gibt es keine Entmündigung, keine Einweisung in geschlossene Anstalten. In jeder Praxis ist *ein Wille*, der sich zuletzt aus Staatlichen Bestätigungen unter Forderungen herleitet." (My italics).

3   Michel Foucault, *Madness and Civilization: A History of Insanity in the Age of Reason* (London: Routledge, 1967).
4   Gilles Deleuze, "Postscript on the Societies of Control," *October* 59 (1992): 3-7.
5   See e.g. Anne-Marie Mai, "The roles of writers in the Danish welfare state," *Forum for World Literature Studies* 4, no. 1, (2012): 86; Anne-Marie Mai, "Velfærdsstatsstudier: kort introduktion til et interdisciplinært skandinavisk forskningsfelt," *European Journal of Scandinavian Studies*, 43 no. 2 (2013): 200-202; Anne-Marie Mai, "Det muliges kunst og det umuliges politik," *TEMP - tidsskrift for historie*, 8 (2014): 65-79; Henrik Dahl and Niels Gunder Hansen, eds., *Velfærdsfortællinger* (Køben-

medicine more specifically.⁶ Indeed, as Peter Simonsen points out, there seems to be a renewed confidence in art and literature as a reliable source of knowledge in investigations of societal matters.⁷ Embedded in existing research on the relationship between literary representations and welfare state development is also the question of how a literary work can be political. On what terms are aesthetic works capable of contributing to political discussions about, for instance, welfare and well-being? Can literature be conceived independently from the context out of which it emerges? Do literary works operate in opposition to, or aligned with, a certain welfare state ideology?

Against this background, my endeavour here is informed by the analytical practice of new historicism and its conception of literature as a cultural poetic.⁸ New historicism is a literary analytical practice paying attention to and acknowledging the cultural and political powers of fiction.⁹ The claim of new historicism is that fiction and literature, as well as other kinds of historical documents, can provide insights into the socio-cultural agendas and social norms of a specific situated historical moment. Fiction always transmits and scrutinizes subjective human experiences, inevitably including reminiscences from the cultural context, the time and place in which it is produced. Thus, novels (like art in general) can be seen as a historical artefact, which I define as a *cultural testimony*, alongside archive material, white papers and other political documents.

---

havn: Gyldendal, 2010); Peter Simonsen, *Livslange liv: plejehjemsromaner og pensionsfortællinger fra velfærdsstaten* (Odense: Syddansk Universitetsforlag, 2014); Tue Andersen Nexø, *Vidnesbyrd fra velfærdsstaten: Den sociale vending i ny dansk litteratur* (København: Arena, 2016); Lasse Horne Kjældgaard, *Meningen med velfærdsstaten: Velfærdsstatsdebat og dansk litteratur 1950–1980* (Roskilde: Roskilde Universitet, 2017).

6   Anne-Marie Mai and Peter Simonsen, eds., *Syg litteratur: litterære tekster om sygdom og sundhedsvæsen* (København: Munksgaard, 2018); Anne-Marie Mai and Camilla Schwartz, "Fiction and Medicine," *Månedstidsskrift for Almen Praksis* 94 (2016): 6-7; Frederik Tygstrup and Knut Stene-Johansen, eds., *Illness in Context* (Amsterdam-New York: Rodopi, 2010); Katarina Bernhardsson, *Litterära Besvär* (Polen: Ellerstöms förlag, 2010); Hilde Bondevik and Knut Stene-Johansen, *Sygdom som litteratur* (Oslo: Unipub, 2011); Mikkel Krause Frantzen, *Going nowhere, slow: scenes of depression in contemporary literature and culture* (København: Københavns Universitet, 2017).
7   Simon Petersen, *Velværelsen: Ny humanistisk velfærdsforskning* (Odense: Syddansk Universitet, 2016).
8   Frederik Tygstrup and Isak Winkel Holm, "Cultural Poetics and The Politics of Literature," in *Ernst Cassirer on Form and Technology: Contemporary Reading*, eds. Aud Sissel Hoel and Ingvild Folkvord (London: Palgrave Macmillan, 2012), 199-213.
9   Louise Montrose, "The Poetics and Politics of Culture," in *The New Historicism*, ed. H. Aram Veeser. (New York/London: Routledge, 1989), Stephen Greenblatt and Catherine Gallagher, *Practicing New Historicism* (Chicago/London: The University of Chicago Press, 2000).

Moreover, literature does not merely reflect historically specific constructions of "the mentally ill": fiction should also be recognized as a political voice in its own right. Conceived in this way, literary praxis is not only affected by but also shapes the society in which it is produced and in which it continues to circulate. The political negotiation of "the mentally ill" citizen, which I suggest the literary works take part in, is not to be understood as a negotiation in any direct way. Rather, it illustrates dominant discourses – *and* produces counterimages of the same discourses. In other words, the works selected exhibit distinct historical approaches to "the mentally ill" by the welfare state, but they also question and problematize not only the state practices that are reflected in these approaches, but also a certain "social totality" of their time.

In "The Dynamics of Social Solidarity: The Danish Welfare State: 1900-2000", Klaus Petersen and Niels Finn Christiansen present a broad analysis of the development of the Danish welfare state in the twentieth century.[10] They divide its development into five larger epochs, which are marked by larger ideological shifts, broader economic structures and, not least, by the political line set by the government of the day. Perceptions of "the mentally ill" and the public practices related to this figure are, as we shall see, clearly shaped by these overall shifts in the political and ideological landscape. Nevertheless, the history of "the mentally ill" also has its own trajectory, one marked by a transfer of responsibility from the family to the state and not least influenced by medical interventions in the field of psychiatry.

My ambition here is to use literature as an empirical source to nuance and extend Petersen and Christiansen's mapping, with a specific focus on "the mentally ill". The first novel, Amalie Skram's *Professor Hieronimus*, was written on the threshold of the twentieth century, prior to what many scholars regard as the real consolidation of the modern welfare state with the great social reforms in the 1930s. The second novel, Tove Ditlevsen's *The Faces*, belongs to the end of what many scholars have called "the golden age" of the welfare state, the period after the Second World War, a time marked by strong economic growth. The third novel, *HHV, FRSHWN* (2019), was written in the twenty-first century and falls outside of Petersen and

---

10 Niels Finn Christiansen and Klaus Petersen, "The Dynamics of Social Solidarity: the Danish Welfare State, 1900-2000," *Scandinavian Journal of History* 26, no. 2 (March 2001): 177-196.

Christiansen's cartography. It speaks to the consequences of how increasing commercialization and marketization from the 1990s onwards has affected not only our perceptions of "the mentally ill" but our modes of living more generally.

In the following sections, I combine synchronic and diachronic perspectives. First, I analyze and contextualize the three novels independently from a synchronic and comparative perspective. I focus on how responsibility with regard to "the mentally ill" has shifted from the family to the state and on how the family as an institution has undergone a transformation in its own right. Each novel thus illuminates how the family and the home constitute an inseparable part of the changing historical context in which "the mentally ill" are constituted in a specific way. Second, employing a diachronic perspective, I draw on Deleuze's notion of "societies of control" to discuss how the identifiable shifts from "insane" to "patient" to "user of psychiatry" illustrated by the literary representations can be linked to broader transformations of the welfare state and to new processes of subjectification.

I. "The insane"

> "I long so terribly to be at home."
>
> "You must try to get over that. Try to persuade yourself that it is best for you to be here".
>
> "No", Else replied irritably, "It was a great mistake for me to come here. My husband would be in despair if he knew how matters are."
>
> Else was now told again that it was her husband who had put her there and that something must have been wrong with her, since she had been brought there.
>
> "Yes", said Else, there had been something wrong with her, but she had not been mad.
>
> "Have you noticed any signs of madness about me?"
>
> "No, but one could never know for certain. There were so many forms of insanity and madness. Those who seemed the most sane were often the worst and when once they had come here –"[11]

---

11   Amalie Skram, *Professor Hieronimus*, translated by Alice Stronach and G. B. Jacobi (London: John Lane, The Bodley Head, 1899 [1885]), 61.

Norwegian-born writer Amalie Skram's semi-autobiographical novel *Professor Hieronimus* (1885), along with the sequel *På Sct. Jørgen* (1885), initiated a wide public debate on conditions in the psychiatric institutions of her time, due to its critique of them. When Amalie Skram's fictional alter ego Else encountered the mental health institution in 1895, she found herself in a trap. At the initiative of her husband, Else was taken away from her home and placed in the mental institution under the custody of the patronizing Professor Hieronimus. As the above quote indicates, the very fact that she had been institutionalized was part of her classification as "mad". The doctor had absolute power and authority and, according to him, her madness consisted primarily in a lack of self-restraint:

> "You have much need to learn self-control. It is want of self-control that you suffer from. I had thought of moving you" – he slapped the palm of the one hand with the short plebeian fingers of the other hand and almost shrieked – "but now you shall stay here" and in a moment he vanished from the cell.[12]

The novel depicts a specific conception of *insanity* as a personal characteristic, behaviour that needs to be tamed or morally disciplined. The treatment consisted above all of isolation. There is an extensive focus on keys and locked doors throughout the novel and Else frequently compares the institution to a prison. All contact with her family is cut off and after her admission the doctor barely communicates with her husband.

The novel has been the object of several analyses accentuating the gendered aspect of "the mentally ill" and analyzing how the term and historical notion of "hysteria" can be seen as a way of pathologizing rebellious women in a male-dominated society.[13] From a contemporary point of view, Else's situation is obviously marked by a misogynist discourse and by her inability to adjust to the bourgeois ideals of family life. Nevertheless, her

---

12 Skram, *Professor Hieronimus*, 131.
13 See e.g. Hilde Bondevik, "Who's Afraid of Amalie Skram? Hysteria and rebellion in Amalie Skrams Novels of Mental Hospitals," in *Illness in Context*, eds. Knut Stene Johansen and Frederik Tygstrup. (Amsterdam/NY: Rodopi, 2010), Unni Langås and Marjorie Lorvik, "The struggle for the body: hysteria and rebellion in Amalie Skram's novel Professor Hieronimus," *Scandinavian Studies* 75 (2003): 55-88; Irene Engelstad, *Sammenbrudd og gjennombrudd: Amalie Skrams romaner om ekteskap og sinnssykdom* (Oslo: Pax, 1989).

explicit critique of her treatment concerns above all the conduct of Professor Hieronimus, whereas her home is represented as a safe place she wishes to return to. For the later comparison with the other two novels, it is worth noting how the boundaries between the home and the institution are sharply separated in Skram's text.

The work was written on the threshold of the twentieth century, a period prior to the great social welfare reforms undertaken by the state in the 1930s. State intervention at this time was generally very limited. As pointed out by Petersen and Christiansen, the ideology in this epoch was informed by a mixture of liberal self-help principles and conservative Christian social ethics.[14] Skram's novel shows how this ideological context also marked the way in which "the mentally ill" were handled. At the dawn of the twentieth century, the large state mental hospitals, which had been built from the mid-eighteenth century, were run by the individual doctors in charge and there was no central administrative control or coordination.

While authority rested with the respective doctors in charge, the family played a central role in the commitment process.[15] As Edward Shorter remarks, during the nineteenth century, individuals with major psychiatric illnesses were increasingly shifted from the family or the poorhouses to the asylums. Shorter explains this shift with reference to a changing pattern of sentiment in family life: "as the family started to consider itself increasingly an emotional unit, disruptive relatives at home began to seem more and more intolerable."[16] By virtue of its physicality and organization, the asylum, as Jette Møllerhøj explains, was seen as an independent part of the treatment strategy: "the core of the treatment was for the mentally ill to be committed and to stay in the calm and isolating institution".[17] The possibilities for a cure were limited at this point in time and the medical treatment consisted most of all in the use of tranquilisers. However, the patient's moral education also played a major role. "The mentally ill", as Møllerhøj formulates it, should:

---

14   Christiansen and Petersen, "The dynamics of social solidarity," 177-178.
15   See e.g. Edward Shorter, *A History of Psychiatry: From the Era of the Asylum to the Era of Prosac* (New York: Wiley & Sons, 1997), 49-50.
16   Edward Shorter, *The Making of Modern Family* (New York: Basic, 1975).
17   Jette Møllerhøj, "Sindssygdom, dårevæsen og videnskab: Asyltiden 1850-1920", in *Psykiatriens historie i Danmark*, ed. Jesper Vaczy Kragh (København: Hans Reitzel, 2008), 101.

be re-regularized and re-educated into a behaviour of order, moderation and self-restraint (...) in the execution of the moral treatment, the character and personal characteristics of the doctor were significant. The doctor in charge should be not just scientifically trained but also superior to the patients morally and spiritually.[18]

In his article "New Answers to Old Questions: Psychiatric Worldviews 1880-1930" (*Nye svar på gamle spørgsmål: psykiatriske trosretninger 1880-1930*), historian Mogens Mellergård asserts that it was primarily the lack of proper treatment possibilities that caused the public conflict between Skram and Pontoppidan (see below).[19] The exercise of discipline was legitimized as a means of therapy, although there was little medical confidence that there could be any real cure. In the so-called "asylum era" from 1850 to 1920, Møllerhøj notes, the psychiatric discipline had not yet been acknowledged as a trusted medical science.[20]

Besides offering a critical perspective on the conditions in the country's mental institutions, Skram's novel also had a political-institutional impact. The chief physician Knud Pontoppidan, who was the doctor in charge of the department where the real Amalie Skram had been hospitalized, had to resign from his position in 1898 due to the harsh criticisms of his professional conduct that Skram's autobiographical novel had evoked. However, Pontoppidan moved to the provinces where he continued his career in the field of psychiatry. He maintained a position as doctor in charge at Aarhus Mental Hospital before returning to the capital and becoming a professor of medicine at the University of Copenhagen three years later.

In conclusion, the "social totality" exhibited in Skram's work, which contributed to the configuration of "the insane", was a regime of discipline, moral regulation and isolation. Yet, Skram's novel also depicts how the boundary between public and private and the division of responsibility between the family and the institution, were clearly separated with regard to how "the mentally ill" were treated. This separation was about

---

18 Møllerhøj, "Sindssygdom, dårevæsen og videnskab," 103.
19 Mogens Mellergård, "Nye svar på gamle spørgsmål: Psykiatriske trosretninger 1880-1930," in *Psykiatriens historie i Danmark*, ed. Jesper Vaczy Kragh (København: Hans Reitzel, 2008), 147.
20 Møllerhøj, "Sindssygdom, dårevæsen og videnskab," 119.

to disappear with the further development of the welfare state. However, in the field of psychiatry, the strategy of isolation, discipline and moral regulation continued for many years, but for different reasons and with new methods. The eugenics movement and theories of degeneration legitimized the continued practice of isolation and regulation with regard to "the mentally ill".[21] As a result, the increasing awareness of citizens' rights and the attention paid to gender and family problems, which Petersen and Christiansen describe as characteristic for the period from 1930 to 1950, did not apply so much to "the mentally ill". One example is the Keller asylums on the small Danish islands of Livø and Sprogø, where the so-called "morally disabled" were isolated. For the women on Sprogø, forced sterilization was a condition of being able to leave. The last of these asylums did not close until 1963.[22]

New theories of heredity and the fear of degeneration also contributed to public investments in medical treatment. This strengthened the view of mental illness as a somatic disease and gradually psychiatry was conceived as an integral aspect of the medical sciences.[23] Yet, as the idea of the dominant state as a new kind of family gained strength in the "Golden Age" of the welfare state, the mentally ill were not just subjected to the aim of being cured, but also to a certain kind of *care*. The ruling principles of universalism in "the golden age" of the welfare state, which included universal social support, also marked the way in which "the mentally ill" were perceived. It is this new "social totality", in which the mentally ill are less "insane" and more "patients" – in the original meaning of the word as "one who suffers" and is eligible to be comforted in a protective institution – that is captured in Tove Ditleven's polemic work *The Faces*.

---

21 K.K. Steincke, who is often referred to as one of the founding figures of the social democratic welfare state, was also occupied with theories of heredity and degeneration and was a strong proponent of eugenics. Enhanced by eugenic thoughts and gendered norms of sexuality and moral conduct, preventive ideas against degeneration were implemented in social reforms from the 1920s onwards, the state thus interfering with domains which had not previously been of public interest. In 1921, Denmark became one of the first countries to ratify a law on sterilization. In 1934, this law was revised to allow forced sterilization and in 1929, the Danish Act on the Formation and Dissolution of Marriage forbade the so-called "morally disabled" to marry. See Lene Koch, *Racehygiejne i Danmark 1920-1956* (København: Nordisk Forlag, 1996).
22 Birgit Kirkebæk, *Letfærdig og løsagtig: kvindeanstalten på Sprogø 1923-1961* (Holte: SocPol, 2004).
23 Jesper Vaczy Kragh, *Det hvide snit, psykokirurgi og dansk psykiatri 1922-1983* (Odense: Syddansk Universitetsforlag, 2010).

II. "The patient"

"Two men in uniform came in and carried her down on a stretcher. With experienced hands they wrapped her in a blanket and carefully carried the stretcher down the stairs. Inside the ambulance one of them sat and held her hand. His mouth was crooked, as if he had facial paralysis. It was as quiet as a cathedral. Hope burned gently in the young man's eyes, which were clear and bright like Søren's. He gave her hand a friendly squeeze and she thought that she would soon be lying in a white bed, surrounded by gentle, kind women with whom she could talk quietly about men and love. In this new place the terror would be gone."

"She knew that there were institutions filled with deformed and monstrous human creatures who were kept hidden from the world and who lived and died without anyone other than the hospital personnel ever seeing them. Had they brought her to that kind of place? She thought of the expression "the locked ward" and longed to go there without having any idea what that term meant: a different place, another reality, where it might be possible to exist."[24]

Tove Ditlevsen is considered one of the great Danish writers of the postwar period. Like Amalie Skram's *Professor Hieronimus*, her semi-autobiographical book *The Faces*, from 1968, is based on her own experiences within the psychiatric system.

Unlike Else's encounter with the dominating and patronizing Professor Hieronimus, Lise Mundus, the protagonist in *The Faces*, experiences friendly and professional warmth on her way to the mental institution in the late 1960s. Lise does not want to be at home and, in contrast to Else, she does not romanticize her family life, which is pictured as corrupt and claustrophobic: her husband has an affair with her housekeeper, who also sleeps with her son. Lise poisons herself with a glass of sleeping pills and calls the doctor on her own initiative. As the quotes illustrate, she allows herself to dream of the mental institution as a parallel world in which she

---

24   Tove Ditlevsen, *The Faces*, translated from the Danish by Tina Nunnally (Washington: Fjord Press, 1991), 58.

can escape her everyday struggles, not least with her family and find another form of existence. Lise does not fear the closed ward because she feels even more cloistered in her own home.

In contrast to the keys and the closed institution in Skram's novel, Ditlevsen's description of the blanket, of the caretaker holding her hand and the hope burning gently in the young man's eyes (compared to her own son's – an indication of a new kind of family), captures a notion of "the patient" as a suffering subject who needs professional care and protection. Even though Lise does not feel protected during her stay at the hospital, the description of her expectations and her first encounter with the welfare-state professionals reflects the idea of the institution as a protective, parallel world and represents a welfare-state approach to "the mentally ill" that differs significantly from that presented in *Professor Hieronimus*.

Everything becomes twisted in Ditlevsen's fictional universe. The boundary between reality and imagination is blurred, like the faces that the main character tries to decipher. Lise's family keeps haunting her as voices through the water pipes and images of her family members merge with the hospital staff. The work questions which world is the most insane: that inside or that outside the hospital ward, the world of the institution or the world of the bourgeois family? Yet, the work also reflects how the boundaries between public and private are effaced and how the respective spaces of the family and the mental institution merge in several ways. It is in the trainee nurse, Miss Arnesen, that Lise finds the most confident support. She is the only one of the care personnel whose face does not change or take on different shapes. She lets Lise smoke and "caresses her sticky hair from her face".[25] Ditlevsen's work exhibits how the welfare state has in many respects become a new kind of caring family for the mentally ill patient.[26]

---

25 Ditlevsen, *The Faces*, 116-118.
26 This development, where the state takes over domains that were previously reserved for the family, Gøsta Esping-Andersen has conceptualized as "the de-familization of the welfare state", a process especially characteristic of the Nordic welfare state models. See Gøsta Esping-Andersen, *The Three Worlds of Welfare Capitalism* (Princeton, NJ: Princeton University Press, 1990). See also Lasse Horne Kjældgaard, "In loco parentis. Affamilialisering i fiktion om den skandinaviske velfærdsstat," in *Velfærdsfortællinger. Om dansk litteratur i velfærdsstatens tid*, ed. Nils Gunder Hansen (København: Gyldendal, 2010).

The novel was written towards the end of "the golden age of the welfare state" a period characterized by economic growth, a strong centralized state and a social-democratic welfare ideology. However, the late 1960s was also a period of cultural rebellion. There was increasing scepticism of all kinds of authority and old structures like "the family" were being challenged and destabilized. It was also a period in which the anti-psychiatric movement was gaining in strength and initiatives like Galebevægelsen ("The mad movement") were established and sought to reshape perceptions of "the mentally ill". Experiments with anti-authoritative forms of care were launched in the mental hospitals. In 1969, the patients in department A at the mental hospital of Sct. Hans were allowed to write in their own medical records. This initiative was in line with the general democratization of the institution, which also offered creative workspaces and art therapy inside the hospital wards. These experiments, however, took place alongside ongoing medical development and treatment.[27]

Despite Ditlevsen's problematization of mental illness as such and of bourgeois family structures in particular, Lise's first encounter with the ambulance and care personnel clearly frames – in all its ambivalence – the contemporary welfare-state ideal of a strong and protective institution taking care of the socially exposed. In this period, the institution functioned as a parallel world in which some of the afflicted were able to live a life shielded from the demands of society in the long term. It is this notion of "the patient" as a suffering human in need of care which, in the wake of the economic crisis of the late 1970s and due to the increasing decentralization and commercialization of public administration and services in the 1990s, came to be replaced with yet another conception of "the mentally ill", namely as "users of psychiatry". Viemose's novel captures this new epoch of the welfare state where care has been replaced by self-care, a movement towards a time when the institution seems absent rather than protective.

---

27 Jesper Vaczy Kragh and Jette Møllerhøj, *Sct. Hans 1816-2016* (Roskilde: Psykiatrisk Center Sct. Hans, 2019), 202.

III. "The user of psychiatry"

"Well, (I controlled a mental breakdown behind St. Paul's Church even before the bus had left and dragged myself up on my monster of a bike and pedaled along Tagensvej following the ass of my son's school bus: sends the boys to school and kindergarten going directly to "the Psych" the little monster in my head shouted with joy), what I wanted to say:

There I stood, speaking to a white coat through a hatch, it obviously wasn't easy to get in here,

Check and check
Check,
Check,
Check,
Yes
no
well
..
And
then
as if by magic ABRA-CA-DA-BRA
the doors opened
and shut behind me BAM!
(The doors on Psychiatric say open and close, open and close,
open and close, open and close,
the doors on Psychiatric say
open and close etc.)"[28]

Hanne Højgaard Viemose's novel *HHV, FRSHWN*, which was nominated for the 2020 Nordic Council Literature Prize, contains clear autobiographical references. In her outreach for the mental institution in 2019, the protago-

---

28 Hanne Højgaard Viemose, *HHV FRSHWN* (København: Gyldendal, 2019), 31-32 (My translation, the work has not yet been published in English).

nist Hanne is not confronted with either a patronizing doctor and a set of keys or a friendly caretaker and a blanket. Instead, she encounters a "white coat" and a questionnaire. She neither longs for nor attempts to escape her family, for it has already dissolved. She has left the father of her two sons, who is struggling with his own depression. Alone with the boys, she longs for an adult person to relate to. However, the doctor and all other professional guidance has been replaced by a piece of paper and just as it seemed difficult to get into a psychiatric hospital, just as quickly she is kicked out of it again. The children's song alluded to in the quoted passage, with the bus doors opening and closing, pinpoints the temporality in the present practices of public mental healthcare. This can be seen as a consequence of the decentralization of the public sector, as mentioned, including the field of psychiatry. The public mental institution of today is neither depicted as a prison, as in *Professor Hieronimus*, nor as an opportunity for a parallel world in which care is central, as in the *Faces*. Instead, it is pictured as a piece of administrative machinery offering hardly any possibility for a long-term stay or personal contact.[29]

Filling out the questionnaire, it is as if Hanne needs to decipher a certain code in order to open up the gates to social support or welfare benefits. There is no doctor or carer present who, by means of a conversation, makes an evaluation based on Hanne's personal account. Her situation is assessed on the basis of her "yeses" and "noes" to a number of predefined questions. This experience can be seen as a consequence of what has been characterized as "the operational revolution" within the discipline of psychiatry that started in the 1960s. It was a process in which "sophisticated descriptions were simplified and shortened into diagnostic manuals, available to the lay public because written in lay language and free of theoretical burden".[30] It also mirrors what Nikolas Rose calls "the checklist approach", a practice "in which individuals are diagnosed with a particular condition if they have exhibited a certain number of behaviours over a specified period of time."[31]

---

29 According a recent report by Sundhedsdatastyrelsen, *Genindlæggelser i det psykiatriske sundhedsvæsen* from January 2017, 23 percent of all admissions are followed up by readmissions and approximately 25 percent of the readmissions take place within the first three days of the first admission.
30 Julie Nordgaard and Josef Parnas, "A haunting that never stops: psychiatry's problem of description," *Acta Psychiatrica Scandinavica* 127, no. 6 (2013): 434-435.
31 Nikolas Rose, *Our Psychiatric Future* (Cambridge: Polity Press, 2019), 7.

In 2019, when Hanne Højgaard Viemose's book was published, "the mentally ill" were no longer perceived mainly as a moral threat to society that required patients to be locked up and disciplined. Nor were "the mentally ill", as reflected in the *Faces,* perceived as patients in need of protection and nursing inside the hospital wards. Rather, "the mentally ill" were addressed as "users of psychiatry".[32] This term appeared for the first time in the Danish context in 1991 and has ever since been frequently used as a substitute for "patient". The following graph illustrates the rise in the use of the term in Danish public newspapers since 1991:[33]

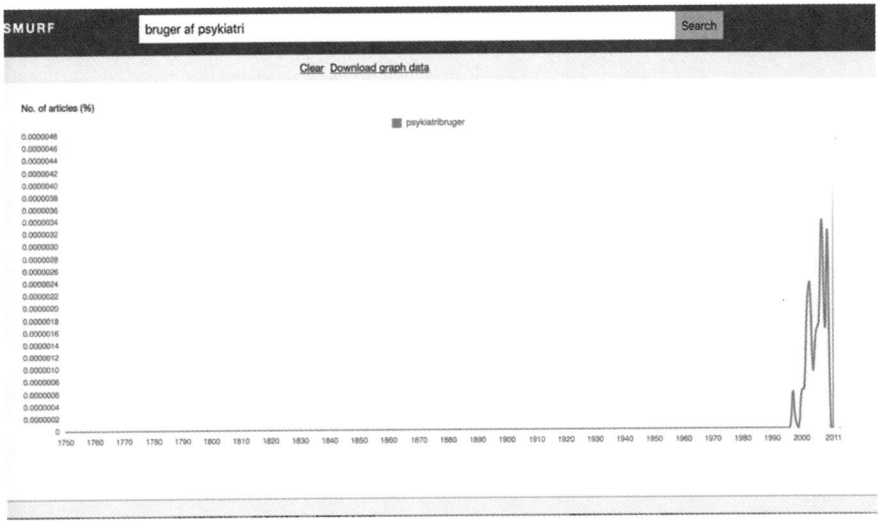

This frequent substitution of "patient" with "user of psychiatry" can be linked to the general ideological shift that informed the introduction of new principles of public management in the public sector in the 1990s. Cowden and Singh have traced this shift from the state and professional

---

32 In English, "user of psychiatry" corresponds to "service user" and can also be translated as "healthcare user". However, I would argue that there is an important difference between these expressions. In the Danish context, the expression has been converted into a noun, "psychiatry-user", which links it more directly to a construction of identity.

33 The expression "user of psychiatry" is not only used in healthcare policies but has also merged into everyday language as a way to avoid using the term "mentally ill". See, for instance, the documentary *Gal eller genial* about the Risskov mental institution, a film made just before the hospital was closed down: https://www.dr.dk/drtv/program/gal-eller-genial_78270

power towards user involvement and citizen choice back to the welfare struggle in Britain in the 1970s and 1980s and the direction set by both Thatcherism and New Labour.[34] Christiansen and Petersen point to a similar shift taking place in the Danish welfare state in the 1990s, where the Social Democratic Party aimed to "lighten the pressure on the public institutions", and they link this to what they call "The Fourth Social Reform":

> This so-called Fourth Social Reform has followed a strategy of "activation" and "self-empowerment" in social policy. On the one hand, trying to empower people through education and training and on the other pressing people out of the social security system through tightening eligibility criteria and shortening the periods.[35]

The term "user of psychiatry" is partly a product of this gradual and overall definitional shift from citizen to service user. However, in the field of psychiatry the "user" term has *also* become intertwined with and further legitimized by, ideologies of recovery and rehabilitation. The recovery ideology stresses that mental illness is not a chronic disease, but something you can "recover from". Fused with neoliberal ideas, the recovery ideology has explicitly been integrated into Danish healthcare policies. As this quote from a public healthcare strategy, *"Towards user involvement in psychiatry: a strategy for user-involvement and cooperation"* (2010), illustrates, the responsibility for recovery (once again) primarily falls on the individual and not on the public social system:

> In the recovery and rehabilitation philosophy, it is absolutely central that if a human suffering from mental illness is to recover, he or she needs to put on the working gloves and participate in and take responsibility for the recovery process. It is not a process anyone else can manage for you.[36]

---

34 Stephen Cowden and Gurnam Singh, "The 'User': friend, foe or fetish? A critical exploration of user involvement in health and social care," *Critical Social Policy* 27, no. 1 (2007): 5-23.
35 Christiansen and Petersen, "The dynamics of social solidarity," 195.
36 Danish health care strategy, *På vej mod brugerinddragelse i psykiatrien – en strategi for brugerinddragelse og samarbejde* (Region Hovedstaden, 2010).

Hanne's meeting with the public healthcare system in 2019 reflects how this new political imaginary of "the mentally ill" as "users of psychiatry" impacts on personal encounters with the welfare-state authorities. In comparison with those depicted in *Professor Hieronimus* and *The Faces*, the mental healthcare institution is not isolating or protective but rather absent and inaccessible. The absent institution is on the one hand a consequence of the fusion of neoliberal politics and the recovery ideology described above. On the other hand, the increasing decentralization is also made possible by the extended use of psychopharmacological treatment, which enables behaviour to be regulated and symptoms to be classified without the need for institutional admission.

Moreover, the inaccessibility and temporality of today's mental healthcare practice can also be explained as part of a general normalization of mental illness. As Nikolas Rose declares, "one might almost say that it is "abnormal" to live one's life without coming into the remit of psychiatry".[37] This normalization of mental illness is reflected in Viemose's work in the way in which the protagonist Hanne's visit to "the psychiatric" is interwoven with her everyday practices. It is not portrayed as a remarkable event, but as something she can fit in between her duties, like a daily routine. The normalization of mental suffering is exquisitely pictured in the sliding movement, described in the quote, from the kindergarten bus to the psychiatric ward and the way in which the meeting with the hospital staff is intertwined with a well-known children's tune. Apart from this one formal encounter with the public healthcare institution, the novel does not explicitly address the question of mental illness as such. Rather, it seems to be omnipresent. The novel opens in the midst of Hanne's (former) husband's psychosis:

> The light was so fiery, it was the summer my ex-husband, my still small boys' father, let's call him Stomur, too obvious? Birnir (Bjørne) then, Hrafn (Ravn), Jussi! (his own wish) rushed around in the all too abrasive nights of Reykjavik in a state of delirium, sleepless with the intentions raging through him, crazy escalating delirium on top: the paranoia (…)[38]

---

37 Nikolas Rose, *Our Psychiatric future* (Cambridge: Polity Press, 2019).
38 Viemose, *HHV, FRSHWN*, 13.

As the writer Niels Frank remarks in his review of the book, the work seems "disturbing" and it is as if the sentences "crack" (*knækker sig*). As Frank also notes, the novel presents us with a person who is unable to maintain boundaries, a person struggling to feel that "someone has a home inside herself."[39] An overall feeling of despair also melts into the language, as witnessed in a headline such as this: "it's going to be a crazy autumn, it was the autumn I met you."[40]

This overall feeling of dissolution, combined with Hanne's impersonal encounter with the welfare state, frames the paradoxes that follow from a conception of "the mentally ill" as "users of psychiatry". We witness a person who is striving unsuccessfully to find protection in a welfare-state society where the responsibility and boundaries are constantly being displaced. Conceived in this way, the subject position pictured in Viemose's work can also be linked to a more general transformation of power dynamics and human subjectivity as described in Gilles Deleuze's text *Postscript on the Societies of Control*, to which I will turn below.

Towards an Era of "dividuals" / non-enclosure?

*"The era of enclosure is over –
and the family as an "interior" is in crisis, like all other interiors."*[41]

In 1992, Gilles Deleuze published a short essay, "Postscript on the Societies of Control", in which he predicts a transition from disciplinary societies in the Foucauldian sense, characterized by the subjectification of citizens through institutions of enclosure, to new kinds of societies that mould their subjects through different mechanisms of control. Deleuze locates the beginning of this transition to the postwar era, when institutions such as the school, the prison, the family and the hospital began to lose their former power and form. According to Deleuze, these sites of enclosure were

---

39   Niels Frank's review in the Danish newspaper *Information*, February 20, 2020: "Niels Frank: Hanne Højgaard Viemoses 'HHV FRSHWN' er en forstyrret roman, man kun kan holde af".
40   Viemose, *HHV, FRHWN*, 89.
41   Deleuze, "Postscript on the Societies of Control".

reshaped and temporarily kept alive through broader welfare reforms. However, at the threshold to the twenty-first century, he envisions a further consolidation of societies of control, which includes new modes of subjectification.

Deleuze's use of the word "control" can at first cause some confusion, as it is also central to Foucault's conception of the disciplinary society. "Control" as the opposite of discipline must therefore be unfolded and understood in relation to the other features of the societies of control that Deleuze emphasizes. Importantly, subjects in societies of control are no longer "man enclosed, but man in debt" and in societies of control "one is never finished with anything…". The changes Deleuze wishes to emphasize concern all areas of life: sports are replaced by internet surfing and simple machines with computers. However, the clearest indication of this societal and social transformation is the changes to the economy:

> Perhaps it is money that expresses the distinction between the two societies best, since discipline always referred back to minted money that locks gold in as numerical standard, while control relates to floating rates of exchange, modulating according to a rate established by a set of standard currencies.[42]

The shift from one society to another, described by Deleuze, is part of a longer process. It is not merely a matter of new forms of power but is also recognizable "in our manner of living and in our relations with others."[43] In the healthcare sector, the changes manifest themselves in:

> the new medicine: "without doctor or patient" that singles out potentially sick people and subjects at risk, which in no way attest to individuation – as they say – but substitute for the individual or numerical body the code of a "dividual" material to be controlled.[44]

---

42 Deleuze, "Postscript on the Societies of Control," 5.
43 Deleuze, "Postscript on the Societies of Control," 5.
44 Deleuze, "Postscript on the Societies of Control," 7.

Deleuze's text was written at a time when the new term "user of psychiatry" had been introduced and was starting to emerge in public healthcare practice. It is remarkable how Deleuze's characterization of a subject in debt and of a subject who is never finished resonates with the transfer of responsibility reflected in current healthcare policies. At present, it is not so much mental deviance as passivity that indirectly stigmatizes. The shift to "user of psychiatry" and the changing healthcare practices that are connected with this new notion can thus be understood as a new mechanism through which the welfare state is able to control and regulate the costly, unproductive and constantly increasing numbers of people who are reaching out to mental healthcare services.

"After all, are we not all individuals?", Charles Taylor asks in his *Modern Social Imaginaries*.[45] At the threshold to the twenty-first century, Deleuze actually forces us to question that claim. Deleuze predicts a development whereby the subject, the citizen in the state, is no longer perceived as an individual but a *dividual*. "Individuals have become *dividuals* and masses, sample, data, markets, or "banks'."[46] Hanne Viemose's description of the subjective encounter with today's public psychiatry seems to confirm Deleuze's predictions. Hanne's experience with the white coat, the questionnaire and the revolving doors of the psychiatric ward reflects a subject with no place to rest, but also a subject who is approached with no regard to individuality, history or context. The protagonist is not met as an individual but encounters an absent and inaccessible healthcare institution. There is an obvious discrepancy between the demand for individual responsibility, as expressed in today's healthcare policies and the conception of the mentally ill citizen as a "divid", as a "data set" or a number in a line of several digits, as shown in Viemose's work.

Deleuze's point is not that societies of control are any worse than disciplinary ones. As he emphasizes, "There is no need to ask which is the toughest or most tolerable regime, for it is within each of them that liberating and enslaving forces confront one another."[47] What Deleuze stresses, however, is the need to think across the economy, social relations and hu-

---

45 Charles Taylor, "Modern Social Imaginaries," *Public Culture* 14, no. 1 (2002): 91-124.
46 Deleuze, "Postscript on the Societies of Control," 5.
47 Deleuze, "Postscript on the Societies of Control," 4.

man subjectivity, including the way(s) in which "the mentally ill" subject is approached and constructed.[48]

Concluding Remarks

Employing literature as a cultural testimony allows us to trace changing conceptions of "the mentally ill" and the relations between these conceptions, mental institutions and healthcare policies. The insight that notions and actions related to "the mentally ill" are always culturally and politically bounded invites critical awareness of the latest changes in vocabulary and the introduction of the term "user of psychiatry" in public healthcare. The present implementation of psychiatric units in somatic hospitals and the increasing decentralization are not just signs of progress and attempts at de-stigmatization, they are also an effect of new methods of political control and subjectification.

As an "insane" at the dawn of the twentieth century, Skram's main character Else, an isolated, concealed and disciplined subject, has to be tamed before she can return to society and to the fold of the patriarchal family. As a "patient" in the "Golden Age" of the centralized welfare state, Tove Ditlevsen's Lise is approached by the hospital staff as a suffering subject and Ditlevsen's novel conveys a time-specific confidence in cure under public care and protection. Simultaneously, the novel echoes a period of cultural revolt and Ditlevsen questions the boundaries between insanity and sanity that are drawn by politics. As a "user of psychiatry" and in sharp contrast to Lise, Hanne, in the work by Hanne Højgaard Viemose, is expected to be responsible for her own situation, not unlike Else. Paradoxically, she is approached as a "divid", with no interest being shown in her personality or record. She is not enclosed or disciplined in any direct way but has to struggle all on her own.

Drawing on Deleuze's notion of "societies of control", the distinct welfare-state configurations of "the mentally ill" I have traced through the three passages, from an "insane" to a "patient" to a "user of psychiatry", can

---

48 The same urge to think across the environment (which covers both nature and culture), social relations and human subjectivity is found in Félix Guatteri's notion of ecosophy in Félix Guattari, *The Three Ecologies*. (NY: Bloomsbury Academic, 2000 [*Les Trois écologies*, Editions Galileé, 1989]).

be seen as part of broader social transformations. The notion of a "user of psychiatry" can be seen as a sign of a general marketization of individuals, which also infiltrates perceptions and constructions of "the mentally ill" citizen. The context or "social totality" in which "the mentally ill" are constituted today is marked by a development whereby institutions – "the hospital" as well as "the family" – seem to be in a process of erosion.

As the literary scholar Anne-Marie Mai emphasizes, "the changes to family life and the relation between state institutions, the family and the individual have been an important welfare theme."[49] In my analysis of "the mentally ill" in the context of the Danish welfare state, it also becomes clear how historically situated dynamics within the family, as well as between the family and public-health institutions, have played a crucial part in the changing constructions of "the mentally ill".

---

49 Mai, "The roles of writers in the Danish welfare state," 86.

The Migrant

A New Legal, Social and Political Category in Welfare State Policy and Debate

Heidi Vad Jønsson

The migrant is one of the most contested figures in contemporary debates over social welfare in Denmark. For decades, the immigration issue has created significant conflicts both between and within political parties and interest groups, as well as in the Danish population at large. New lines of differentiation have been drawn in Danish party politics in the wake of the continuous politicization of immigration and new ideological positions (e.g. welfare nationalism) have emerged in this process. A highly diverse figure in contemporary political debates, the migrant appears simultaneously as a legal category (e.g. convention refugee), a new social group (central to debates over ghettoization) and not least a political target group governed by both integration policy and immigration policy. But how, we may ask, did these different categorizations of the migrant and their diverse layers of meaning emerge in the context of the Danish welfare state?

Several studies have explored the various impacts of immigration on the welfare state. A growing body of social-science literature points to immigration as a factor potentially undermining trust in society.[1] While this is perhaps less problematic in liberal welfare regimes characterized by a balance between state and market that favours the latter, social trust is at the very foundation of universal welfare states (e.g. the Scandinavian welfare states). This is also implied in those studies that explore the historical impact of immigration on the development of the welfare state at the beginning of the twentieth century; such studies have also identified trust as a causal mechanism explaining the variation in welfare regimes. According to this literature, welfare-state development in the United States did not experience the same turn to universal provision as the one that affected Scandinavian welfare states, since the American population was highly diverse and thus less homogenous than was the case in northern Europe.[2] In these studies, both immigration as a phenomenon and the migrant as a figure are treated as factors that destabilize welfare states.

Other studies of immigration focusing on Scandinavian welfare states have explored shifting discourses and stressed that the way in which immigration is debated has an effect on perceptions of migration-related issues.[3] While the studies mentioned above seek to theorize social trust as a social phenomenon and as such give it a more prescriptive character, the numerous discourse analyses tend to be more descriptive in their output. By analyzing developments over time, this literature argues that discourses of immigration are constantly being reconstructed and that over time immigration comes to be attached to various other issues, such as the labour market, unemployment, crime and racism, as well as opposition to racism.[4]

---

[1] Ruud Koopmans, *Assimilation oder Multikulturalismus? Bedingungen gelungener Integration* (Lit Verlag, 2017); Wim Van Oorshot, "Solidarity towards immigrants in European welfare states," *International Journal of Social Welfare* vol. 17, no. 1 (2008): 3-14.

[2] Alberto Alesina and Edward Glaeser, *Fighting Poverty in the US and Europe: A World of Difference* (Oxford: Oxford University Press, 2004); Cybelle Fox, *Three Worlds of Relief: Race, Immigration and the American Welfare State from the Progressive Era to the New Deal* (Princeton: Princeton University Press, 2012); Will Kymlicka and Keir Banting, *Multiculturalism and the Welfare State: Recognition and Redistribution in Contemporary Democracies* (Oxford: Oxford University Press, 2006).

[3] Lærke Klitgaard Holm, *Folketinget og udlændingepolitikken, diskurser om naturaliserede Indvandrere og flygtninge 1973-2002* (Ph.D. thesis, AMID, Aalborg Universitet, 2006); Lars Jørgensen, *Hvad sagde vi! ...om "De Andre". Den udlændingepolitiske debat i Folketinget 1961–1999*. (Ph.D. thesis Roskilde Universitet, 2006); Kirsten Hvenegård-Lassen, *På lige fod: samfundet, ligheden og folketingets debatter om udlændingepolitik 1973-2000* (Ph.D. thesis Københavns Universitet, 2002).

[4] See, for example, Jacob Gaarde Madsen, *Mediernes konstruktion af flygtninge og indvandrerspørgsmålet* (Aarhus: Aarhus Universitetsforlag, 2004).

However, this literature does not analyze the migrant as a figure in the Danish welfare state. In the growing number of studies that track developments in migration policy, immigrants and refugees appear as a new group whose conditions, entry into and presence in Denmark are politicized, regulated and politicized again. By focusing on the policy process, the migrant is implicitly treated as a target group for social policy measures.[5] The process of constructing the migrant as a political target group is thus implied in these studies, which identify specific institutions (e.g. political parties, labour movements, social movements etc.) as important arenas for the politicization of immigration.[6] However, it is not entirely clear how the migrant is constructed as a figure.

Hence, exploring how the migrant was ascribed meaning by Danish welfare institutions and their policy-makers from the golden days of the welfare state to the neoliberal age, this chapter draws on insights from the growing field of migration welfare studies. This period of the welfare state is especially interesting to explore with regard to the category of the migrant. Even though the Danish welfare state dates back to at least 1892, with the introduction of old age pensions and distinctions between the deserving and undeserving poor, migrants were always categorized as outsiders. Migrants living in Denmark were at risk of deportation if they were found to be without means. Throughout the first decades of the twentieth century, migrants were categorized as neither citizens nor as denizens, but rather as margizens.[7] Migrants did not belong to the new social category of the deviant poor. The migrant only became a key figure in the welfare state with the latter's expansion from a system of mainly social rights to a type

---

[5] These include Grete Brochmann and Anniken Hagelund, eds., *Immigration Policy and the Scandinavian Welfare State 1945-2010* (Cham: Palgrave Macmillan, 2012); Jørn Henrik Petersen, Klaus Petersen and Niels Finn Christiansen, eds., *Dansk Velfærdshistorie vol. 1-6* (Odense: Syddansk Universitetsforlag, 2010-2014).

[6] Grete Brochmann and Anniken Hagelund, eds., *Immigration Policy and the Scandinavian Welfare State 1945-2010* (Cham: Palgrave Macmillan, 2012); Heidi Vad Jønsson, *Fra lige muligheder til ret og pligt: Socialdemokratiets integrationspolitik i den moderne velfærdsstats tidsalder* (Odense: Syddansk Universitetsforlag, 2018); Karen Nielsen Breidahl, *Når staten lærer: En historisk og komparativ analyse af statslig policy læring og betydningen heraf for udviklingen i den arbejdsmarkedsrettede del af indvandrerpolitikken i Sverige, Norge og Danmark fra 1970 til 2011* (Ph.D. thesis, Department of Political Science, Aalborg Universitet, 2012); Mats Wickström, *The Multicultural Moment: The History of the Idea and Politics of Multiculturalism in Sweden in Comparative, Transnational and Biographical Context, 1964–1975* (Ph.D. thesis, Åbo Akademi, 2015).

[7] Yasemin Soysal, *A Theory of Denizenship* (Ph.D. thesis, University College London, 1994).

of state that aimed at reducing inequalities by providing free and equal access to social services such as health care (e.g. the Hospital Act of 1946) or day care (gradually expanded in the 1960s and 1970s).

In this period, the universalist principle became the dominant framework for the expansion of welfare. In this process, the question of how to address those who were not covered by the welfare state's social and economic security schemes and therefore were not included in the welfare society became a salient topic in Danish welfare policy. According to the British social researcher Richard Titmuss, the welfare state is a system of social services for everybody from everybody, but with rising immigration in the postwar years, national, universal welfare states were confronted with a new dilemma: who is everybody in a globalized world?[8] This question represented an ongoing dilemma for the universal Danish welfare state, one that remains unanswered.

The rest of this chapter unfolds an analysis of the migrant as a key political actor in the welfare state with a focus on how this figure was negotiated and ascribed meanings in the main phases of the welfare state.[9] Hence, the ideational and institutional changes to the Danish welfare state constitute the analytical grit, while the migrant – a figure on the margins of the welfare state – is the analytical object. The process of constructing the migrant as a legal, social and political category is thus the analytical focus of this chapter.

Guest and Worker: an Economic necessity

The 1960s are known as the golden days of the welfare state, but they were also a period of dramatic economic growth.[10] While the postwar years had been marked by limited economic growth, the economic boom of 1958 to 1973 led to both growth in prosperity and higher levels of welfare. Unemployment was lower than ever before and while debates over welfare in the years leading up to the Second World War had been focused on fighting unemployment as one of its main topics,[11] the problem was now quite the

---

8   Richard Titmuss, "Universalism versus Selection," in *The Welfare State reader*, second edition (Cambridge: Polity Press, 2006), 30-39.
9   See introduction.
10 Jørn Henrik Petersen, Klaus Petersen and Niels Finn Christiansen, eds., *Dansk Velfærdshistorie vol. 4: Velfærdsstatens storhedstid*, (Odense: Syddansk Universitetsforlag, 2012).
11 Jørn Henrik Petersen, Klaus Petersen and Niels Finn Christiansen, eds., *Dansk Velfærdshistorie vol. 3:*

opposite: unemployment was low in an economy with hitherto unseen high growth rates. This labour shortage represented a new problem for Denmark's economy and even though the gradual expansion of day-care facilities paved the way for women's entry into the paid labour market, certain sectors were unable to hire qualified labour. One example was one of Denmark's main export sectors, pig production, where a lack of qualified slaughterhouse workers, combined with the over-production of fattener pigs, led to a so-called "slaughter pig backlog" in 1963.[12]

The solution to the labour shortages in this particular sector was to import Spanish slaughterhouse workers. However, by the mid-1960s policy-makers and labour-market parties became very aware that the labour shortage was not a single sector problem, but a general challenge and potentially a serious threat to the Danish economy and the ongoing expansion of the welfare state. Moreover, the industrial sector was experiencing similar difficulties in recruiting both skilled and unskilled workers and the Danish Employers' Association demanded political initiatives to open up the Danish labour market to foreign guestworkers. Legally, migrants were able to come to Denmark and apply for a job and afterwards for a work permit, but the trade unions were very reluctant to agree to foreign labour being brought in, especially if immigration were to continue in what was a highly liberal system with only a few regulations.[13] By the mid-1960s, the Social Liberal Minister of Trade, Hilmar Baunsgaard, was making it quite clear that something needed to be done. In June 1964, he argued for the need either to expand the labour force or to lower the level of production:

> Everything indicates that the labour shortage will be a problem in Denmark for years to come. This can be solved in two ways. We can either align production with the existing labour force or we can expand the labour force. By choosing the latter, we can secure a higher level of production and higher growth rates.[14]

  Velfærdsstaten i støbeskeen (Odense: Syddansk Universitetsforlag, 2012).
12 Bent Jensen, *De Fremmede i dansk avisdebat fra 1870'erne til 1990'erne* (København: Spektrum, 2000).
13 Henrik Zip Sane, *Billige og villige? Fremmedarbejdere i fædrelandet ca. 1800-1970* (Farum: Farums Arkiver og Museer, 2000); *Indvandrerne i Danmarks historie: Kultur og religionsmøder* (Odense: Syddansk Universitetsforlag, 2007).
14 Quoted from Jensen, *De Fremmede*, 398.

The rationale behind Baunsgaard's statement was that importing labour was a decisive measure to prevent the bottleneck that was threatening the Danish economy. The Labour Organization (LO) recognized that labour shortages were a problem but were very reluctant to agree to expanding the labour force using foreign labour.[15]

From the point of view of the labour movement, automatization and investments in more efficient production machinery were preferred to importing foreign labour, which might undercut wages. This position was not due to national chauvinism, but based on the the labour movement's raison d'être, namely to protect organized labour against unorganized and very possibly cheaper labour.[16] In his parliamentary statement about the economic situation in 1965, Baunsgaard stated:

> As stressed by the Minister of Economy, we expect that production growth rates will be lower today than in previous years, since we do not have a labour force reserve. This situation, of course, calls for investments in the rationalization and automatization of industry, but at the same time it brings to our attention the importance of dicussing the option of importing foreign labour. Labour importation is obviously not unproblematic, but we cannot do nothing simply because the discussion might be unpleasant.[17]

The employer's organization, the DA (Dansk Arbejdsgiverforening), was unsurprisingly very much in favour of importing labour, since its members were reporting growing difficulties in hiring qualified workers, especially in the construction and production sectors. The conflict between the employers' interests and the political ambition to maintain high growth rates on the one hand and the labour movement's demands to protect organized labour on the other dominated the debates and shaped how migrants were characterized in this period.

---

15 Karen Nielsen Breidahl, *Når staten lærer: En historisk og komparativ analyze af statslig policy læring og betydningen heraf for udviklingen i den arbejdsmarkedsrettede del af indvandrerpolitikken i Sverige, Norge og Danmark fra 1970 til 2011* (Ph.D. thesis, Department of Political Science, Aalborg Universitet, 2012).
16 Sane, *Billige og villige*.
17 Folketingstidende 1964/65, *Forhandlinger*: 2076.

These discussions continued throughout the 1960s and in June 1969 the Social Liberal Minister of Labour, Lauge Dahlsgaard, appointed a commission to investigate the conditions for foreign workers in Denmark. While stressing in the mandate that "Foreigners only work in sectors where it has not been possible to employ Danish workers and thus their [guest workers] labour is considered desirable",[18] the minister also recognized that, even though importing foreign labour was an economic necessity, the existing liberal practice was not unproblematic. In the following couple of years, the commission suggested various regulatory mechanisms to ensure greater control of labour immigration (entry regulations), all of which were gradually incorporated. Labour immigration continued under increasingly more restrictive regulations dictating the conditions for issuing work permits, but the debate did not stop there. On the contrary, the employers' organization continued to argue that foreign labour was crucial to the Danish economy. This position was voiced quite explicitly by Jens Fisker, member of the DA, in 1970:

> We need a labour force reserve to replace the one that is disappearing and guestworkers are especially welcome. Compared to a reserve of unemployed or housewives, guestworkers will not cost much for society. If we do not need the [imported] labour, we can just deport it. This will mean that the economic burden of maintaining a labour force reserve [in times of recession] will rest upon the guestworker personally or on his home country. The guest worker will rarely bring his wife and family to Denmark and hence our economy can grow faster, since it will not be necessary to invest in additional kindergartens, schools, family housing projects or other social investments that would accompany family migration. Finally, the guestworker is especially welcome since we only need a few investments in housing and machinery to put them to work – guestworkers do not mind irregular working hours.[19]

From the employers' perspective, guestworkers were an economic asset and a necessity. However, Fisker and DA were also very much aware of the

---

18 Niels Elkær Hansen, *Betænkning om udenlandske arbejderes fohold til Danmark: Afgivet af det af arbejdsministeriet den 17. Juni 1969 nedsatte udvalg* (København: Arbejdsministeriet, 1971), 3.
19 Jens Fisker, "Velkommen Mustafa", *Arbejdsgiveren* (1970).

social problems that might be caused by the unregulated immigration of guestworkers, which is why, in the same article, Fisker argued for a national immigration policy. To this end, the federation of trade unions, Landsorganizationen i Danmark LO,[20] and the DA agreed on the need for a national guestworker policy, but continued to argue over the means. Should membership of a union be mandatory for guestworkers, or should this remain voluntary? The unresolved question was whether guestworkers should be seen as labour (a tradable commodity) or as workers with rights that would be ensured by union membership.

In discussing how to resolve the growing labour shortage, guestworkers were ascribed the dual classification of labour or worker. While the employers' organization and the Social Liberal (Radikale Venstre) government[21] mainly viewed guestworkers as imported labour, LO stressed the need to transform the categorization of the migrant from the passive category of labour to the active category of worker. As stressed in a report by the DASF (Dansk Arbejdsmands- og Specialarbejderforbund/The Danish Union for Semi-skilled Worker), Denmark needed an immigration policy that would regulate immigration, ensure that guestworkers became members of a union and allow unions to ensure that salaries were in accordance with the collective agreements. In addition to traditional labour-market issues, the DASF stressed that guestworkers were a vulnerable group at risk of exploitation, especially in the housing market and therefore they needed Danish lessons and various leisure-time activities, all of which should be provided by unions and localities with substantial economic support from those employers who employed them.[22]

Hence, the DASF categorized the migrant as both an active worker whose rights should be protected and a guest in need of special welfare initiatives.[23] The debates over the implicit question of who the guestwork-

---

20 LO, now FH (Fagbevægelsens Hovedorganization), is the federation of trade unions established in 1898 as De Samvirkende Fagforbund, which changed to LO (Landsorganizationen i Danmark) in 1967.
21 The Social Liberal Party (Radikale Venstre) leader Hilmar Baunsgaard was prime minister in a coalition government with the liberals (Venstre) and the conservatives (Det Konservative Folkeparti) in 1968-71.
22 Carl Damsted Andersen, *Samme Vilkår: DASF udvalgsrapport om Fremmedarbejderproblemet* (København: DASF, 1970).
23 Images of guest workers were highly gendered as all illustrations in the report pictured male workers.

er was and what his/her role was in Danish society ended quite abruptly when the oil crisis hit Denmark in the autumn of 1973. As a consequence of the new economic situation, which was causing growing unemployment, the Social Democratic Minister of Labour, Erling Dinesen, completely stopped issuing new work permits and restricted the possibilities for renewing existing permits.[24] The guestworker period came to an end, but immigration to Denmark did not – on the contrary. In the years following this very brief period of bringing in guestworkers and the spontaneous immigration of migrant workers, immigration continued under new conditions and new categories of migrants gradually became part of the Danish welfare state and of social policy debates. Hence, while the category "guestworker" became less central to the debates on migrant welfare in the years following 1973, a new key figure gradually emerged in social policy debates: the immigrant. In the same process, the main area of discussion also changed. Whereas guestworkers were ascribed meaning in debates between two clearly opposing parties, LO and DA, new arenas for defining the migrant as a welfare-state figure came to dominate in the years following 1973.

Permanent Immigrant or Temporary Migrant? The Economic Crisis of Welfare

As already noted, the economic boom of the 1960s came to an abrupt end with the first oil crisis in the autumn of 1973, when an economic recession and high unemployment became important issues in debates over social policy.[25] In this context, guestworkers changed into immigrants both legally (in terms of residence permits) and as figures in debates on social policy. Immigration was a marginal political topic in the national debate, but it became much more salient locally.[26] This was especially the case in Ishøj, a small suburban municipality close to Copenhagen, which had already had a highly diverse population since the early 1970s. Many guestworkers

---

24 Sane, *Billige og villige*.
25 Thorsten Borring Olesen, *De Danske Ministerier: Anker Jørgensens Tid 1972-1982* (København: Gad, 2017).
26 Christoffer Green Pedersen, *Partier i nye tider* (Aarhus: Aarhus Universitetsforlag, 2011); Heidi Vad Jønsson, "Immigrant Policy Developing in Copenhagen and Ishøj in the 1970s," *Scandinavian Journal of History*, 38:5 (2013): 590-911.

chose to move to the new welfare suburbs that were being built to create high-quality homes for the Danish middle and working classes.²⁷

The reality was, however, that very few families living in Copenhagen chose to move to the new apartments in large concrete buildings. As a consequence, Ishøj municipality advertised in magazines to attract guestworkers living in Copenhagen's slums.²⁸ In the years that followed, guestworkers moved to Ishøj with their families and by 1974, a large proportion of Ishøj's population had migrant backgrounds.²⁹ In this context, the Social Democratic mayor, Per Madsen, persistently argued that guestworkers were in fact immigrants who were going to remain in Denmark permanently. In addition, Madsen stressed that immigrants' social conditions differed from those of Danish nationals when it came to access to welfare services. Hence, locally "the migrant" ceased to be a narrow issue of the labour market and was being treated as a new social category in the Danish welfare state. While Ishøj municipality argued that guestworkers were not temporary imported labour, but permanent immigrants with social problems that could not be dealt with by existing welfare policies, the guestworker category was maintained in national debates, policy documents and newspapers.³⁰

However, in 1979, the immigrant became attached more explicitly to the welfare state when the left-wing party VS (Left Socialists) held a debate in parliament on the social conditions of immigrant families.³¹ In this debate, Preben Wilhjelm (VS) emphasized that migrants were in a vulnerable position in Denmark. First of all, he argued that the guestworkers who had arrived in Denmark during the economic boom had been hit harder by the economic recession following 1973: "De har den højeste arbejdsløshed".³² Secondly, the legal status of foreigners was very insecure, since they were at risk of administrative deportation.³³

---

27 Mikkel Høghøj and Silke Holmqvist, "Da betonen blev belastende: Den emotionelle kamp om Gellerupplanen i 1960'erne og 1970'erne," *TEMP – tidsskrift for historie*, vol. 16 (2018): 124-144.
28 Jønsson, "Immigrant Policy".
29 Ishøj Kommune, *Indvandrerrapport II* (Ishøj: Ishøj Kommune, 1978).
30 See http://labs.statsbiblioteket.dk/smurf?q=indvandrer.g%C3%A6stearbejder
31 Jørn Henrik Petersen, Klaus Petersen and Niels Finn Christiansen, eds., *Dansk Velfærdshistorie vol. 5: Velfærdsstaten i tidehverv*, (Odense: Syddansk Universitetsforlag, 2014).
32 Folketingstidende 1979/80, 2. Samling. *Forhandlinger* sp. 692.
33 Karen Andersen, *Gæstearbejder - udlænding - indvandrer - dansker! Migration til Danmark i 1968-78* (København: Gyldendal, 1979).

Even though the question of migrants' legal position was linked to entry policy (the regulation of residence permits and deportation), this issue became important for the framing of the migrants in the Danish welfare state, as their uncertain legal position regarding the right to residence had consequences for their social rights. Migrants were entitled to social benefits, but in theory they could be deported if they were proved to need long-term social assistance.[34] Even though this passage in the social legislation was interpreted very loosely and was not sanctioned, the very risk of deportation represented a problem in terms of migrants' position in society in general and in relation to the welfare state in particular.[35]

In addition to these issues, VS stressed that migrants lived in poor housing conditions, had poor access to education and were not sufficiently covered by the social schemes of the Social Democratic welfare state.[36] Hence, they saw the migrant as a figure who was exploited by the capitalist system and they questioned the existing welfare system's ability to solve the problems of this so-called "new proletariat".[37] In the 1979 debate, the Social Democratic Prime Minister Anker Jørgensen acknowledged that migrants were a vulnerable group whose legal position in society should be improved by new regulations governing the existing system relating to deportation. Furthermore, Jørgensen emphasized that migrants should have full social rights and be covered by the existing system of social and economic security.[38] But while the left-wing parties argued for special initiatives to protect migrants from exploitation, the Social Democratic government maintained that migrants' social problems should be solved by the existing welfare system. Hence, in the eyes of the left-wing parties, the migrant was given a minority status and the political answer to migrants' social problems was a minority policy that would entail full social rights, legal protection against administrative deportation and the ability to maintain and develop their cultural lives.[39]

---

34 Andersen, *Gæstearbejder*.
35 Andersen, *Gæstearbejder*.
36 Folketingstidende 1979/80, 2. samling. *Forhandlinger* sp. 692ff.
37 In this period, the left-wing parties were critical of the social democratic welfare state. See Jørn Henrik Petersen, Klaus Petersen and Niels Finn Christiansen, eds., *Dansk Velfærdshistorie vol. 5: Velfærdsstaten i tidehverv*, (Odense: Syddansk Universitetsforlag, 2014).
38 Jønsson, *Fra lige muligheder til ret og pligt*.
39 On multicultural policies, see Wickström, *The multicultural moment*.

A quite different attitude to the migrant dominated the Social Democratic position. As Anker Jørgensen implied in his parliamentary address, equal treatment of all citizens in similar situations was the very foundation of the Social Democratic welfare state, a factor that also shaped the government's immigrant policy:

> the period after arrival will now for the greater part of the migrant population be an integration period where they have to adjust to Danish society. This quite clearly raises several problems. It has been suggested that a special public authority should be created to address and solve these integration-related problems. I will, however, use his opportunity to stress that the government's policy is still that foreigners' problems should not be managed by a special authority, but rather be dealt with by the same institutions and authorities as used by Danish nationals.[40]

At least two different migrant categories were invoked in the 1979 debate. First, there was the migrant as a minority figure requiring a minority policy with special institutions that could secure minority rights. Second, there was the figure of the new welfare citizen, whose social problems were to be solved by the existing system. These two figures came to dominate the debate in the following decades, when immigration became a much more heated topic. However, one other migrant figure was also constructed in the late 1970s: that of the problematic immigrant. This figure was part of the media debate throughout the 1970s, a period when immigration was linked to crime,[41] but from a welfare-state perspective the problematic immigrant became key only when the radical right-wing party Fremskridtspartiet (the Progress Party) made a rather extreme proposal for a parliamentary decision in 1979. Under the heading "Tyrkerdrænet"[42], party leader Mogens Glistrup demanded cancellation of the social contracts that had been made with Turkey and Yugoslavia in 1976. These contracts had been

---

40 Folketingstidende 1979/80, 2. Samling. *Forhandlinger* sp. 696.
41 Jacob Gaarde Madsen, *Mediernes konstruktion af flygtninge og indvandrerspørgsmålet* (Aarhus: Aarhus Universitetsforlag, 2004); Jensen, *De Fremmede*.
42 The term "Tyrkerdrænet" suggested that Turkish guest workers were an economic deficit and thus "drained" the Danish welfare system.

made to ensure guestworkers had a minimum of entitlements to social benefits corresponding to the number of years they had worked and paid taxes in Denmark.[43] As the Minister for Social Affairs explained:

> These bilateral agreements are to ensure that nationals from other countries are guaranteed the right to recieve social pensions correponding to the work effort and tax payments they have made while in Denmark. Whether they wish to recieve social pensions in Denmark or in their home country is optional. Founded on the principle of reprocitiy, Danish nationals are also guarateed equal social rights corresponding to the social legislation in those countries that are included in the bilateral agreements.[44]

In justifying his parliamentary motion, Glistrup argued that social contracts would lead to the immigration of migrants from poorer countries increasing and would in effect pose a threat to the Danish welfare system and the Danish economy: "Når fidusen rygtes, vil enhver tyrkisk landsby med respekt for sig selv sende folk til Danmark for at se, om man ikke kan komme med til denne nye guldkalvdans. Et sådant truende digebrud for dansk økonomi må afværges, før truslen tager alvorligt fat."[45] The motion was not debated in parliament, as its wording ("Tyrkerdræn") was considered improper. Nonetheless the motion represented a view of the migrant as a potential threat to the Danish nation and the Danish welfare state, creating a migrant figure that came to dominate the debates over migrant welfare in the years that followed.

Hence, by 1979, in the Danish welfare state the migrant was not one key figure, but three opposing figures. Left-wing parties called migrants a minority and argued for a multicultural policy based on minority rights.[46]

---

43 Heidi Vad Jønsson, "A new inequality in the Danish Welfare State", in *Marginalized Groups, Inequalities and the Postwar Welfare State: Whose Welfare?*, eds., Monika Baar and Paul van Trigt (London: Routledge, 2019) 174-192.
44 Folketingstidende 1979/80. Tillæg A sp. 5829.
45 Folketingstidende 1979/80. Tillæg A sp. 5829.
46 Multicultural policies were introduced in Sweden in the 1970s and were thus one among more optional policy directions in this formative period. See Mats Wickström, *The Multicultural Moment: The History of the Idea and Politics of Multiculturalism in Sweden in Comparative, Transnational and Biographical Context, 1964–1975* (Ph.D. thesis, Åbo Akademi, 2015).

Right-wing parties drew the quite opposite picture of the migrant as an unwelcome intruder in the Danish welfare state, a guest who had "outstayed his welcome" and an outright threat to Danish society. In between these two opposing positions was the Social Democratic view of the migrant as a new welfare citizen with the same welfare rights and obligations as Danish nationals. In this view, the migrant was seen as a social category with new sorts of difficulties, such as language and cultural barriers, which had to be addressed and solved by the existing welfare system.

These three positions set the framework for migration debates in the following decades when new types of migrant category, such as refugees and asylum-seekers came to dominate the debate on migrant welfare.

Refugees, Asylum-seekers and the Formation of new Subcategories

After the 1960s, the category of migrant changed both as a concept and in its content. While the guestworker was seen as either passive labour or active worker depending on the context (LO/DA), the immigrant gradually emerged as a new citizenship category in the 1970s and was now loaded with three competing definitions: a threat, a minority or a new welfare citizen. This provided the basis for debating immigration when a new group of migrants, in the form of refugees, gained increasing attention.

Refugees were not a new group in Denmark, but they attracted increased attention in the 1980s for several reasons. First, in 1983 a new Aliens Act was passed after years of heated debate over the legal position of migrants in Denmark.[47] The Act introduced a legal right to a residence permit when the conditions defined in the law had been fulfilled. In addition, a board of appeal and other initiatives to prevent administrative deportation without the right to appeal were introduced to strengthen migrants' legal rights.[48] Furthermore, migrants' social rights were reinforced as the ability to deport non-Danish nationals who were in need of long-term social assistance was now removed.[49] The new Aliens Act represented a total

---

47 Peter Christensen, "Udlændingeloven 1983-2009", *Grænser for solidaritet: indvandrerpolitik i dansk og europæisk perspektiv*, eds. Mette Bock and Jens Holger Schjørring (København: Anis, 2010).
48 Niels Wium Olesen, *De danske ministerier: Poul Schlüters Tid 1982-1993* (København: Gad, 2017).
49 Heidi Vad Jønsson and Klaus Petersen, "Indvandring og integration' in *Dansk Velfærdshistorie vol.*

reform of the existing system and was based on the principles of legal protection, which meant that the migrant was now ascribed meaning as an individual with the right to legal protection to the same extent as Danish nationals. This push towards improving migrants' social rights and legal protection came from the centre-left and left-wing parties, whereas the Liberals and especially the Conservatives now in government preferred to continue with the administrative assessment of individual cases.[50]

As an effect of these developments, the migrant was given two additional meanings, causing the debates on immigration and the role, rights and position of the migrant in the Danish welfare state to become even more fuzzy. Even though the discussions mainly acknowledged Denmark as a society based on the rule of law, they also shaped these reconstructions of the immigrant in the welfare state, who was now defined as a citizen whom the welfare state must protect and who must at the same time be protected from the state through improvements to the migrant's legal position. Hence, the already rather blurred image of the migrant was reinforced when refugees became part of the discussion.

Different groups of refugees had entered Denmark throughout the twentieth century in various circumstances.[51] In the years following the Second World War, refugees were treated as a special group in need of protection under international law. More specifically, the UN's Refugee Convention (1951), which was ratified by Denmark in 1952, described in detail who refugees were and emphasized their basic human rights.[52] This meant that refugees' social rights in Denmark must be equal to those of Danish nationals.[53] Hence, refugees who came to Denmark were granted protection and included as new citizens in the existing welfare system. While refugees who came to Denmark in the 1950s and 1960s mainly consisted

---

5: *Velfærdsstaten i tidehverv*, Jørn Henrik Petersen, Klaus Petersen and Niels Finn Christiansen, eds., (Odense: Syddansk Universitetsforlag, 2014).
50 Wium Olsesen, *De danske ministerier*; Anne Brøcker, "Udlændingelovgivning i Danmark 1983-86: Faktorer i den politiske beslutningsproces," *Politica* 22, no. 3 (1990): 332-345.
51 See for example Cecilie Banke, *Et menneske uden pas er ikke noget menneske: Danmark i den internationale flygtningepolitik 1933-1939* (Odense: Syddansk universitetsforlag, 2005); Garbi Schmidt, *Nørrebros indvandringshistorie 1885-2010* (København: Museum Tusculanum, 2015); Østergaard, *Indvandrerne i Danmarks historie*.
52 Gil Loescher, "UNHCR's Origins and Early History: Agency, Influence and Power in Global Refugee Policy," *Refuge* vol. 33, no 1. (2017): 77-86.
53 See UN Refugee Convention, Chapter IV: Welfare: https://www.unhcr.org/3b66c2aa10.

of expatriates and small groups of persecuted refugees from the Soviet Union, the situation changed in the 1970s in the wake of the Vietnam War. The UNHCR played a key role in making arrangements for the relocation of Vietnamese refugees and in 1978 the Danish state agreed with the UNHCR that it would receive five hundred refugees a year. Hence, this subcategory became one of several refugee categories that were debated using different and competing logics. Whereas migrants who were granted a residence permit as refugees were protected by the UN's Refugee Convention, the conditions and social rights of other categories of migrants (e.g. immigrants, asylum-seekers, marriage migrants etc.) became a heated topic in Denmark throughout the 1980s.

While quota refugees were both protected by the UN Convention and received asylum in Denmark as an effect of bilateral agreements, the legitimacy granted to other groups of refugees and their conditions were debated much more intensely. The 1983 reform was to a great extent the product of a discussion of migrants' legal protection, especially in connection with deportation, but it also included legal rights to residence permits under those conditions stated in the legislation.[54] As the number of asylum-seekers had already risen just a year after the passing of the new Aliens Act, the debate shifted from deportation and migrants' legal protection to entry policy and residence permits.[55] In these debates, a new category of migrants – asylum-seekers – was now the centre of attention. During the 1980s, Denmark continued to receive UNHCR quota refugees, but in discussions on immigration, so-called "spontaneous asylum-seekers" gradually became key figures in a very heated and emotional debate. The three migrant categories that took shape in the 1979 debates were reinforced in the highly emotional climate that came to dominate immigration debates from the mid-1980s.

This happened in a context of intensified criticism of the welfare state when the neoliberal logics of privatization and marketization were formulated as a response to the continued economic recession and high unemployment. In connection with the immigration issue, the role of the welfare state was questioned. While the Social Democratic government

---

54 Folketingstidende 1982/83, Tillæg C: 609-632.
55 Anne Brøcker, "Udlændingelovgivning i Danmark 1983-86: Faktorer i den politiske beslutningsproces," *Politica* 22, no. 3 (1990): 332-345.

had recognized that the inequalities experienced by different groups of migrants should be remedied through social policies, the Conservative-Liberal coalition that entered office in 1982 took the quite opposite position. As Minister of Interior Britta Schall Holberg (V) stressed in her presentation of the government's immigration policy, migrants had a personal responsibility to become part of society. Integration was thus seen as an individual obligation rather than a matter for the state.[56] In the years that followed, debates on migration in Denmark were focused on a number of conflicts which became more and more outspoken.

First of all, there was a fierce debate over the number of asylum-seekers, refugees and immigrants that Denmark could and should receive. Secondly, the question of culture created new lines of conflict between the political parties, social movements and interest groups. The left-wing parties, the Social Liberals and some within the Social Democratic Party argued that Denmark had an international responsibility and that the number of newcomers was not a problem. They saw the lack of equal opportunities as the most important immigration-related issue.[57] This position was debated throughout the 1980s, when the Social Democratic Party in particular was marked by internal conflicts over the migration issue and from the mid-1980s split into at least two factions. One faction represented localities that viewed immigrants as a new social group whose integration was costly for those localities that had received a large number of immigrants and now also refugees. In addition, immigrants' cultural backgrounds entered into debates over the problems and challenges pertaining to immigration. The second faction consisted of the Social Democrats in Parliament, who stressed with increasing intensity that the number of refugees was not a problem and should not be regulated. As party leader Svend Auken stressed in an internal meeting: "This is also a question of moral leadership",[58] thereby emphasizing that Denmark had a moral obligation to accept refugees and that refugees had the right to become part of society. As for the question of culture, the social democrat Birte Weiss stressed that migrants' cultural backgrounds and cultural diversity were not problems, but rather enriched Danish society.[59]

---

56   Folketingstidende 1982/83 "Forhandlinger", 8978 ff; 9665ff.
57   Jønsson, *Fra lige muligheder til ret og pligt*.
58   Jønsson, *Fra lige muligheder til ret og pligt*, 94-97.
59   Birte Weiss, "Tyrken i Ishøj", *Politiken* March 8 1989.

Hence, in the eyes of the centre-left parties, migrants were not *a* social problem, but a group that *had* social problems related to their special situation as newcomers in a society that did not provide them with adequate opportunities to integrate. More specifically, the ability to learn Danish, receive an education and learn about Danish society should be increased, whereas migrants' cultural backgrounds should not be seen as part of the problem. Hence, the migrant figure of the 1980s appeared as a refugee in need of protection and a welcome new citizen with social problems and limited social resources.

A diametrically opposite view of the migrant was that represented by the right in Danish politics. From this part of the political spectrum, the very numbers of asylum-seekers and refugees were a threat to Danish culture and the Danish nation state. Migrants as a group were singled out as problematic figures in Danish society and within the migrant category different logics of problematization were attached to refugees, asylum-seekers and immigrants. Quota refugees were in Denmark as the result of negotiations with the UNHCR and were therefore categorized in line with the logic of human rights and Denmark's international responsibilities. However, in the 1980s, the image of the refugee changed quite substantially as migrants started coming to Denmark and applying for asylum at the Danish border. This new group of migrants were categorized as "spontaneous asylum-seekers", as they were not part of the regulated UNHCR quota system, nor were they recognized as other refugees.[60]

As the Aliens Act of 1983 gave asylum-seekers the legal right to stay in Denmark while their case was being assessed by the Danish authorities, the growing numbers of asylum-seekers gave rise to a debate concerning not only whether Denmark should accept refugees, but also over the legitimacy of the legal definition of a refugee and its potential consequences. Hence, while left-wing parties, interest groups and large stakeholders in Danish refugee policy, such as Danish Refugee Aid (Dansk Flygtningehjælp) categorized refugees within a framework of human rights and internal obligations, the political right and new right-wing movements classed

---

60 The United Nations High Commissioner for Refugees: UNHCR was established in 1950 and played a key role in international refugee policy and the relocation of refugees. See Loescher, "UNHCR's Origins and Early History."

both refugees and especially asylum seekers with reference to the context of the nation state.

A highly influential voice in this debate was the priest Søren Krarup, who in 1987 initiated a campaign against the 1983 Aliens Act by arguing that accepting refugees would "eventually lead to the end of the Danish nation."[61] This campaign was taken up by a rather small but nonetheless highly visible organization, Den Danske Forening (The Danish Organization), which persistently protested against refugees' legal claims to residence permits, arguing that migrants (refugees, immigrants etc.) from cultures that differed in significant ways from Danish culture posed a threat to the the Danish nation state.[62] Hence, from this perspective, the migrant was constructed as a cultural threat and as a bearer of values that were incompatible with so-called Danish values.

This position was also reflected in parliamentary debates where the Progress Party (Fremskridtspartiet) questioned the legitimacy of asylum-seekers by introducing a new label: "convenience refugee", thereby emphasizing a distinction between refugees who were recognized as such and those who were not. The criteria for this distinction centred around a new logic of culture and religion. As Fremskridtspartiet argued in a legislative proposal:

> Due to the existing taxsystem and respressive regulations, we end up exporting our own visionary countrymen (especially the young and/or dynamic ones) who were supposed to improve economic growth and prosperity in Denmark. Meanwhile, the revenues from the unbearable plunderings of taxation are thrown away on the continuous entry of convenience refugees, who arrive unrestricted by airline from the Middle East, and who are culturally worlds apart from ourselves.[63]

While the Progress Party (Fremskridtspartiet) represented an extreme position on both immigration and the welfare state as an anti-immigration and anti-welfare state party, the logic of culture and religion was also quite

---

61 See Jensen, *De Fremmede*; Jønsson, *Fra lige muligheder til ret og pligt*.
62 The magazine *Danskeren*: http://www.dendanskeforening.dk/side534.html
63 Folketingstidende 1979/80 2. Samling, Tillæg A: 5827-5830.

prevalent among the Conservatives and Liberals, both of whom had voiced concerns over the increasing numbers of asylum-seekers from countries far away from Denmark and cultures that were considered very different from Danish. Already in 1983, the Conservative Minister of Justice Erik Ninn-Hansen voiced his concern over a possible connection between increased immigration and "racial unrest".[64]

Hence, the migrant was a highly contested figure in Danish political debates and a category that was negotiated in a sensitive and emotional context stretched out between different logics of the Danish state. Liberals and Conservatives regarded the migrant as a potential threat to the nation state, while the more extreme right-wing parties and movements claimed there was an actual threat to both the nation state and the welfare state from immigration. In strong opposition to this position were the left-wing parties and social movements associated with the centre-left parties (Social Democratic Party and Social Liberal Party), which treated the migrant as an individual who should enjoy equal social rights and legal protection. Hence, to a great extent this group drew on the idea of Denmark as a welfare state emphasizing universalism and equality and as a progressive state with international responsibilities. In this perspective, the migrant was seen as an individual who must be protected by the welfare state and equally importantly a potential victim of discrimination and racism. Hence, the anti-discrimination logic also affected how the migrant was classified regardless of his or her legal status as an asylum-seeker, refugee or immigrant.[65]

In addition to the cross-party negotiations and conflicts over various migrant categories, intra-party conflicts made the categorization even more complex. The Social Democratic Party was split over opposing views on the migrant, drawing on the competing logics of numbers being a problem either for social cohesion or local economies. Hence, the immigration debate centred around the question of whether migrants were a social, cultural and economic problem due to their increasing numbers, or whether they had social problems due to a lack of induction schemes, limited social and economic resources and/or discriminatory policies such

---

64 Quoted from Jensen, *De Fremmede*, 447.
65 Ishøj Foreningen mod Fremmedhad is an example of an anti-racist movement that was established in opposition to the local policy. See Jønsson, "Immigrant Policy".

as the housing policy introduced in Ishøj municipality.[66] By the beginning of the 1990s, the migrant was being reduced to a set of legal categories as refugee, asylum-seeker, the social-political categories of immigrant and descendant and a number of political categories that also included a very "colourful palette" of new concepts with polemical connotations, such as "convenience refugee" or Muhammadan.

These different categories all emerged during the 1980s and drew on competing and opposing logics, turning the migrant into a highly diversified category that attracted increasing attention as immigration became a more important political issue. This was not least because of increasing awareness of this very heated topic among voters in a context in which voting on issues had an impact on party politics that the parties themselves had to respond to.[67]

Welfare Reforms: Migrants as a Political Target Group

By the early 1990s, the migrant was thus a fuzzy and highly contested figure with multiple layers of categorization that were constantly being renegotiated and ascribed new layers of meaning. As immigration became an ever more heated topic, categorizing migrants more narrowly as a political target group became a pressing issue. This process was mainly pushed by two factors. First, the debate over how many refugees Denmark could and should accept continued, an issue that became even more pressing in the wake of the Yugoslav Wars, which put thousands of people to flight, thereby creating even greater pressure on the Danish asylum system. By the mid-1990s, 18,000 refugees from the former Yugoslavia were in Denmark with a new type of residence permit: "temporary protection", which meant that refugees granted asylum under these conditions were only given protection in Denmark for a limited number of years.[68] In addition to this sizea-

---

66 See Niels Ufer, *Set fra Ishøj* (København: Informations Forlag, 1988); Jønsson, "Immigrant Policy".
67 Issue voting came to dominate the political scene from the 1970s onwards. See Christoffer Green Pedersen, *Partier i nye tider* (Aarhus: Aarhus Universitetsforlag, 2011).
68 For an analysis of Danish asylum policy, see Kathrine Vitus and Signe Smith Nielsen, eds., *Asylbørn i Danmark: En barndom i undtagelsestilstand* (Copenhagen: Hans Reitzels Forlag, 2011); Thomas Gammeltoft-Hansen and Hans Gammeltoft-Hansen, "Retten Til at Søge: Om FN's Menneskerettighedsdeklaration Art. 14 og EU's Asylpolitik," In Eva Ersbøll et al eds., *Denne Verden Fortjener at Blive Forandret* (København: DJØF Forlag, 2007), 67-89.

ble group of refugees, the entry of so-called "spontaneous asylum-seekers" continued as an increasing number of Somalis entered Denmark in the wake of Somalia's civil war. Whereas the refugees from Yugoslavia were problematized due to their numbers (the right-wing position) or their limited ability to participate in Danish society (the left-wing position), the legitimacy of the Somalis as refugees was questioned in tabloid newspapers like *Ekstra Bladet*, which in a series of feature articles claimed that Somali "refugees" were not refugees, but immigrants who had come to Denmark to capitalize on the generous Danish welfare system.[69] In this way, the tabloid press fuelled the ongoing debate over the legitimacy of different categories and groups of refugees by introducing a new label, "fake asylum-seeker" (*fupasylansøger*). Hence, the categorizations that had been heavily negotiated in the 1980s were reproduced and attached to different groups of refugees in the 1990s, thereby shaping the process of transforming the various refugee categories into specific political target groups in immigration policy governed by the Aliens Act.

Secondly, when a new Social Democratic government inspired by third-way social democracy entered office in 1993, several reforms to the welfare state were introduced in the period from then until 2001. Under a slogan proclaiming the "right and duty to welfare", Prime Minister Poul Nyrup Rasmussen stressed the importance of all citizens fulfilling their duties to work and pay taxes and claiming their rights to welfare benefits and services.[70] Hence, active labour market policies (ALMP) became the overall framework for reforms to Danish social policy in what became known as "the age of activation".[71] In this context, immigrant integration became mainly a question of labour-market participation.[72]

While migrants categorized as foreigners were already a political target group for immigration policy and the Aliens Act, the migrant did not become a separate target group in welfare policies until the introduction of the first Integration Act, passed by Parliament in 1998. In this

---

69 Jørgensen, *Hvad sagde vi!*
70 Jørn Henrik Petersen, *Pligt & ret – Ret &pligt* (Odense: Syddansk Universitetsforlag, 2014).
71 Jørgen Goul Andersen, "Universalisation and de-universalisation of unemployment protection in Denmark and Sweden," in *Welfare State, Universalism and Diversity*, eds., A. Anttonen, L. Haikio and K. Stefansson, (Cheltenham: Edward Elgar Publishing, 2012), 162-186.
72 Grete Brochmann and Anniken Hagelund, eds., *Immigration Policy and the Scandinavian Welfare State 1945-2010* (Cham: Palgrave Macmillan, 2012).

new welfare legislation, the different migrant categories of newly arrived immigrants and refugees were now defined as unique new social persons with both the right and the duty to integrate into Danish society.[73] The Integration Act specified that newly arrived immigrants and refugees had the right to become part of Danish society, as well as an equal duty to participate in integration programmes that would enable their labour-market participation.[74] Hence, the migrant was now more narrowly defined as a target group in both immigration and integration policies. This shift from a fuzzy and contested category to a political category became an important benchmark for the immigration debates that continued and intensified in the twenty-first century.

By the turn of the millennium, the immigration issue had moved to the top of the political agenda, becoming a decisive election issue in the 2001 parliamentary election. Even though the migrant remained a contested figure, the institutionalization of the migrant as a political target group in immigration and integration polices shaped the migration debate in the following decades. As economic growth and labour shortages came to dominate the first decade of the twenty-first century, a dual immigration policy was developed to attract specific groups of migrant workers.[75] At the same time, integration policies were increasingly designed to target so-called non-western immigrants.[76] In both cases, migrants were clearly defined as a political target group, but how to integrate migrants and regulate immigration remained highly controversial issues.

Migrant Categories in the Danish Welfare State, 1960s to 2000s

As we can see from the foregoing, the migrant has been a highly contested figure in Denmark for the past half-century. The category of migrant has been reconfigured in three phases. In the years of the booming economy and welfare-state expansion, the migrant was narrowly linked to labour-

---

73 Jønsson, *Fra lige muligheder til ret og pligt*.
74 Jønsson, *Fra lige muligheder til ret og pligt*.
75 Patrick Emmenegger, Silja Häusermann, Bruno Palier and Martin Seeleib-Kaiser, *The Age of Dualization* (Oxford: Oxford University Press, 2012).
76 See Jønsson, *Fra lige muligheder til ret og pligt*.

market issues under the label of guestworker. This category was ascribed a dual meaning as either passive labour with a high degree of commodification as the underlying assumption, or an active worker whose membership of a union was crucial to avoid the consequences of commodification (wage pressure) and to enable guestworkers to become active (but temporary) members of society. This dual meaning of the migrant was challenged in the 1970s and 1980s, when refugees became a heated and highly emotional political issue. Several competing perceptions of the migrant consequently appeared. Hence, in this period of criticism of the welfare state, an economic recession and increasing immigration by asylum-seekers, the migrant was ascribed meaning as a legal category pertaining to international law (the UN Refugee Convention) as well as the Danish Aliens Act. In addition, the migrant became a politically contested figure with opposed meanings both across the political spectrum and within the political parties. Hence, in the second phase of categorization, the status of migrant was subject to constant renegotiation and became an important symbolic figure in social policy debates. The fuzzy and multiple layers of meanings were to some extent accumulated as the migrant became a political target group in the third phase of categorization. The contested nature of the migrant continued, but with the introduction of a new welfare policy in 1998 stressing the importance of integration. Social policy debates were now shaped by this new institution of welfare policy, which became an important benchmark for the ongoing debate over the migrant in the twenty-first century.

The Patient

Citizen, Consumer and Partner in Health Governance

Anja Svejsgaard Pors, Kirstine Zinck Pedersen and Peter Kjær

In this chapter, we contribute to the unpacking of institutional changes of the welfare state by examining how the patient is configured as a key political actor in the Danish healthcare system.[1] By analyzing the configuration of the patient, we show how the patient is enacted as part of particular rationalities of governance both at the level of national policymaking and at the level of a welfare institution, exemplified at a single hospital. As a discursive figuration, the patient is not exclusively related to the specificity of the doctor-patient relation - rather, the patient has a much wider remit as part of a configuration of the ways in which certain problems of healthcare organization and management are perceived. The analysis of how the patient is inscribed in healthcare problems and solutions point

---

1 The chapter builds on two previously published articles by the authors on patient discourses in Danish healthcare. The introductory sections and diachronic analysis draws on Kirstine Zinck Pedersen and Peter Kjær, "The new patient": the emergence of a political persona," *International Journal of Public Sector Management* 30, no. 1 (2017): 85-98. The synchronic analysis builds on Anja Svejgaard Pors, "Constructions of the patient in healthcare communications: six patient figures", *Journal of Health Organization and Management*, 30, no. 2 (2016): 279-298.

to historically changing authority relations and intersecting governance ideals either within concrete organizational contexts or within the healthcare system and the welfare state at large.

Our ambition is to show how the patient is neither a formal political actor nor simply an expression of a broad ideology of new public management; rather, we study the patient in the context of particular historical and organizational ideals. We unpack and contextualize the mobilization of the patient by analyzing how diverse representations of the patient are discursively enacted in Danish healthcare policy and organization. For this purpose, our analytical strategy is both diachronic and synchronic. We study, diachronically, the emergence of the patient in two key historical healthcare policy debates: the debate on healthcare effectiveness and controlling public expenditure one the one hand and the debate on healthcare quality and service-optimization on the other. The analysis takes its point of departure in the beginning of the 1970s, when the Danish welfare state is consolidated through social reforms that secure, among other things, free access to healthcare. Moreover, a structural reform lays the ground for a coordinated fiscal governance of the healthcare sector for the first time. Due to the fiscal crisis in the 1970s, the state is required to formulate and consolidate a national health policy that displays problems and solutions in welfare governance.

Here, for the first time, the patient is addressed as part of the solution, i.e. as a responsible key political actor in governance of the welfare state. This part of the analysis is based on a discourse analysis of national-level health policy documents from the 1970s to 2000. We show that, in the course of the two debates, two new patient figures are formulated: the socio-economically responsible citizen and the demanding consumer, respectively.

We then study, synchronically, the mobilization of the patient in organizational documents attached to a Danish hospital's locally developed policy program. We here trace how the patient is enacted in a range of co-existing discursive figures: within the same program, the patient is figured as an affective individual, as a consumer with rights and choices and as a collaborating resource. The program thus constructs the patient as a flexible figure able to fit a variety of specific organizational problems and potential solutions.

All together, the analysis tells stories of changing authority relations between patients, professionals, healthcare institutions and welfare state in which health governance discourses display the patient as a flexible management tool and thus a key political actor in the formation of the Danish welfare landscape.

Background

In recent decades, rising costs and marketization have challenged the very rationale of healthcare organizations. Once viewed as highly specialized organizations dedicated to treating patients through expert knowledge, public healthcare organizations today are also seen as service providers, offering services to customers whose needs cannot simply be stipulated a priori by healthcare professionals.[2] Today, healthcare organizations must meet very specific patient needs, empower patients and simultaneously free resources. In this landscape, improving efficiency and the quality of care have become a question of identifying and meeting growing demands by engaging with patients in new ways; i.e. the patient has become a key figure in healthcare policy and organization.

The current focus on the patient is manifested in the massive preoccupation with "patient-centredness" among healthcare professionals, patient advocates and healthcare researchers who highlight the need and practical means for reconfiguring the doctor-patient relationship.[3] Thus, over the past three decades, patient-centredness has swept across our "Western" societies as a movement to humanize healthcare the aim

---

2   Peter Kjær, Anne Reff Pedersen and Anja Svejgaard Pors, "A Discursive Approach to Organizational Health Communication," in *Oxford Handbook of Health Care Management*, eds. Ewan Ferlie, Kathleen Montgomery, Anne Reff Pedersen (Oxford: Oxford University Press, 2016), 302-324; Ewan Ferlie, Liz Cairncross, and Andrew M. Pettigrew, "Introducing market-like mechanisms in the public sector: The case of the National Health Service," in *Perspectives on Strategic Change*, eds. Luca Zan, Stefano Zambon and Andrew M. Pettigrew (Kluwer Academic, 1993), 235-256.

3   Jozien Bensing, "Bridging the gap: The separate worlds of evidence-based medicine and patient-centered medicine," *Patient Education and Counselling*, 39 (2000): 17–25; Donald M. Berwick, "What "patient-centered' should mean: Confession of an extremist," *Health Affairs* 28 no. 4 (2009): 555-565; Nicola Mead and Peter Bower "Patient-centredness: a conceptual framework and review of the empirical literature," *Social Science and Medicine* 51, no.7 (2000): 1087-1110; Moira Stewart, *Patient-Centered Medicine: Transforming the Clinical Method* (London: Sage, 1995); Margaret Gerteis, Susan Edgman-Levitan, Jennifer Daley and Thomas L. Delbanco, *Through the Patient's Eyes: Understanding and Promoting Patient-Centered Care* (London: Wiley, 2002).

developing a broader and more holistic approach to healthcare, to problematize the so-called "sovereign authority" of professional expertise and to highlight the basic mutuality of this relation and the actual or potential agency of the patient in producing his or her own health. Patient-centred care has therefore also been strongly associated with a quest for patient empowerment.[4] These debates have primarily been concerned with the patient-provider nexus, although it is occasionally acknowledged that there may be political or organizational interests at stake in the mobilization of the patient.[5]

Public organization and management studies concerning patient-centred care expand the field of inquiry from the clinical encounter to the overall political, institutional and organizational context. These studies often consider patient involvement and patient-centredness as an expression of the rise of New Public Management tropes with a focus on individual choice and patient preferences as a distinct move towards consumerism and marketization within healthcare.[6] Thus, patient-centred healthcare has merged with marketization ideals, according to which the demands and choices of patient-cum-consumers could spur healthcare organizations to maximize efficiency.

There seems to be a gulf between such critical observations and the enthusiasm with which many patient advocates and healthcare professionals embrace patient-centredness. Recent work has attempted to challenge this gulf by disentangling the relationships between clinical norms and practices, on the one hand and wider policy or organizational ideals, on the

---

4   Inger Holmström and Marta Röing, "The relation between patient-centredness and patient empowerment: A discussion on concepts," *Patient Education and Counseling* 79 (2010): 167-172; Isabelle Aujoulat, William d'Hoore and Alain Deccache "Patient empowerment in theory and practice: Polysemy or cacophony?", *Patient Education and Counseling* 66 (2007): 13-20.
5   Paulina Bravo, Adrian Edwards, Paul James Barr, Isabelle Scholl, Glyn Elwyn and Marion McAllister. "Conceptualising patient empowerment: a mixed methods study," *BMC Health Service Research* 15 (2015): 252-259; Holmström and Röing, "The relation."
6   Sharon C. Bolton, "Consumer as king in the NHS," *International Journal of Public Sector Management* 15, no. 2 (2002): 129-139; Lars Nordgren, *Från patient till kund - Intåget av marknadstänkande i sjukvården och förskjutningen av patientens position* (Ph.D. thesis, Lund: Ekonomihögskolan, Lunds Universitet, 2003); Ellen Kuhlmann, *Modernising Health Care: Reinventing professions, the state and the public* (Bristol: The Policy Press, 2006); Agneta Ranerup, "Transforming Patients to Consumers: Evaluating National Healthcare Portals," *International Journal of Public Sector Management* 23, no. 4 (2010): 331-339; Alex Mold, "Making the patient-consumer in Margaret Thatcher's Britain," *The Historical Journal* 54, no. 2 (2011): 509-528.

other. Research in this direction has been started by Dent and Pahor and associates,[7] who study how different models for patient involvement have been implemented in a number of European countries.[8] Policy researchers have also begun to examine the historical configuration of the patient to highlight how such configuration should be viewed in historical and political contexts.[9] Our study adds to this conversation, as well as to discussions within the Danish history of the welfare state and, more specifically, the history of the Danish healthcare system – an area within which scholars have only paid sporadic attention to the patient.[10]

Method and analytical Handholds

Our analysis is founded on the insight that, in political and organizational debates of problems and solutions, new types of agency or identity are being defined. A growing body of literature shows how policy and strategy-making processes constitute agency rather than simply reflecting it.[11] In

---

7   Mike Dent and Majda Pahor, "Patient involvement in Europe – a comparative framework", *Journal of Health Organization and Management* 29, no 5 (2015): 546-555.
8   See also Inga-Lill Johansson, Lars Noren and Ewa Wikstrom, "Patient-centred care: the Nordic position," *International Journal of Public Sector Management* 23, no. 4 (2010).
9   Nick Fox and Katie Ward, "Health identities: from expert patient to resisting consumer," *Health* 10, no. 4 (2006): 461-79; Nancy Tomes, "Patients or Healthcare Consumers: Why the History of Contested Terms Matters," in *Putting the Past Back in: History and Health Policy in the United States*, eds. Rosemary A. Stevens, Charles E. Rosenberg and Lawton R. Burns (New Brunswick, USA: Rutgers University Press, 2006), 83-110; David Armstrong, "Actors, patients and agency: a recent history," *Sociology of Health & Illness* 36, no. 2, (2014): 163–174.
10 Kurt Jacobsen and Klaus Larsen, *Ve og Velfærd: Læger, Sundhed & Samfund gennem 200 år* (København: FADLs forlag, 2017); Jørn Henrik Petersen, Klaus Petersen and Niels Finn Christiansen, eds., *Velfærdsstaten i tidehverv. Dansk velfærdshistorie, vol. 5, 1973-1993* (Odense: Syddansk Universitetsforlag, 2013); Jørn Henrik Petersen, Klaus Petersen and Niels Finn Christiansen, eds., *Hvor glider vi hen? Dansk velfærdshistorie, vol. 6, 1993-2004* (Odense: Syddansk Universitetsforlag, 2014); Signild Vallgårda. *Sygehuse og Sygehuspolitik i Danmark. Et bidrag til det specialiserede sygehusvæsens historie, 1930-1987* (Copenhagen: Jurist- og Økonomforbundets Forlag, 1992); Signild Vallgårda, "The rise, heyday and incipient decline of specialization: Hospitals in Denmark, 1930-1990," *International Journal of Health Services* 29, no. 2 (1999): 431-457; Allan Krasnik and Karsten Vrangbæk, "Reformer og reformprocesser," in *Sundhedsvæsen og sundhedspolitik*, eds. Signild Vallgårda and Allan Krasnik (København: A Munksgaard, 2016), 123-154.
11 James G. March and Johan P. Olsen, *Rediscovering Institutions: The Organizational Basis of Politics* (New York: Free Press, 1989); Maarten A. Hajer, *The Politics of Environmental Discourse: Ecological Modernization and the Policy Process* (Oxford: Oxford University Press, 1995); Jon Pierre and B. Guy Peters, *Governance, politics and the state* (Basingstoke, UK: Macmillan, 2000); Norman Fairclough, *Language and Power* (London: Longman, 2001).

particular, we are inspired by early governmentality studies' aim to discern how subjects are created at certain points in history as solutions to particular problems.[12] By studying the inter-connection of subjectivity and governance, particular patient figures such as consumers and partners should be understood as means of restructuring and governing organizations and, on a larger scale, the welfare state. Making the patient governable, then, is also a way of governing the healthcare organizations of which the patient is part; not least the health professionals who are expected to respond to the activated patient in new ways. We use the analytical concept of *figuring* to highlight how various patient figures with shifting attributes (as "responsible citizen", "consumer", "partner" and so forth) become inscribed into the governance of healthcare organizations and practices.[13]

Our study builds on a combination of diachronic historical and synchronic organizational analysis. While the diachronic analysis has a longitudinal perspective and emphasizes the gradual construction up of policy problems, solutions and patient figures, the synchronic analysis examines a small "slice" of discourse over a limited timespan within a single healthcare institution.

The diachronic analysis investigates expectations to the patient in health policy discourse in the context of official policy documents that address the development of the field of healthcare in Denmark between 1970 and 2000.[14] The synchronic analysis examines organizational documents collected as part of an ethnographic fieldwork at a Danish university hos-

---

12   Michel Foucault, "Governmentality," in *The Foucault Effect: Studies in governmentality*, eds., Graham Burchell, Colin Gordon and Peter Miller (Chicago: University of Chicago Press, 1991), 87-104; Nikolas Rose, "Governing 'advanced' liberal democracies," in *Foucault and political reason*, eds. Andrew Barry, Thomas Osborne and Nikolas Rose (London: Routledge, 1996), 37-64; Mitchell M. Dean, *Governmentality: Power and rule in modern society* (London: Sage, 1999).

13   Peter Kjær and Anne Reff Pedersen, eds., *Ledelse gennem patienten – nye styringsformer i sundhedsvæsenet* (København: Handelshøjskolens Forlag, 2010); Ranerup, "Transforming Patients"; Johansson, Noren and Wikstrom, "Patient-centred care"; Signild Vallgårda, "Appeals to Autonomy and Obedience: Continuity and Change in Governing Technologies in Danish and Swedish Health Promotion," *Medical History* 55, no.1 (2011): 27–40.

14   See Kirstine Zinck Pedersen, "Patienten som diskurspolitisk styringsredskab," in *Ledelse gennem patienten – nye styringsformer i sundhedsvæsenet*, eds. Peter Kjær and Anne Reff Pedersen (København: Handelshøjskolens Forlag, 2010), 27-45; Pedersen and Kjær, ""The new patient": the emergence of a political persona," *International Journal of Public Sector Management* 30, no. 1 (2017): 85-98. We identified a total of 35 national-level policy documents that address problems related to healthcare governance. After a first summary reading, 10 documents were selected for further study. See appendix.

pital conducted in the period 2007-2011. These are documents connected to the hospital's locally developed program "The Perspective of the Patient" and the analysis traces how the patient is constructed as a figure across different types of documents.[15] The four documents include a communication policy from 2006, a 'Plan for the Perspective of the Patient 2007-2008", a 'Handbook for Health Professionals on Patient Information" from 2009 and the leaflet "Information on Planned Caesareans", developed in 2008 and published in 2009 is an example of an output of the program.[16] Each of the selected documents in the diachronic as well as the synchronic analysis were subjected to a three-step process discursive analysis. First, we mapped the objectives and problems in each document. Second, we focused on how various actors, including patients and healthcare professionals, were positioned as solutions to the problems. Third, we focused particularly on the expectations of and constitutions of patients. After analyzing each document, we compared problematics, solutions, positioning of actors and patient-related expectations across documents to look for systematic differences and similarities (see appendix for our initial analysis).[17]

In the following diachronic analysis we present two major discourses discerned in the national policies. Each discourse comprises a distinct set of problems and solutions and a distinct set of expectations vis-à-vis patients: Both discourses can be found in present-day health policy debates, but historically, the discourse on effectiveness and fiscal control has preceded the discourse on quality and service-optimization.

Diachronic analysis: Two discourses on the Patient and Public Healthcare
Controlling public expenditure: The rise of the responsible citizen
In the beginning of the 1970s, the idea of the welfare state was consolidated through social reforms that established equal rights to education, health and social welfare. In 1970, a large structural reform established 275 munici-

---

15 See Anja Pors, *Iværksættelse af kommunikation – patientfigurer i hospitalets strategiske kommunikation*; Pors (Ph.D. thesis, Copenhagen: Copenhagen Business School, 2012); Pors, "Constructions of."
16 See appendix.
17 All quotes from policy documents in this paper have been translated from Danish to English by the authors.

palities and 14 counties within Denmark. Both levels were given the authority to raise taxes and the counties were given the overall responsibility for the development of hospital services. With the reform, state authority in the field of healthcare was delegated to the counties while the state continued to co-fund healthcare services and monitored the overall expansion of healthcare services. The 1970 reform was motivated by the need to create a stronger organizational (and fiscal) foundation for the expansion of public services. The 1960s and early 1970s was a period of heavy public investment in healthcare, welfare services and infrastructure and the new counties were seen as the key vehicles for the investment in hospitals. Within a few years, however, the seemingly uncoordinated or uncontrollable rise in public expenditure emerged as a crucial political challenge that was amplified with the 1970s economic recession. Gradually, healthcare – especially hospitals – became a pressing national policy issue in relation to expenditures. In addressing these issues, the welfare state gradually adopted a more active stance, e.g. engaging in formal annual budget negotiations with Amtsrådsforeningen (the National Federation of Counties) and by sponsoring investigations into healthcare prioritizations, healthcare costs, productivity and hospital management, among other issues.[18]

It was on the basis of this problematization of cost control in the public sector that health policy became a national concern in Denmark in the 1970s. Until then, Danish health policy had been characterized by a large degree of political consensus and a limited governmental control through framework laws that put the medical profession in charge of not only treatment but also the organization and management of the healthcare sector. The first major national policy documents that marked a change in this attitude were the two "Perspective Plan" reports from 1971 and 1973 produced by working groups appointed by the Danish Government to discuss the long-term expansion of the public sector.[19] The plans moderately articulated a wish to establish the necessary conditions for economization and prioritization; consequently, for instance, preventive

---

18 For this history, see for instance Jacobsen and Larsen, *Ve og Velfærd*, part 5, chapter 4. Petersen, Petersen and Christiansen, *Velfærdsstaten i tidehverv,* chapter 5; Vallgårda, *Sygehuse og Sygehuspolitik i Danmark;* Vallgårda. "The rise, heyday, and"; Krasnik and Vrangbæk, "Reformer og reformprocesser".

19 The Danish Government, *Perspektivplanlægning 1970-1985: Redegørelse fra den af regeringen i november 1968 nedsatte arbejdsgruppe* (Copenhagen: H. J. Schultz Forlag, 1971). The Danish Government, *Perspektivplan-redegørelse 1972-1987* (Copenhagen: Statens Trykningskontor, 1973).

healthcare was discussed as a way to of achieving major health policy goals. However, the reports did not question the authority of the doctors as the primary authorities in relation to the identification of needs and allocation of resources in healthcare, which left unresolved the articulated wish for more fiscal control of the sector.

In 1977, a Health Prioritization Committee (Sundhedsprioriteringsudvalget) published a report entitled "Report on the conditions for an overall prioritization of efforts in hospital care and disease prevention". As the title suggests, the committee sought to establish a shared foundation for prioritization and better resource utilization. In doing so, they directly challenged the doctor as the ultimate authority and expert – also in matters of cost control and prioritization. While the committee emphasized the overall problems of resource allocation and prioritization in the healthcare system, they also – for the first time – considered the role of mobilizing patients/citizens in relation to healthcare expenditure. Preventive healthcare, which was ultimately positioned as an individual responsibility, was considered to have important potential for relieving the healthcare system of pressure in terms of costs:

> It is necessary that the entire population develop a greater understanding and awareness of individual responsibility - and the importance of individual efforts - for the health condition. In other words, it is of the utmost importance that the individual person really understands that he/she has a responsibility for his/her own health condition and that one cannot always count on the healthcare system being able to restore health in the case of illness.[20]

The committee formulated two expectations of the patient/citizen: first, to ultimately take responsibility for own health and to act accordingly and second, to adjust expectations in terms of healthcare services in order to accept that there were limits to the capacity of the healthcare system. This discourse of health promotion now positioned patients as responsible individuals capable of acting in relation to their own health condition and

---

20 Ministry of the Interior, *Betænkning om grundlaget for en overordnet prioritering af indsatsen inden for sygehusbehandling og sygdomsforebyggelse* (Sundhedsprioriteringsudvalget, Betænkning no. 809, København: Indenrigsministeriet, 1977), 30.

in relation to the healthcare system as an entity with finite resources at its disposal. It further emphasized the importance of health-information and education with the aim of, for instance, warning against "alcohol and drug abuse, tobacco smoking, promoting road safety and safety at work."[21] Later reports, such as that from the Healthcare Coordination Committee, echoed these new expectations by focusing upon the governmental need to ingrain "reasonable attitudes"[22] in the population and to motivate the "correct application of the healthcare system."[23] In the so-called Productivity Committee's (Produktivitetsudvalget) report from 1984, such expectations translated into clinical practice:

> The aim is, as far as possible, to activate and involve patients in the examination, treatment and care. In practice, this means that the patient should, as far as possible, be able to handle at least some of the tasks that have traditionally been included in the care routines.[24]

A few years later, the so-called Lotz report even argued that the free public Danish health system had a "confusing effect" on citizens, who were likely to "be of the impression that the costs are lower than what is actually the case, which encourages greater use of the services than if the actual cost was stated to the citizen."[25] Therefore, it was suggested that the actual costs of individual services be made public so citizens would be better informed about the economic consequences of their consumption of healthcare services.

In these early health policy discourses, the patient is articulated in relation to governmental strategies of cost containment. The patient is represented as a responsible individual whose conduct can be directed, not least through targeted information, to enhance governmental objectives:

---

21 Ibid., 19.
22 Ministry of the Interior, *Samordning i sundhedsvæsenet: Betænkning fra det af Indenrigsministeriet nedsatte Samordningsudvalg for sundhedsvæsenet* (Betænkning no. 1044, København: Indenrigsministeriet, 1985), 210.
23 Ibid., 211.
24 Ministry of the Interior, *Sygehusenes organization og økonomi: Betænkning fra Indenrigsministeriets produktivitetsudvalg* (København: Indenrigsministeriet, 1984), 35.
25 Ministry of Interior, *Amtskommunalt udgiftspres og styringsmuligheder: Betænkning fra det af Indenrigsministeren nedsatte udvalg om amtskommunalt udgiftspres og styringsmuligheder* (Lotz-betænkningen, Betænkning no. 1123, København: Indenrigsministeriet, 1987), 37.

in this case, both individual well-being and societal cost control. In fact, these two are seen as coterminous and mutually enhancing. Thus, in the Productivity Committee, the importance of responsibilizing the patient through education and counselling is emphasized, by enhancing individual capacities for self-government and also marshalling governmental resources more economically through shorter hospital stays and fewer treatments.[26] Similarly, the aforementioned report on healthcare coordination emphasized the use of information to enable patients to "assume responsibility for initiatives both in relation to one's own life style and in relation to contacts to health and social services."[27]

In relation to healthcare governance, this role of the patient involves a new division of responsibilities where the patient is not only responsible for his/her own (future and present) well-being but also for balancing individual needs with the overall capacity of the healthcare system. To be a "patient" is thus to be both a responsible individual, maximizing one's own health and an agent of economization, assisting the state in utilizing its resources more efficiently and effectively. Within this particular rationality of governance, therefore, the patient is represented as an ally of the state in a struggle to contain healthcare costs – in a situation where doctors have been severely challenged as the ultimate authorities in relation to health prioritization and cost containment.

Increasing the quality of care:
The rise of the demanding consumer

From 1990 and onwards, the emphasis on expenditure was supplemented by an interest in healthcare quality. Quality was no longer considered a function of investment but was viewed as a distinct issue in itself. On the one hand, quality emerged as a concern within the hospital sector itself in connection to experiments with various forms of organized quality improvement that emphasized changes in professional practice and organizational routines. On the other hand, capacity problems, waiting lists and related concerns led to strong public outcries about access to care and the ability of hospitals to respond to patient needs.[28]

---

26 Ministry of the Interior, *Sygehusenes organization*.
27 Ministry of the Interior, *Samordning i sundhedsvæsenet*, 172.
28 For this history see for instance Jacobsen and Larsen, *Ve og Velfærd: Læger, Sundhed & Samfund gennem*

In response to these issues, the state was once again positioned as a key actor. The Ministry of Health, the National Health Agency and other state institutions engaged politically in the field of quality, first by formulating distinct policy goals, targets and quality assurance systems, second by addressing issues of renewal within healthcare in a number of policy reports and investigations and third by reconsidering the overall governance of the healthcare sector.

Cost containment remained a key health policy concern throughout the 1980s in Denmark. However, by the early 1990s, years of fiscal restraint had resulted in capacity problems in the hospital sector, which were manifested in significantly increased waiting times for treatment.[29] This led to a gradual shift in the emphasis in governmental discourses on healthcare, where the capacity of healthcare providers to meet expectations became a key political matter of concern. The government increased investments in healthcare, but tied investment to the achievement of specific national policy goals and performance criteria such as throughput, waiting times and patient choice. As such, health governance entailed a focus not only on achieving policy goals but also on meeting patient demands in terms of service levels and quality. One 1994 committee report on hospital economy stated that there was now a "mismatch between patient expectations and the ability of hospitals to meet such expectations".[30] The immediate issue seemed to be exactly the same as the previous expenditure discourse. Now, however, expectations were viewed as a positive "competitive" force:

> The citizens' wish for a higher service level will, other things being equal, lead to a pressure on the hospital sector in the coming years. Everywhere in the hospital sector one works to develop better service (...) A common feature of such initiatives is that they do not necessarily lead to higher hospital expenditures. In contrast, organizational development will often lead to a more economically rational operation.[31]

---

200 år, Part 6, chapter 3; Petersen, Petersen and Christiansen, eds. *Hvor glider vi hen? Dansk velfærdshistorie, vol. 6, 1993-2004* chapter 5; Krasnik and Vrangbæk, "Reformer og reformprocesser."

29 Karsten Vrangbæk, *Markedsorientering i sygehussektoren: Opkomst, udformning og konsekvenser af frit sygehusvalg* (Ph.D. thesis, København: Københavns Universitet, Institut for Statskundskab, Licentiatserien, 1999).

30 Ministry of Health, *Rapport fra Udvalget vedrørende sygehusvæsenets økonomi* (København: Statens Information, 1994), 215.

31 Ibid., 81.

Similarly, a health policy whitepaper approached user demands as:

> a positive pressure on the healthcare sector which needs to be handled constructively and which creates new opportunities and challenges in the relation between patient and provider.[32]

This influences the patient figure. While the ideal behaviour was previously articulated as moderation in their use of and expectations towards the healthcare system, patients were now expected to develop individual preferences regarding healthcare services and actively express these preferences by demanding and choosing services as consumers on a market. In line with the internationally growing spread of New Public Management (NPM) ideas and tools, quality and patient choice became the main tropes that encapsulated this reframing of health governance and the new articulation of the patient figure. Thus, on the one hand, a national strategy for quality development called for increased and improved measurements of quality, including those of the immeasurable fields.[33] To measure the immeasurable, the patient figure was mobilized as both the source and the recipient of quality measurement and service-optimization. Patient satisfaction surveys were to be integrated into measurements of quality, but the national strategy also envisioned the direct involvement of users in the definition of quality of care.

As for the rhetoric of patient choice, it presumed the use of competition among healthcare providers as pressure that would lead to improvement. A report from the Hospital Commission in the late 1990s, for example, stated, "Free choice thereby provides an incentive for the hospitals to continuously improve their services – to create the best treatments possible."[34] Here, national quality indicators were developed to assist patients in making informed choices among providers.

---

32 Ministry of Health, *Sundhedspolitisk redegørelse 2000* (København: Sundhedsministeriet, 2000), 8.
33 Danish Health and Medicines Authority, *National strategi for kvalitetsudvikling i sundhedsvæsenet* (København: Sundhedsstyrelsen, 1993).
34 Ministry of Health, *Udfordringer i sygehusvæsenet: Betænkning fra Sygehuskommissionen* (Betænkning 1329, København: Sundhedsministeriet, 1997), 5.

In this quality discourse, the patient figure was elaborated as a demanding consumer of healthcare services epitomized in the ideal of "the new patient":

> "The New Patient" is becoming increasingly well informed, seeking his/her own information about treatment opportunities domestically and abroad and making increasing demands on the content of healthcare services.[35]

As in the expenditure discourse, information was a central part of mobilizing "the new patient". However, while the earlier expenditure discourse stressed health information and health education as a one-way mechanism from the state to the public, the quality discourse foregrounded information (or more often "communication") not simply as means to educate the patient but rather to mobilize the patient's healthcare knowledge and experience for the sake of developing the overall system, e.g. via user involvement of various sorts.

This shift in the constitution of the patient figure had a number of implications for healthcare governance. First, the patient was mobilized as a disciplining pressure from below on healthcare providers who were in turn represented as needing to become more flexible and quality oriented. Second, the patient was situated not simply in a relationship with his/her local healthcare provider but also as an agent for the overall governance of the public healthcare system. This marks not only a change in expectations of the patient but also a shift in the governing rationality of the state. The immediate target of governance is no longer the patient or the public directly but rather the healthcare system, at a distance, through the increased pressure of the demanding consumer.

It is important to note that the new concern with quality sits alongside and does not displace the preoccupation with economization. Rather, it seems that the question of economization is now redefined in significant ways. By becoming a consumer of healthcare who makes choices in a market, the patient is positioned as a force of quality improvement and service optimization, as well as of the efficient allocation of scarce resourc-

---

35 Ministry of Health, *Sundhedspolitisk redegørelse 2000*, 8.

es within the sector. In the guise of an autonomous individual seeking to maximize his/her own health outcomes, the patient is equally represented as an active agent of economization, as a force challenging the professional autonomy of the doctor to "know best" and, through his/her acts of choice in a market for healthcare, as the arbiter of quality within the sector.

Synchronic Analysis: Three Patient Figures in Organizational Discourse

In the following paragraphs, we shift from a diachronic to a synchronic mode and from national policy to a locally developed policy program at a single hospital. Whereas the reading in the diachronic analysis focuses on how different patient figures become established over time, the synchronic analysis reads across documents within the same programme. Our analysis of the programme "The Perspective of the Patient" unpacks how expectations of the patient intersects in discourses throughout the four selected organizational documents. Here, we identify three simultaneous patient figures that instigate different authority relations and are configured to pose a particular set of demands on healthcare organization: 1) The affective individual, 2) The consumer with rights and choices, 3) The collaborating resource.

The affective individual

> Patients often express their need for health professionals to be able to relate to their fear of pain, insecurities and other feelings or existential reflections connected with their disease and treatment. These feelings and thoughts should be articulated, even in the leaflets, because it helps patients dare to talk about the subjects, if they need to.[36]

Disease is only mentioned a few times in the documents. Instead, the patient is often described from a holistic approach as a person with individual needs related to psychosocial aspects of the disease. The affective individual is emotionally affected by the trajectory at the hospital and comes across as

---

36 Handbook, 20.

vulnerable and alienated – described in the Handbook in such terms as "sensitive", "without preconditions", "nervous", "scared", "wondering", "worried". Written information, illustrative graphics and photos of situations experienced along the way are viewed as opportunities to "set the stage for openness and dialogue"[37] and thus "overcome fear."[38] The hospital's written information should "encourage patients to ask you and your colleagues about details that surprise them or any other issue on their minds."[39]

Although the affective individual is understood as sensitive and vulnerable it would be wrong to assume that the patient is understood as passive in the traditional understanding of the patient role.[40] Rather, patients are expected to communicate and express their emotions and fears and they are expected to be receptive to the holistic emotion management of the psychosocial approach. Moreover, the affective individual is understood to be in need of *individualized* care. Here, the patient's ability to express such individual desires, needs and wishes becomes the precondition for the healthcare professionals' provision of care, safety and security for the affective individuals.

The consumer with rights and choices

Throughout the documents, the patient is configured as a consumer with rights and choices who:

> ... has a right to knowledge and insight [...] All patients have a right to know and understand their diagnosis and treatment. Written and oral patient communication is highly prioritized.[41]

Conversely, "Rules and requirements [are] justified, so that patients understand why they have to follow them."[42] Thus, as a rational and active right-bearing individual, the patient has the right to be treated individually, including the right to protect him/herself against exposure (e.g. to

---

37 Communication Policy.
38 Handbook, 21.
39 Handbook, 5
40 Talcott Parsons "The Professions and Social Structure," in *Essays in Sociological Theory*, ed. Talcott Parsons (New York: The Free Press, 1964 [1951]), 34-49.
41 Communication Policy, 2.
42 Handbook, 13.

decline information) and the right to choose between health services treatments: "You are invited to take part in making the decision about whether to have a planned caesarean."[43] By addressing the patient's options, the hospital signals responsiveness to patients preferences: "If you wish, a paediatrician can examine your child before you are discharged. After your discharge, you can have your child examined at the hospital (...) You can also have your general practitioner examine your child."[44] For this reason, the healthcare professionals – and the information they deliver – must give "a clear idea of tests and treatments and the options available to patients."

The consumer "is involved in making decisions regarding examinations and treatment to the extent desired."[45] Treatment is referred to as an offer to the patient – and professionalizing the communication can make the offer more reliable and trustworthy, while also "giving patients an overview and signalling professional quality."[46] In this way, healthcare services and their communicative wrapping are largely constructed as products to be sold to critical consumers. In alignment with the historical discourse on the demanding consumer, expectations formed as rights and choices call for a more quality-oriented attitude from the healthcare professionals. At the same time, this configuration of the patient as a critical, inquisitive consumer also allocates certain demands and obligations to the patient, who is expected to make individual choices and take part in planning his/her trajectory – and more specifically to act as a collaborating resource in his/her own treatment and in organizational development.

The collaborating resource

Throughout the documents, the patient is portrayed as an empowered figure managing her own treatment and thereby enhancing (organizational) efficiency because she is responsible for her own treatment and recovery.

> Within six hours of the caesarean, you should try to get out of bed and get your body going after the surgery. It is a good idea to take a walk in the maternity unit as soon as possible. In the days after the operation, you should alternate between sitting, walking around and resting in bed.[47]

---

43 Leaflet, 3.
44 Leaflet, 13.
45 Communication Policy.
46 Handbook, 16.
47 Leaflet, 10

However, the patient is not only a potential resource in relation to her own health and trajectory, but also a resource for organizational development. The patient is seen as having potential resources to optimize treatment and trajectories.

> "Listen to the patients': A project in which five patients were interviewed about their hospitalizations. They talked about how they experienced doctors' and nurses' oral communication. They were also asked if they had an overview of the medication they received. Moreover, they were asked to share their best experience with their hospitalization and to give staff advice for improvement. The goal was to let patients act as experts in the experience of their own trajectory. The broadcast was welcomed by several department heads, who found it inspiring."[48]

The "Listen to the patients" project described in the Plan portrays the patient as a collaborating partner for organizational development. The argument is that the patient is a source of knowledge: a competent expert with whom the hospital can discuss and negotiate and to whom the hospital has a duty to provide the information required for her to manage her own treatment and recovery. One of the patients – a so-called patient ambassador – is cited as follows in the Handbook:

> It is important to make leaflets available online, so patients can get acquainted with information before they meet the doctor. This allows the conversation with the doctor to be more focused. Many physicians complain that patients attend consultations with printouts from the web, including all sorts of information that is not relevant to the patient. Thus, a hospital has to make understandable and appropriate information available. This creates a good starting point for a constructive dialogue.[49]

---

48 Plan, 13.
49 Handbook, 23

In this context, the patient is a potential resource for the organization. By making information available to patients, the hospital becomes more focused and effective in its work: "... a well-informed patient is better able to follow the advice and instructions you give as a health professional."[50] Thus, the patient is articulated as a proactive partner who reads the information provided and asks questions so that he or she can be clearly and fully informed about what to do when and who in return has a range of expectations of the healthcare services provided.

> After giving birth, you might have questions that this leaflet does not answer. If you wish, you can have a consultation with the midwife or doctor present at your delivery.[51] Feel free to ask the healthcare professionals if you have any uncertainties […] Please let us know if you need more [painkillers].[52]

The patient is presented as a dialogue partner who is mobilized as a responsible participant in the trajectory.

The Plan designates patients as "equal fellow human beings and collaborators."[53] Simultaneously, patienthood renders the patient an analytical object that can help develop hospital services when used properly. Qualitative interviews, user surveys, focus groups or more informal forms of involvement and participation provide endless sources of organizational opportunities for improvement. As a resource, the patient is seen as a rational individual – an empowered expert patient helping to optimize processes through self-treatment and feedback. Treatment experiences turn the patient into a qualified resource whose feedback and comments can be used when information is reviewed and organizational services are developed.[54]

As shown in the analysis of the three documents, the patient figures interweave and overlap, as illustrated in the example below:

---

50 Handbook, 4.
51 Leaflet, 3.
52 Leaflet, 10.
53 Plan, 13.
54 Handbook, 7.

People pictured on the front of the leaflets: The image must create confidence by showing the good contact enjoyed between healthcare professional and patient and must emphasize that patients are active participants in their treatment.[...] Leaflets provide patients with an overview and signal professional quality.[55]

Here, the figurations of the patient as an affective individual, collaborator and consumer intersect: in a few words, taking care of the emotional patient's need for information becomes associated with an engaged participant who is a potential resource for the hospital in the healthcare market.

Discussion and Concluding Remarks

In our diachronic analysis of national level health policy documents, the identified patient figures are indicative of governing rationalities of the welfare state: The empowerment of patients coincides with a renewed emphasis on the need for strengthening overall coordination and development and challenging the authority of doctors and healthcare organizations. The challenging of professional expertise and intermediary levels of government, alongside an emphasis first on patient responsibility and patient involvement and later on patient choice and engagement, are indicative of the processes through which the importance of central state institutions is boosted. Thus, in line with insights from governmentality studies, the patient can – whether as a responsible citizen or as a demanding consumer – be understood as an agent of governance that enhances the authority of the state while the state maintains or gains a capacity to govern healthcare both from below and from above.[56] In the Danish context, this process implies not a privatization of public services but rather governance arrangements that rely on a particular alliance between citizens and the state regarding public sector renewal. This also implies that "the patient" in this particular sense has not always been around, i.e. the patient as an agent of healthcare governance is a historical specific figure.[57]

---

55 Handbook, 14 and 16.
56 Rose, "Governing 'advanced' liberal democracies"; Dean, *Governmentality*.
57 See also Tomes, "Patients or Healthcare Consumers"; Mold, "Making the patient-consumer"; Armstrong, "Actors, patients and agency."

More specifically, it is a figure who, in the Danish context, appears together with the first political attempts to strengthen management within Danish hospitals in the late 1970s and early 1980s, where specific challenges in the Danish healthcare system paved the way for the birth of the responsibilized patient.

In our synchronic analysis of organizational level documents, the mobilization of the patient serves more concrete organizational purposes with apparent references to general public management trends and governance ideals, such as the ideal of partnership or user-involvement. However, the particular figurations of the patient also serves as managerial tools in the concrete management and organization of the particular hospital. The different patient figures within the same program indicate that the relationship between the various figures is cumulative rather than mutually exclusive, as seems to be the case in our diachronic analysis. The figures each respond to particular managerial problems and – in each their way – contribute to an understanding of the patient as an agent to be responded to and engaged with in different ways. The various versions of the patient figure exist side by side and ascribe value to the patient in the form of resources, needs, rights and duties. Simultaneously, the patient figures pose demands on the organization and the healthcare professionals. Besides treating and curing the patient, hospitals and professionals are providers of holistic individualized emotion management alongside a more strategic service- and quality-oriented attitude and, not least, the capacity to enact patients' potential resources in relation to both their own treatment and organizational development.

The national health policies' mobilization of the patient is primarily a story about the changing authority relations between the state, healthcare institutions and professionals. In contrast, the synchronic analysis is largely a story about how more local managerial program in healthcare institutions change organizational authority-relations and task-specifications, not least by multiplying the demands put on the healthcare professionals and expectations of patients' behaviour.

This combination of a diachronic and synchronic analytical strategy has provided us with the opportunity to study how the mobilization of the patient is contextually dependent on particular problems and solutions historically, at particular times and within a singular organizational context. Our dual analytical strategy has also allowed us to combine the study of the discursive formation of the patient as a political figure – and the discourse-ruptures that take place within the first decades of this formation – with a more contemporary focus on how dissimilar and potentially conflicting patient figurations co-exist side-by-side in the representations of diverse organizational strategies and objectives. While this signals an increased complexity in the discourse of hospital organization compared with national health policy, it also indicates a more complex contemporary health political landscape in which a layering of health management discourses offer a wide pallet of diverse, overlapping and potentially contradictory patient figures as managerial tools and solutions to a variety of policy or organizational problems.

The focus on the historical, contextual and political attributes of the patient can help us nuance the debate on the connection between citizens and public management ideals. At first sight, dominant representations of the development of international public management models or paradigms resembles the sequence although not quite the timing we have proposed in this paper. Pollitt and Bouckaert's classic text-book, for instance, describes a rational, planning discourse up until the 1970s, taken over by a New Public Management discourse until the late 1990s, followed by a more unspecific contemporary "third wave" – sometimes referred to as New Public Governance or Public Value Management – focusing on value-creation, network, partnership, co-creation, transparency and trust.[58] Within this historical framework, however, the first mobilization of the users of services as political figures is part and product of New Public Management, where ideals of consumer choice and empowerment are mobilized to create more responsive (and competitive) public organizations.[59] This seems to have been the case in Britain, for instance, where the patient-consumer was introduced under Thatcher's conservative rule in the late 1970s.[60] However, in Denmark the duty-based idea of the responsible and activated patient appeared as a political figure before the (in many ways opposite) NPM-inspired idea about the patient as a right-bearing consumer was introduced

---

58 Christopher Pollitt and Geert Bouckaert, *Public Management Reform – A Comparative Analysis – into the age of austerity* (Oxford: Oxford University Press, 2017).
59 E.g. Bolton, "Consumer as king in the NHS."
60 Mold, "Making the patient-consumer."

into healthcare. Thus, although "the birth" of the new, activated patient figure is relatively concurrent in Denmark and in Britain, the attributes of this figure are specific to the particular policy problems of the healthcare political context.

Our synchronic analysis of the organizational mobilization of the patient shows how on an organizational level different aspects of the patient figure are merged. The patient-centred program is not inhabited by distinct, mutually exclusive rationales or logics and it is not clear whether the patient figures should be understood as attempts to manage the patient and the organization as a whole. The analysis shows how, within the same program, the patient can be portrayed in a number of active figurations to be managed and negotiated with, and of whom the hospital expects a certain degree of control and management. Overall, the patient oscillates between being a rhetorical centre and a variety of more specific figures: an affective individual, a consumer with rights and choices, as well as a collaborating partner securing organizational efficiency and development.

An important research agenda that needs further attention is the question regarding the links between political and organizational discourses of the patient and actual clinical practice or patient attitudes. Such links, or potential discrepancies, have not been the focus of this study. However, it is nonetheless indeed remarkable that all the described figurations of the patient have a very particular set of features in common: they are all active and resourceful – competent, responsibilized, demanding – and with this they claim a certain type of response from the health system and health professionals, they meet. Even the affective patient figure poses demands on the health professionals calling for individualized psycho social management alongside treatment as the core tasks of the hospital. With the activation of the patient, the health system becomes governable. This categorization, however, captures the displacements of the patient figure in the passive patient role,[61] as a possibly recalcitrant and inactive receiver, a sick body or even an information-resistant, and/or irresponsible patient. In line with Clarke's identification of silent actors, such patient figures and their concrete illnesses seem, not surprisingly, to be missing from the political and managerial attempts to mobilize and activate the pa-

---

61 Parsons, "The Professions and Social Structure."

tient in governing healthcare organizations.[62] Thus, the identified patient figures of our analysis create a partly imaginary reality, solely inhabited by capable patients, whereas the space for the sick patient is diminished. Accordingly, Parsons' analytical identification of the sick role from 1951 still has critical potential.

---

62 Adele E. Clarke, *Situational Analyses: Grounded Theory After the Postmodern Turn* (Thousand Oakes, CA: Sage, 2005).

Appendix:

Table 1. Policy documents for diachronic analysis

Document	Problems	Suggested solutions	The patient
Perspective Plans I and II (1971, 1973)	Rising health costs	Increased central steering	A passive recipient of healthcare services
Health Prioritization Committee (1977)	Lack of prioritization in healthcare sector	A holistic assessment of healthcare, coordination, cost-awareness, prevention	A responsible and informed citizen
Productivity Committee (1984)	Lack of productivity in the hospital sector	New incentives for health professionals; mobilization of patient resources	A responsible and active patient willing to utilize own resources
Healthcare Coordination Committee (1985)	Lack of coordination (and cost effectiveness)	Coordination between hospital and primary sector; education of and information to citizens	A citizen with "reasonable" expectations related to healthcare services
The Lotz committee (1987)	Expenditure pressure and lack of steering at regional level	New clinical management structures; information about cost of treatment to citizens	An economizing and modest citizen
National strategy for quality development (1993)	Need for quality development and service improvement	Making quality measurable through data collection and patient-satisfaction surveys	A health service user who articulates personal preferences and needs
Committee concerning hospital economy (1994)	Lack of responsiveness, quality and efficiency in healthcare delivery	Market-based solutions such as free-choice and performance management	A demanding service user who puts pressure on the healthcare system
The hospital commission (1997)	Problems of steering, management, service, quality and waiting times	Activity-based funding, division of labour, choice, quality indicators, patient centredness	An information-seeking, demanding and actively choosing service user
Health policy white paper (2000)	New pressures for higher quality, user satisfaction, information	User orientation, free choice, contact persons, communication, patient rights, patient pathways	'The new patient': A knowledgeable user with rights

Table 2. Organizational documents for synchronic analysis

Document	Problem	Solution (method)	The patient
Communication policy	Lack of quality in communication, co-ordination and focus on the patient	Patient involvement and communication as integrated practice	• The affective individual • The consumer with rights and choices • The collaborating resource
Plan	Health professionals' attitude. Inefficiency caused by unclear roles and responsibility	More and better written information effected by managing, formalizing and optimizing organizational infrastructure	
Handbook	Inefficiency and dissatisfied patients	Recipes such as standards and concepts for information, e.g. leaflet production	
Leaflet	Patients' lack of knowledge about procedures and options	Procedures and roles are explicit and understandable to the patient	

# The Entrepreneur

The Invention of a Pedagogical Ideal of Societal Behaviour

Clara Lyngholm K. Mortensen

In recent decades, the entrepreneur has become a pedagogical ideal of societal behaviour in the Danish welfare state. This development has been promoted politically through the implementation of entrepreneurship in the Danish education system. The concept of the entrepreneur is inextricably linked to the concept of entrepreneurship, where the latter can be said to incapsulate the societal behaviour of the former. Thus, understanding the dissemination of the concept of entrepreneurship is fundamental to grasping how the entrepreneur has been articulated and implemented as a pedagogical citizen ideal.[1] Therefore, the concept of entrepreneurship

---

[1] Part of the chapter is based my article "Udbredelsen af begrebet entreprenørskab – fra økonomisk begreb til pædagogiseret borgerideal, *Temp*, forthcoming, 2021.
In Danish, the words "iværksætter" and "entreprenør" both mean entrepreneur when translated into English. Therefore, the entrepreneur as a citizen ideal includes and draws on both words in a Danish context. This chapter will not focus on the difference between the connotation of these words in Danish, but on the overall dissemination of the citizen ideal of "the entrepreneur," where the concept of "entrepreneurship" is a key analytical tool. In contrast to the concept of the entrepreneur, the relatively recent linguistic introduction of the concept of entrepreneurship in Danish

will function as an analytical prism, which will enable us to figure the entrepreneur as a citizen ideal.

Thirty years ago, the concept of entrepreneurship was nowhere to be found in Danish education policy, but in the late 2000s it became ubiquitous in strategies for the Danish education system, as outlined in the inter-ministerial policy paper *Strategi for Uddannelse i Entreprenørskab* (Strategy for Education in Entrepreneurship) from 2009: "Entrepreneurship must be integrated in primary and lower secondary school and in post-secondary education and it must be implemented in the syllabus for higher education."[2] The political understanding was thus that entrepreneurship could and should be learned by all citizens, which emphasizes that the implementation of entrepreneurship was part of promoting and disseminating a specific pedagogical citizen ideal – the entrepreneur. But where did this understanding of the concept come from and what did it entail in more specific terms?

In Danish academic scholarship and debate, the recent comprehensive reforms and new strategies in the education system have been linked to the emergence of the competition state, understood as a state in which political imperative and legitimacy depend on mobilizing and optimizing the competitiveness of the state.[3] This debate, to which this chapter will contribute, intensified after Ove K. Pedersen's publication of *Konkurrencestaten* (The Competition State) in 2011.[4] Pedersen argues that the logic

---

makes it possible to follow the dissemination of the citizen ideal closely linked to the concept in an empirically time-limited source material.

2   Ministeriet for Videnskab, Teknologi og Udvikling, Økonomi- og Erhvervsministeriet, Undervisningsministeriet og Kulturministeriet, *Strategi for Uddannelse i Entreprenørskab* (København: Forsknings- og Innovationsstyrelsen, 2009), 5; all quotes from policy documents in Danish have been translated into English by the author.

3   Jens Erik Kristensen, Hans Siggaard Jensen and Ove Korsgaard, "Globalisering og livslang læring," in *Pædagogikkens Idehistorie*, eds. Ove Korsgaard, Jens Erik Kristensen and Hans Siggaard Jensen (Aarhus: Aarhus Universitetsforlag, 2017), 366; Ove Kaj Pedersen, *Konkurrencestaten* (København: Hans Reitzel, 2011), 12.

4   The notion of the "competition state" has been used in international analysis since the late 1990s, see e.g. Philip G. Cerny, "Paradoxes of the Competition State: The Dynamics of Political Globalization," *Government and Opposition* 32, no. 2 (1997): 251-274 and Joachim Hirsch, *Der nationale Wettbewerbsstaat: Staat, Demokratie und Politik in globalen Kapitalismus* (Berlin: Edition ID-Archiv, 1995). Several researchers and commentators have added both descriptive and normative input to the Danish debate, see e.g. Knud Illeris ed. *Læring i konkurrencestaten – kapløb eller bæredygtighed* (København: Samfundslitteratur, 2014); Søren Kaj Andersen and Ove Kaj Pedersen eds. *Konkurrencestaten og dens kritikere* (København: Jurist- og Økonomiforbundet, 2017); Jørn Henrik Petersen, *Fra Luther*

of the competition state unfolded most clearly in the education system, where "the opportunistic personality" was allegedly the ideal.[5] However, Pedersen does not connect the prevalence of entrepreneurship with the opportunistic person, even though the ideal he identifies clearly resonates with the entrepreneur as a citizen ideal. In addition, the empirical evidence provided by Pedersen regarding the opportunistic personality is extremely limited.[6] Through an empirical investigation of the transformation and dissemination of the concept of entrepreneurship – and thereby the ideal of the entrepreneur – this chapter aims to provide a deeper understanding of transnational dynamics and national developments which have driven the change of the Danish welfare state in recent decades.

In Danish historical research, the dissemination of the concept of entrepreneurship and the political focus on the implementation of entrepreneurship in the education system is largely unexplored. Only few contributions, mostly within the pedagogical field, have analyzed how the emergence of the Danish competition state might be connected with the entrepreneur as a citizen ideal.[7]

One of these contributions is *Pædagogikkens Idéhistorie* (The History of Ideas in Pedagogy) from 2017 in which Jens Erik Kristensen, Ove Korsgaard and Hans Siggard Jensen comment on the entry of a number of concepts into the Danish education system. The authors see the concept of entrepreneurship as part of the human capital theory put forward by Theodore W. Schultz and Gary S. Becker from the Chicago School of Economics and thus argue that the concept became disseminated in line with an increased political focus on optimizing Danish competitiveness on a global scale.[8] The authors base their arguments on empirical findings in reports from transnational organizations, which, the authors argue, have played a vital

---

    til *Konkurrencestaten* (Odense: Syddansk Universitetsforlag, 2016); Martin Bøje Møller Rasmussen, *Konkurrencestatsministeren: til forsvar for den danske konkurrencestat* (København: DJØF Forlag, 2019).
5 Pedersen, *Konkurrencestaten*, 170, 188.
6 Pedersen, *Konkurrencestaten*, 169-203.
7 See e.g. Dorte Christiane Iversen, "Nyt dannelsesideal i kølvandet på entreprenørskabsparadigmet," in *Entreprenørskabsundervisning*, eds. Anne Kirketerp and Linda Greve (Aarhus: Aarhus Universitetsforlag, 2001), 81-90; Birthe Lund, "The Enterprising Self: Innovationsevne og entreprenørskab i et dannelsesperspektiv," in *Læring og Erkendelse*, eds., Maziar Etemadi, Merete Wiberg, Michael Paulsen and Søren Harnow Klausen (Aalborg: Aalborg Universitetsforlag, 2009), 109-136.
8 Kristensen et al., "Globalisering og livslang læring," 377, 379.

role in shaping Danish education policy.[9] Following this lead, this chapter will examine the influence of the transnational organizations while broadening the analytical optics and taking a more empirical approach in order to bring into focus the connection between the dissemination of the concept and Denmark's transition to a competition state.

To empirically examine the dissemination of the concept of entrepreneurship, a diverse range of source material is used, consisting of generally four types of sources: 1) scientific primary literature, 2) reports from transnational organizations, 3) policy papers from Danish ministries and government agencies and 4) Danish newspaper articles. The ambition has been to identify the sources which were the first to use the concept of entrepreneurship in an educational policy context. Newspaper articles have been included to gain a broader understanding of when and by whom the concept has been disseminated in Denmark.

Against this empirical background, the chapter presents three arguments. The first argument is that it was the academic disciplines, in particular economic theory and business management and the transnational organizations, such as the World Bank, The Organization for Economic Co-operation and Development (OECD) and the European Commission (EU-Commission), that were instrumental in bringing the new educational-political concept of entrepreneurship to Denmark. The second argument is that, alongside Danish think tanks and consulting companies, these transnational organizations exerted pressure on the Danish government that contributed to bringing entrepreneurship on the education policy agenda. The third argument is that entrepreneurship became implemented and widespread in the Danish education system because the concept encapsulates and promotes a citizen ideal that meets the Danish competition state's imperative on growth – the entrepreneur.

The chapter begins by outlining a number of historical definitions of entrepreneurship and the entrepreneur in the international literature, which will be used as heuristic tools in the investigation of how the concept has transformed into a citizen ideal in recent decades. Then follows three parts, which correspond to the arguments above and sketch a dissemination process comprised of three phases. The first part examines the

---

9   Kristensen et al., "Globalisering og livslang læring," 361.

role of transnational organizations in transferring the concept of entrepreneurship to Denmark. The second part focuses on when and by whom the concept became disseminated in Denmark, as well as how it became part of the education policy agenda. The third part examines which political expectations were attached to the concept and how these expectations contributed to disseminating the concept as a citizen ideal in the education system.

International Literature on the Concept of Entrepreneurship

The limited amount of international literature, which has historically examined the concept of entrepreneurship, can broadly be divided into two fields: one field examines the changing definitions of the concept, while the other seeks to explain the underlying mechanisms behind the popularity of the concept, most often from a critical approach inspired by Michel Foucault.

In the descriptive field, Robert Hébert and Albert Link's *A History of Entrepreneurship* (2009) provides one of the most comprehensive and detailed contributions. They focus on the development and significance of the concept in economic literature and describe how modern ideas of entrepreneurship can be traced back to the Irish-French economist Richard Cantillon in the early 1800s, after which the concept was taken up and further developed by many economists worldwide.[10] Hébert and Link point out that the Austrian economist Joseph Schumpeter's definition of entrepreneurship, as it is presented in *Theorie der Wirtschaftlichen Entwicklung* (The Theory of Economic Development) from 1911, has been pivotal for the dissemination of the concept and laid the foundation for numerous later definitions.[11]

---

10   Robert Hébert and Albert Link, *A History of Entrepreneurship* (London: Routledge, 2009), 5-7.
11   Hébert and Link, *A History of Entrepreneurship*, 67; Pierre Dardot and Christian Laval, *The New Way of the World: On Neoliberal Society* (New York: Verso, 2013), 117; Tomas Marttila, *The Culture of Enterprise in Neoliberalism: Specters of Entrepreneurship* (New York: Routledge, 2013), 9; Jens Erik Kristensen, "Viljen til innovation – en idehistorisk og samtidsdiagnostisk kommentar til tidens innovationsstrang og - tvang," *KvaN* 32, no. 92 (2012): 58; Magnus Hoppe, "The Entrepreneurship Concept: A short introduction," *Högre Utbildning* 6, no. 2 (2016), 96; Louise Li Langergaard, "Entreprenøren som figur under neoliberalismen: Kapitalisme, individ og velfærdsorganisering," *Slagmark – Tidsskrift*

Schumpeter defined the entrepreneur as an innovator who generates economic development by making "new combinations" in production.[12] According to Schumpeter, entrepreneurship is the driving force in the economy and functions as a time-limited form of "creative destruction" which creates disequilibrium in the market and thus ensures economic development.[13] Schumpeter launched this argument as a critique of the focus maintained by neoclassical economics on the market as static and in equilibrium.[14]

Additionally, Hébert and Link argue that the economists Ludwig von Mises and Israel Kirzner, who like Schumpeter belonged to the Austrian School, redefined the concept in influential ways.[15] Mises and Kirzner both maintained that entrepreneurship is crucial to the economy, but challenged Schumpeter's understanding of entrepreneurship as a time-limited act.[16] Instead, focusing on the act of human choice, Mises argued that all individuals are *always* entrepreneurs in the actual economy.[17] Mises' student Kirzner translated this into an understanding of entrepreneurship as the human characteristic of alertness to perceived profit opportunities — a characteristic that is either present or not.[18]

Mises and Kirzner's understanding of entrepreneurship have been the subject of some critical research inspired by Foucault's lecture series at the Collège de France in 1979, which has been compiled in *The Birth of Biopolitics* (2008). In his analyses of the intellectual systems of neoliberalism, Foucault described, with particular reference to the Chicago econo-

---

for Idéhistorie 74 (2016), 162; Catherina Juul Kristensen and Søren Voxted, "Indledning. Innovation og entreprenørskab," in *Innovation & Entreprenørskab*, eds. Catherina Juul Kristensen and Søren Voxted (København: Hans Reitzles Forlag, 2011), 10.

12   Hébert and Link, *A History of Entrepreneurship*, 72; Langergaard, "Entreprenøren som figur under neoliberalismen," 162.

13   Joseph A. Schumpeter, *The theory of economic development*, trans. Redvers Opie (London: Transaction Publishers, 1983 [1911]), 75, 78; Robert Hébert and Albert Link, "In search of the meaning of entrepreneurship," *Small Bus Econ* 1 (1989): 41.

14   Hébert and Link, *A History of Entrepreneurship*, 67; Suna Løwe Nielsen, Kim Klyver, Majbritt Evald and Torben Bager, *Entreprenørskab i teori og praksis: Paradokser i spil* (Kolding: Iværksætterakademiet IDEA, 2009), 36.

15   Hébert and Link, *A History of Entrepreneurship*, 84-89.

16   Hébert and Link, *A History of Entrepreneurship*, 84-89; Ludwig von Mises, *Human Action: A Treatise on Economics* (Auburn: The Ludwig von Mises Institute, 1998 [1949]), 249.

17   Mises, *Human Action*, 253.

18   Israel Kirzner, *Competition and Entrepreneurship* (Chicago: University of Chicago Press, 1973), 14-15; Hébert and Link, *A History of Entrepreneurship*, 86-89.

mist Becker, entrepreneurship as a specific neoliberal understanding of "homo economicus".[19] This means that each individual is an entrepreneur of himself in eternal competition with other individuals to exploit profit opportunities, which outlines the entrepreneur as a citizen ideal.[20] In relation to this, Pierre Dardot and Christian Laval argue in *New Way of the World* (2013) that Mises and Kirzner's understanding of entrepreneurship represents a subjectification of the market, in which entrepreneurship takes the form of a neoliberal self-government that is strengthened and shaped by the market economy.[21] This chapter will not present a critical Foucauldian analysis, but it will draw on the insights regarding the relationship between entrepreneurship and neoliberalism, as neoliberalism is understood as the underlying ideological complex behind the logics of the competition state (neoliberalism is here defined as the extension of market mechanisms to all spheres of our private and political lives, fostered and enforced by the state).[22]

The American historian Angus Burgin also employs insights from the critical literature in his article "The Reinvention of Entrepreneurship" from 2018, which examines the sudden popularity of the concept of entrepreneurship in the second half of the twentieth century.[23] Like Dardot and Laval, Burgin argues that American management guru Peter Drucker played a crucial role in "democratizing" the concept through management literature from the 1950s onwards.[24] Like Mises and Kirzner, Drucker understood entrepreneurship as the ability to seize the opportunities created by change: "[…] and this defines entrepreneur and entrepreneurship – *the*

---

19 Michel Foucault, *The Birth of Biopolitics: Lectures at the Collège de France, 1978-1979* (New York: Palgrave Macmillan, 2008), 226.
20 Foucault, *The Birth of Biopolitics*, 226; Angus Burgin, "The Reinvention of Entrepreneurship," in *American Labyrinth: Intellectual History for Complicated Times* eds. Raymond Haberski Jr. and Andrew Hartman (London: Cornell University Press, 2018), 165.
21 Dardot & Laval, *The New Way of the World*, 106-107, 111.
22 See e.g. Pedersen, *Konkurrencestaten*, 19-31. Neoliberalism originated as a political ideology and movement in the interwar period and was institutionalized with the so-called Mont Pèlerin Society in 1947. Since then, neoliberalism has divided into different branches and is today a plural phenomenon; see Niklas Olsen, "The Mont Pèlerin Society: neo-liberalismens fødsel og mutationer 1930-2000," *Kritik* 45, no. 206 (2012): 2; Jacob Jensen and Niklas Olsen, "Hvad er neoliberalisme? – Redaktionelt forord," *Slagmark – Tidsskrift for Idéhistorie* 74 (2016): 9-22.
23 Burgin, "The Reinvention of Entrepreneurship," 164-165.
24 Burgin, "The Reinvention of Entrepreneurship," 174; Dardot and Laval, *The New Way of the World*, 118-119.

entrepreneur always searches for change, responds to it and exploits it as an opportunity."[25] However, Drucker differed from the earlier economic definitions by arguing that management was crucial for the creation of an entrepreneurial society permeated by a spirit of enterprise.[26] According to Drucker, the ideal of the entrepreneur was the constant readiness to change, which was to be enhanced by management.[27]

Additionally, in line with Hébert and Link, Burgin argues that, alongside Drucker, the Chicago economist Theodore Schultz was crucial in expanding the scope of entrepreneurship by incorporating the concept into his neoclassical theory of human capital.[28] Schultz extended the concept to include activities outside the market and anyone who is capable of increasing their human capital – whether a housewife or a student – is consequently an entrepreneur.[29] Schultz empirically documented that education can increase individuals' entrepreneurship, understood as the ability to deal successfully with economic disequilibria.[30] Thus, entrepreneurship became achievable for everyone, making the entrepreneur an ideal applicable for all citizens. Burgin points out that the concept was subsequently picked up by the social-psychological discipline in the 1960s.[31] It happened in the wake of the publication of *The Achieving Society* (1961) written by psychologist David McClelland, which examines how entrepreneurship, understood as a behavioural trait, affects economic growth.[32]

Inspired by the method of Burgin, this chapter will analyze the dissemination of the concept of entrepreneurship across different spheres

---

25 Peter Drucker, *Innovation and Entrepreneurship* (New York: Routledge, 1985 [2015]), 25; and Dardot & Laval, *The New Way of the World*, 118-119.
26 Drucker, *Innovation and Entrepreneurship*, 33; Dardot and Laval, *The New Way of the World*, 118-119.
27 Burgin, "The Reinvention of Entrepreneurship," 173-174; Dardot and Laval, *The New Way of the World*, 118-119; Drucker, *Innovation and Entrepreneurship*, 25.
28 Burgin, "The Reinvention of Entrepreneurship," 174; Hébert and Link, *A History of Entrepreneurship*, 82.
29 Burgin, "The Reinvention of Entrepreneurship," 174; Hébert and Link, *A History of Entrepreneurship*, 81-82.
30 Theodore W. Schultz, "The Value of the Ability to Deal with Disequilibria," *Journal of Economic Literature* 13, no. 3 (1975): 843.
31 Burgin, "The Reinvention of Entrepreneurship," 175.
32 David C. McClelland, *The Achieving Society* (Princeton: Van Nostrand, 1961); Burgin, "The Reinvention of Entrepreneurship," 175; Bo Carlsson, Pontus Braunerhjelm, Maureen McKelvey, Christer Olofsson, Lars Persson and Håkan Ylinenpää, "The evolving domain of entrepreneurship research," *Small Business Economics* 41, no. 4 (2013): 918.

of knowledge. To unpack the transformation of the content of the concept in these different spheres of knowledge, the derived historical definitions will be used as heuristic tools in the analysis. For this purpose, the definitions are summarized below in Figure 1.

Entrepre-neurship	Schumpeter	Mises	Kirzner	Drucker	Schultz	McClelland
What is it?	An innovative action	A description of all agents in an economy	A human characteristic	An ability strengthened by management	An ability strengthened by education	A behavioural trait
Who does it apply to?	The man of action	Agents in an economy	Persons with the specific characteristic	Everyone can have	Everyone can learn it	Persons with the specific trait

Figure 1: Overview of definitions of entrepreneurship.

The Role of Transnational Organizations in Promoting and Disseminating Entrepreneurship

The 1980s and 1990s saw an increasing academic awareness of the concept of entrepreneurship, as reflected in the establishment of a number of interdisciplinary journals devoted to the theme.[33] In the same period, the concept of entrepreneurship gained ground outside academia, as transnational organizations began to embrace it.[34] This development happened at the same time as the emergence of the competition state and the increased dominance of neoliberal ideas, which reflected the new global economic world order allegedly heralded by the collapse of the Soviet Union in 1989.[35]

The concept of entrepreneurship was seemingly first applied by a transnational organization in a 1989 report by the OECD's Center for Educational Research and Innovation (CERI).[36] The OECD, which was originally

---

33   Carlsson et al., "The evolving domain of entrepreneurship research," 920.
34   Carlsson et al., "The evolving domain of entrepreneurship research," 920; Kristensen et al., "Globalisering og livslang læring," 359-367; Pedersen, *Konkurrencestaten*, 46-51; Mark Olssen and Michael Peters, "Neoliberalism, higher education and the knowledge economy: from the free market to knowledge capitalism," *Journal of Education Policy* 20, no. 3 (2005): 313–314.
35   Kristensen et al., "Globalisering og livslang læring," 364-365; Ove Kaj Pedersen, "Konkurrencestaten og dens uddannelsespolitik – baggrund, intentioner og funktionsmåder" in *Læring i konkurrencestaten – kapløb eller bæredygtighed*, ed. Knud Illeris (København: Samfundslitteratur, 2014), 17; Pedersen, *Konkurrencestaten*, 22.
36   OECD, *Towards an "enterprising' culture: A challenge for education and training*, OECD/CERI educational monograph no. 4 (Paris: OECD, 1989), 1, 37.

established with a purely economic-political focus, came with the establishment of CERI in 1968 to play a crucial role in shaping the education policies of its member states.[37] The report *Towards an "Enterprising" Culture* from 1989 stated that: "the phenomenon of change and the many and varied impacts of such change on all aspects of people's lives and on society's institutions [...] point to the need for "being enterprising'."[38] Following Drucker's notion of change, OCED emphasized the future demand for citizens who are able to adapt to constant societal changes.[39] In addition, the report suggested that "enterprise learning" should be implemented in the education systems of member states to promote "being enterprising" and "entrepreneurial skills"[40] among citizens. Thus, OECD described entrepreneurship as skills that can be strengthened through education by changing the methods of work and pedagogical practice in the education systems, which outlines how the entrepreneur as a citizen ideal was pedagogical.[41]

During the same period, the concept of entrepreneurship was included in the World Bank's report *World Development Report: The Challenge of Development* from 1991, which focused on the macroeconomic conditions for economic growth.[42] The report made explicit the understanding that states' growth and development depend on entrepreneurship: "[...] the key to rapid development is the entrepreneur. Governments need to serve enterprise, large and small, not supplant it."[43] This view of entrepreneurs leans on the understanding of entrepreneurship promoted by Austrian

---

37 Vera G. Centeno, "The Birth of the OECD's Education Policy Area," in *The OECD's Historical Rise in Education: The Formation of a Global Governing Complex*, ed. Christian Ydesen (Cham: Springer International Publishing AG, 2019), 64-65; Matthias Schmelzer, *The Hegemony of Growth: The OECD and the Making of the Economic Growth Paradigm* (Cambridge: Cambridge University Press, 2016), 207; Christian Ydesen, *The OECD's Historical Rise in Education: The Formation of a Global Governing Complex* (Cham: Springer International Publishing AG, 2019); Christian Ydesen and Karen Egedal Andreasen, "Koblinger mellem økonomi og uddannelse: et rids af dansk transnational uddannelseshistorie," *Educare* 1 (2019): 18-42; Martin Marcussen, *OECD og idéspillet: game over?* (Copenhagen: Hans Reitzel, 2002).
38 OECD, *Towards an "enterprising' culture*, 5.
39 OECD, *Towards an "enterprising' culture*, 1, 5, 8.
40 OECD, *Towards an "enterprising' culture*, 1, 5, 7.
41 OECD, *Towards an "enterprising' culture*, 1, 5, 7, 8, 37; Magnus Hoppe, "Policy and entrepreneurship education," *Small Business Economics* 46, no. 1 (2016), 17.
42 The World Bank, *World Development Report: The Challenge of Development* (New York: Oxford University Press, 1991), 1, 7, 69.
43 The World Bank, *World Development Report*, 70.

economists such as Mises and Kirzner, which highlights innovative actions and risk-taking as distinctive features.[44]

The report from the World Bank followed in the footsteps of the OECD's emphasis on the positive effect of education on entrepreneurship.[45] Thus, the World Bank and the OECD both promoted an understanding of entrepreneurship based upon that of Schultz, as evident from the direct reference to Schultz's human capital theory in the World Bank's report *Priorities and Strategies for Education* from 1995.[46] Schultz's understanding also appeared in the OECD's report *Lifelong Learning for All* from 1996, which stated that education can improve students' entrepreneurial skills.[47] Entrepreneurship was thus understood by the OECD and the World Bank as a growth-stimulating ability that could be cultivated through education.

In the report *Fostering Entrepreneurship* from 1998, it is explicitly set out that entrepreneurship was a key concept in the OECD's growth agenda:

> Entrepreneurship is central to the functioning of market economies. Entrepreneurs are agents of change and growth in a market economy and they can act to accelerate the generation, dissemination and application of innovative ideas. [...] Entrepreneurs not only seek out and identify potentially profitable economic opportunities but are also willing to take risks to see if their hunches are right.[48]

The OECD's definition emphasizes the opportunistic role of the entrepreneur and resonates with Kirzner's understanding of the concept. In the report, the OECD described the importance of creating a culture that "support[s] risk-taking and individual reward."[49]

On the basis of these reports, it can be concluded that the basic understanding of the concept rested on the definitions of the Austrian economists, where innovative actions were weighted in combination with a

---

44 The World Bank, *World Development Report*, 57.
45 The World Bank, *World Development Report*, 57.
46 The World Bank, *Priorities and Strategies for Education: a World Bank Review* (Washington D.C.: The World Bank, 1995), 27, 99.
47 OECD, *Lifelong Learning for All* (Paris: OECD, 1996), 100.
48 OECD, *Fostering Entrepreneurship* (Paris: OECD, 1998), 11.
49 OECD, *Fostering Entrepreneurship*, 13.

risk-averse opportunistic behaviour. In addition, Schultz's human capital theory was incorporated when the concept was translated into concrete policy initiatives and recommendations, highlighting education as the key to increased entrepreneurship, which outlines the pedagogical citizen ideal. Together, the reports paint a picture of the entrepreneur as a citizen, who is innovative, risk-averse and possesses a constant drive for "lifelong learning", thus being able to constantly optimize one's own human capital and thereby adapt to the ever-changing labour market.[50] In all the reports, the rationale behind increasing the role of entrepreneurship in the education system was the expectation that the economy was becoming a knowledge economy, as elaborated in the OECD's report *The Knowledge-Based Economy* from 1996, in which the overall conclusion was that future growth depended on the level of education within the nation states.[51] Hence, entrepreneurship became an instrument for the OECD and the World Bank to achieve the goal of increased growth.[52]

During the 2000s, this understanding of the concept was also invoked by the EU Commission, which, with the so-called Oslo Agenda for Entrepreneurship Education in 2006, focused on how EU countries could increase and stimulate entrepreneurship in practice.[53] The recommendation was that entrepreneurship education should be implemented in education systems throughout the EU.[54] Thus, the concept of entrepreneurship went from describing a specific economic action for a limited period of time, as Schumpeter argued, to more diffusely describing a range of abilities that could and should be learnt by all. This understanding of the concept follows Schultz's human capital theory as well as Drucker's management focus and outlines how the entrepreneur was promoted as an ideal of societal behaviour applicable to all.

---

50 Kristensen et al., "Globalisering og livslang læring," 370; Magnus Dahlstedt and Andreas Fejes, "Shaping entrepreneurial citizens: A genealogy of entrepreneurship education in Sweden," *Critical Studies in Education* 60, no. 4. (2019): 462-632.
51 OECD, *The Knowledge-based Economy* (Paris: OECD, 1996), 14; Kristensen et al., "Globalisering og livslang læring," 369.
52 As shown by Matthias Schmelzer, OECD played pivotal role in making an economic growth paradigm, see Schmelzer, *The Hegemony of Growth*.
53 EU-Commission,"Entrepreneurship Education in Europe: Fostering Entrepreneurial Mindsets through Education and Learning," *The Oslo Agenda for Entrepreneurship Education in Europe*, October 26-27, 2006 (Brussels: European Commission, DG Enterprise and Industry), 5.
54 EU-Commission, "Entrepreneurship Education in Europe," 5; Sarah Robinson and Per Blenker, "Tensions between rhetoric and practice in entrepreneurship education; an ethnography from Danish higher education," *European Journal of Higher Education* 4, no. 1, (2014), 80.

In several of the reports, the transnational organizations explicitly pointed out that Denmark needed to promote entrepreneurship to a much greater extent if the country was to cope successfully with the transition to a knowledge economy: In a report from 1991, The World Bank criticized how Denmark in the decades after the Second World War regulated the capital market and expanded the public sector to such an extent that entrepreneurship has had difficult conditions.[55] In 1999, the Global Entrepreneurship Monitor (GEM) began an international monitoring of entrepreneurship, in which Denmark was placed in the group with low-level entrepreneurship.[56] In 2000, the OECD published a Regulatory Reform Review, which pointed out a number of economic barriers that hampered entrepreneurship in Denmark.[57] In 2002, Denmark received a warning from the OECD that Denmark's growth could be reduced due to a lack of entrepreneurship.[58]

In addition to disseminating a specific understanding of the concept, the transnational organizations thus play an active role in highlighting and criticizing Denmark's failure to live up to recommendations in the field. This chapter argues that the criticism levelled at Denmark contributed to put entrepreneurship on the Danish education policy agenda.

The Dissemination of the Concept of Entrepreneurship in Denmark

Since the beginning of the nineteenth century, the concept of the entrepreneur has been used in the Danish language to describe a person who performs building and construction work.[59] The usage of the concept of the entrepreneur is thus nothing new, but the understanding of a connection between entrepreneurship and growth, as promoted by the international organizations, was in the 1980s still novel in the Danish academic disci-

---

55 The World Bank, *World Development Report*, 36.
56 Global Entrepreneurship Monitor, *National vurdering af iværksætteraktivitet, Danmark 1999* (Kolding: CESFO, Syddansk Universitet, 1999), 6.
57 OECD, *OECD Reviews of Regulatory Reform: Regulatory Reform in Denmark* (Paris: OECD, 2000), 61-62.
58 TV2, "OECD: Danmark risikerer lavvækst," April 29, 2002.
59 Jens Christensen, *Entrepreneurship i vidensamfundet* (Aarhus: Aarhus Universitetsforlag, 2005), 21; for an example hereof see *Fyens Stifts Kongelig allene privilegerede Adresse-Avis og Avertissements-Tidende*, January 9, 1810.

pline of economics. The first work focusing on the concept in the Danish academic discipline of economics can be traced back to the year 1988 and in the succeeding years more work was published on the concept of entrepreneurship.[60] This indicates that there has been a knowledge exchange across the Atlantic, where the Danish economists, with a delay of several decades, adopted the economic theory of the Chicago school and not least the Austrian tradition, whose theorists were employed by American universities and resident in the United States.[61]

During the same period, other spheres of knowledge began to embrace the concept of entrepreneurship and the Danish business schools in particular played an important role in the dissemination of the concept. In 1989, researchers Henrik Herlau and Mette Mønsted from the Copenhagen Business School offered a course in entrepreneurship.[62] The course was held 42 years after the first course in entrepreneurship was offered at Harvard Business School in 1947.[63] In the 1990s and 2000s, Danish business schools continued to offer courses in entrepreneurship and from the mid-1990s other universities in Denmark also began to focus on entrepreneurship.[64] Since then, the scope of teaching entrepreneurship has increased massively, with as many as 224 courses in entrepreneurship offered at Danish universities in the academic year 2011/2012.[65] The business schools' focus on entrepreneurship led to a large body of literature, which translated insights from economic theory into practical guidelines for entrepreneurship, largely following Drucker's understanding of the concept.[66]

---

60 For the earliest identified usage, see Jørgen Ravn Elkjær, "Entreprenøren og foretageren i økonomisk teori," *Nationaløkonomisk Tidsskrift* 126 (1988): 96-111; Jørgen Ravn Elkjær, "Entreprenørbegrebet," *Nationaløkonomisk Tidsskrift* 130 (1992): 309-315; John Kjeldsen, *Bidrag til udvikling af en egentlig entrepreneurteori* (Aarhus: Handelshøjskolen i Aarhus, 1991); Jørn Henrik Petersen, "Plan og marked - marked eller plan?," *Nationaløkonomisk Tidsskrift* 129 (1991): 84-97.
61 Hébert and Link, *A History of Entrepreneurship*, 84.
62 *Politiken*, "Slut med kluntede råd til opfindere," August 19, 1989.
63 Carlsson et al., "The evolving domain of entrepreneurship research," 917.
64 *MetroXpress*, "Akademikere skal være selvstændige" January 16, 2003; *Jyllands-Posten*, "Navne i noter" October 20, 2000; *Erhvervsbladet* Morten Hansen, "Revisionsfirma sponsorerer professor" November 30, 1999.
65 Fonden for Entreprenørskab, *Entreprenørskab fra ABC til Ph.D.*, (Odense: Fonden for Entreprenørskab – Young Enterprise, 2012), 103.
66 Kristian Philipsen, *Innovation: entreprenørskab og intraprenørskab* (Odense: PRAXIS – Nyt Teknisk Forlag, 2015); Nielsen et al., *Entreprenørskab i teori og praksis*; Henrik Herlau and Helge Tetzschner, *Fra jobtager til jobmager* (Frederiksberg: Samfundslitteratur, 1995).

The concept of entrepreneurship has consequently been part of various spheres of knowledge in Denmark since the late 1980s, where Danish academics in economic theory began to use it. From the beginning of the 1990s, business schools and later other universities, adopted the concept both in the form of teaching entrepreneurship and in the literature of the discipline. However, according to the Danish newspapers' use of the term, it was not until the early 2010s that the concept was integrated into everyday language. Below is an illustration of the development in the number of articles in Danish newspapers that have used the term, since the first article in 1989 reported on Herlau and Mønsted's course.[67] That the concept was until the 2010s reserved for the academic disciplines and thus did not formed part of the Danish newspapers' vocabulary, raises the question of when and how entrepreneurship became part of the political agenda in Denmark.

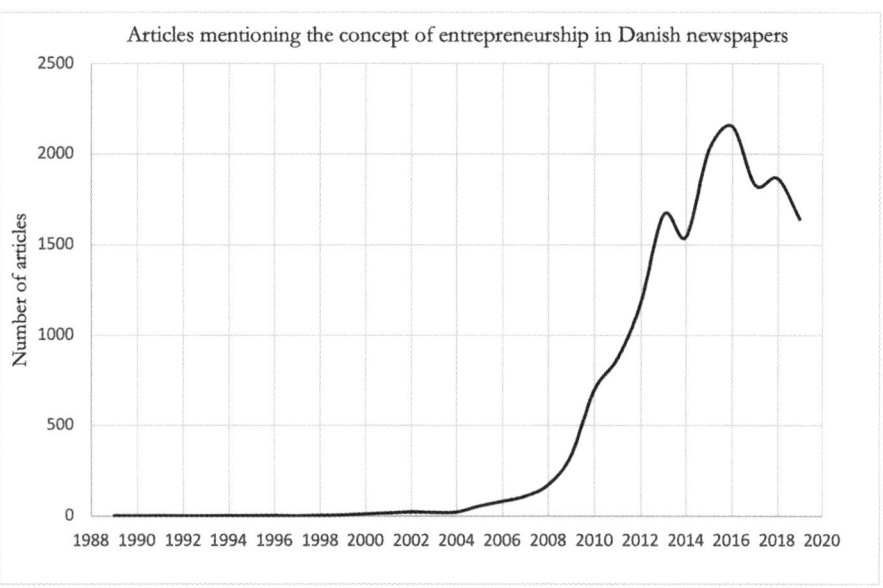

Figure 2: The number of articles using the concept of entrepreneurship from 1989-2019. The articles have been identified by searching for "entrepreneurship" in the database Infomedia.

---

67   *Politiken,* "Slut med kluntede råd til opfindere" August 19, 1989.

Entrepreneurship on the Political Agenda in Denmark – a Citizen Ideal in the making

The first time the use of concept of the entrepreneur can be identified in a Danish policy-paper is in *Innovative iværksættere – kompetence og kapital* (Innovative entrepreneurs – competence and capital) from 1996, which was written by a working group put together by the Ministry of Research.[68] In the policy-paper, four different ideal types of entrepreneurs were described.[69] Common for the ideal types was the Schumpeterian notion of developing something new in a market context.[70] For example, one of the four types was described as a highly skilled person who developed new products by using technological knowledge.[71] In the paper, there was no explicit mention of entrepreneurship, but the concept as well as a number of other concepts, such as competence and lifelong learning, subsequently became more common in Danish policy-papers. This development resonates with the so-called "learning and competence policy turn", which influenced the Danish education system in the 1990s.[72]

In 2000, Forskningsrådet (the Danish Research Council) published the policy-paper *Det globale vidensmarked* (The Global Knowledge Market), which described entrepreneurship as a specific culture, the goal of which was to ensure Denmark's competitiveness: "The purpose is to help ensure that Danish companies and research institutions have the opportunity to develop the entrepreneurial and innovative culture that is a prerequisite for maintaining competitiveness in both the research system and in

---

68   Forskningsministeriet, *Innovative iværksættere - kompetence og kapital*, Arbejdsgruppen om innovative iværksættere og nyttiggørelse af forskningsresultater og opfindelser (København: Forsknings-ministeriet, 1996).
69   In Danish the word "iværksættere" was used, while one of the four ideal types was described with the Danish word "entreprenør"; Forskningsministeriet, *Innovative iværksættere - kompetence og kapital*.
70   Forskningsministeriet, *Innovative iværksættere - kompetence og kapital*.
71   Forskningsministeriet, *Innovative iværksættere - kompetence og kapital*.
72   Kristensen et al., "Globalisering og livslang læring," 360-361. There is some Danish literature focusing on the concept of competence and the politcal attention toward it; see e.g. Jens Erik Kristensen and Stefan Hermann, "Kompetenceudvikling – Psykologisk inderliggørelse på dåseform?," *Psyke & Logos* 25, no. 2 (2004): 494-515; Stefan Hermann, *Et diagnostisk landkort over kompetenceudvikling og læring – pejlinger og skitser* (København: Danmark Pædagogiske Universitetsforlag, 2008); Laura Louise Sarauw, *Kompetencebegrebet og andre stileøvelser: Fortællinger om uddannelsesudviklingen på de danske universiteter efter universitetsloven 2003* (Ph.D. thesis, University of Copenhagen 2011).

business."⁷³ Following this, the paper announced a project which aimed to secure the establishment of courses in entrepreneurship.⁷⁴ This focus on education in entrepreneurship, as well as the notion of an entrepreneurial culture, strike a chord with the message in the OECD's reports and not least Drucker's enterprise spirit.⁷⁵ Seemingly, the broader and more diffuse understanding of the concept which the transnational organizations helped to promote had also found its way to Denmark at the turn of the millennium.

Thus, in Denmark the concept of entrepreneurship became part of the political agenda more or less 10 years after the World Bank's criticism of Denmark's macroeconomic conditions. The criticism and the pressure that the transnational organizations exerted on Danish politicians was intensified in the late 1990s and during the 2000s by forces in the Danish business community, think tanks and consulting companies: Kompetencerådet (The Competence Council), which was established under the auspices of the private think tank Mandag Morgen, stated as early as in 1998 that Denmark was under pressure, as "The transition from industrial society to knowledge society requires a fundamental new understanding of society's opportunities and challenges - a completely new diagnosis."⁷⁶ The expectation of Kompetencerådet was that "[…] leadership and entrepreneurial spirit will emerge stronger from this decade. But also that we have a long way to go yet before it is good enough."⁷⁷ In 2000, the consulting company Rambøll Management published the study *Frontløberlande i den nye økonomi* (Frontrunner countries in the new economy), where one of 10 pieces of advice for Denmark laid out in the report was: "Strengthen entrepreneurship and globalization in companies."⁷⁸ The same logic was repeated in *Den danske strategi* (The Danish Strategy) from 2004, published by Innovationsrådet (The Innovation Council), which replaced the Competence Council at the independent think tank Mandag Morgen.⁷⁹ In *Den*

---

73 Danmarks Forskningsråd, *Det globale videnmarked – en udfordring for offentligt-privat samspil* (København: Forskningsministeriet, 2000), 30.
74 Danmarks Forskningsråd, *Det globale videnmarked*, 31.
75 Dardot and Laval, *The New Way of the World*, 118.
76 Kompetencerådet, *Kompetencerådets rapport 1998* (København: Mandag Morgen Strategisk Forum, 1999), preface.
77 Kompetencerådet, *Kompetencerådets rapport 1998*, 5.
78 Rambøll Management, *Frontløberlande i den nye økonomi – Benchmarking af Danmark.com*. (Aarhus: PLS Rambøll Management, 2000), 7.
79 Kristensen et al., "Globalisering og livslang læring," 373.

danske strategi, it was emphasized that: "Danish entrepreneurship is weak - that is, the ability to create new companies and make them grow."[80] In continuation of this, the Innovation Council also criticized the Danish tax system, which "[...] distorts the economic incentive structures".[81]

Fundamental to the critique referred to above was the understanding of entrepreneurship as a tool for creating growth, an understanding which was echoed in the criticism from the Danish business community, which entered the debate in the mid-2000s. The then chairman of Dansk Erhverv (the Danish Chamber of Commerce), Poul-Erik Pedersen, wanted more teaching in entrepreneurship in 2008: "Entrepreneurship must to a much greater extent be a very fundamental value in the Danish education system."[82] In the same year, the then Minister of Education, Bertel Haarder, and Director of Dansk Erhverv, Christian T. Ingemann, wrote a joint debate piece in the Danish newspaper *Berlingske Tidende* where they argued that education in entrepreneurship should be implemented in primary school, as they believed that the skills which entrepreneurship entails will be crucial for the future Danish labour market.[83] In the piece, they described how a new strategy should ensure: "that more young people open their eyes to their inner entrepreneur by encouraging abilities such as independence, creativity, business understanding, courage and motivation to start something new."[84]

The Danish think tanks, consulting companies as well as the public debate thus reinforced the pressure established by the transnational organizations to implement entrepreneurship in the education system. Venstre (the Liberal Party) and Det Konservative Folkeparti (The Conservative Party), who from 2001 and in the following 10 years formed the Danish government (VK-government), incorporated the criticisms in their policy through the ambition of launching a number of reforms that would

---

80 Innovationsrådet, *Den danske strategi: Danmarks muligheder i det globale videnssamfund* (København: Mandag Morgen nr. 36, 2004), 8.
81 Innovationsråde, *Den danske strategi*, 15.
82 *Dansk Erhvervs Avis,* Poul-Erik Pedersen: "Fremtidens arbejdsmarked tilhører entreprenørerne" January 23, 2008.
83 *Berlingske Tidende*, Bertel Haarder and Christian T. Ingemann: "Debat: Fremtidssikring ii: Flere skal tænke mere selv" July 19, 2008.
84 *Berlingske Tidende*, Bertel Haarder and Christian T. Ingemann: "Debat: Fremtidssikring ii: Flere skal tænke mere selv" July 19, 2008.

restructure the Danish economy and society.[85] Central to the VK-government's policy was that it became the task of the education system to promote the societal behaviour of the entrepreneur by implementing entrepreneurship education.

In the government's policy document *Better Education* from 2002, entrepreneurship was identified as one of five areas of focus for the government, a decision which was justified on the basis of ensuring future growth.[86] In the government's publication, *Et samfund med plads til det frie initiativ* (A society with space for free initiative) from 2003, the securing of "the future's culture of independence" was written together with a larger societal critique. To the government, promoting entrepreneurship signified that "Rules and systems that have taken the initiative away from the Danes must be removed."[87] These political initiatives were in line with the neoliberal marketization of the time, a development in which the state had to create conditions which ensured that the citizens could act rationally and follow economic incentives. *Et samfund med plads til det frie initiative* illustrates how the VK-government's political embrace of entrepreneurship was part of a particular policy consisting of specific ideas for transforming the Danish society into a more competitive society.

As a follow-up to the publication *Better Education* from 2002, the government published *Innovation, Entrepreneurship and a Culture of Independence in the Danish Education System* in 2004, which identified the education system as the spearhead in optimizing Denmark's competitiveness: "Denmark must become part of the European elite in entrepreneurship. Enterprise and innovation are essential to maintaining and improving Denmark's position in the global market and the global community. […] The education system is central to this development."[88] The policy document stated that the purpose of the strategy was "[…] to foster a culture of entrepreneur-

---

85   In *Konkurrencestaten,* Pedersen also points to the fact that the VK-government incorporated the critique of the Danish education system into the government's policies, but Pedersen does not pay attention to how central the concept of entrepreneurship was to this development, see p. 189.
86   The Government, *Better Education* (København: Undervisningsministeriet, 2002), 4.
87   The Government, *Et samfund med plads til det frie initiativ* (København: Schultz, 2003), 9; in the publication, the Danish word "iværksætteri" was used.
88   Undervisningsministeriet and Ministeriet for Videnskab, Teknologi og Udvikling, *Innovation, Entrepreneurship and a Culture of Independence in the Danish Education System* (København: Undervisningsministeriet, 2004), 3.

ship in the education sector".[89] Entrepreneurship was again described as a culture, as was the case in the policy document *Det globale videnmarked* from the Danish Research Council in 2000, a definition so vague that the real meaning of the term is difficult to encapsulate.[90] Nevertheless, the understanding that education should foster this specific form of culture is clear, drawing connections to Schultz's human capital theory and the OECD's report *Fostering Entrepreneurship* from 1998.

From the mid-2000s and onwards, a political understanding prevailed that Denmark's future competitiveness depended on entrepreneurship, an argument used to legitimize economic reforms as well as a restructuring of the education system with the overall aim to disseminate the entrepreneur as a pedagogical citizen ideal. The VK-government's agenda met support from both sides of the political spectrum and was partly continued when Socialdemokratiet (the Social Democratic Party), Radikale Venstre (the Danish Social-Liberal Party) and Socialistisk Folkeparti (the Socialist People's Party) took power in 2011.[91]

In policy documents and in the public debate, where the Danish business community, think tanks and consulting companies played active roles, it can be stated that entrepreneurship was defined as both a culture, an inner behavioural trait and a value. Common for these broad definitions was that they were all based on an expectation that education would be able to increase entrepreneurship, thereby creating innovative, independent and adaptable citizens who could secure growth in the future Danish labour market. The mentioning of entrepreneurship as a behavioural trait, following McClelland's understanding, underlines how the entrepreneur was a citizen ideal in the making during the 2000s. The importance of the education system for the dissemination of entrepreneurship and thereby for the diffusion of the entrepreneur as a citizen ideal testifies to the fact that Schultz's human capital-inspired understanding of entrepreneurship, which was promoted by the OECD in particular, had become dominant in Danish politics.

89 Undervisningsministeriet & Ministeriet for Videnskab, Teknologi og Udvikling, *Innovation, Entrepreneurship and a Culture of Independence*, 9.
90 Danmarks Forskningsråd, *Det globale videnmarked*, 31.
91 See e.g. Ministeriet for Forskning, Innovation og Videregående Uddannelse, *Danmark – Løsningernes Land* (København: Ministeriet for Forskning, Innovation og Videregående Uddannelse, 2012).

Thus, an overall picture can be formed of the dissemination process of the concept of entrepreneurship, in which both the academic disciplines and the transnational organizations have played an important part, as illustrated below in Figure 3. The entry of the concept into Denmark can be traced back to the late 1980s in the academic disciplines, while during the 2000s, the concept was embedded in a political agenda of increased growth and optimization of Danish competitiveness. Hence, the government followed recommendations from transnational organizations, Danish consulting companies and think tanks and began, from the mid-2000s, to focus on implementing entrepreneurship education throughout the Danish education system.

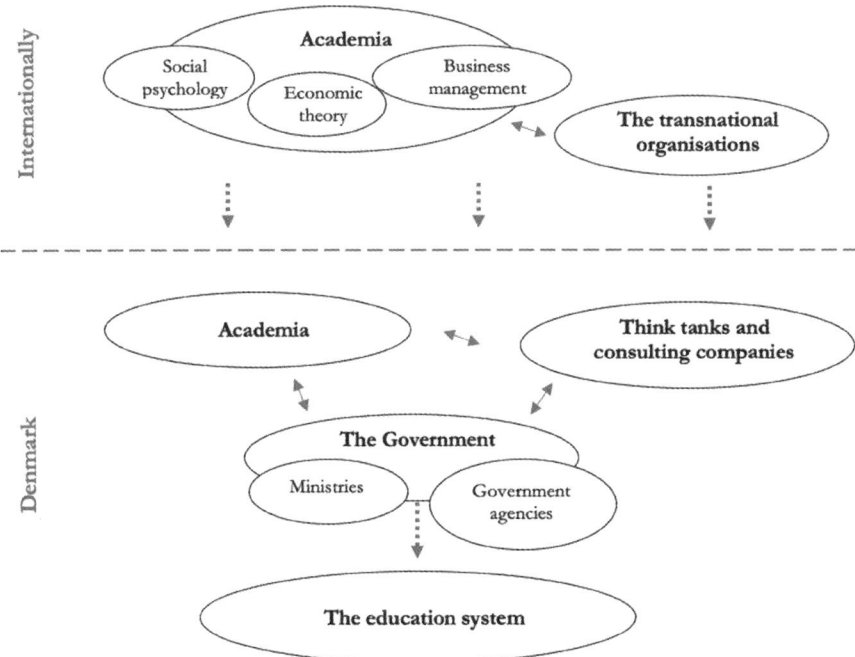

Figure 3: Illustration of the circulation of the concept of entrepreneurship across the different spheres of knowledge.

Education in Entrepreneurship – the Dissemination of a Citizen Ideal

To investigate which political expectations the concept was charged with when entrepreneurship was launched in the Danish education system, the inter-ministerial policy document, *Strategi for uddannelse i entreprenørskab* (Strategy for education in entrepreneurship) prepared by the Ministry of Science, Technology and Innovation, Ministry of Economic and Business Affairs, Ministry of Education and Ministry of Culture in 2009, is taken into consideration.

In April 2005, the VK-government established Globaliseringsrådet (the Globalization Council), which, with "globaliseringsstrategien" (the Globalization strategy), set the course for Denmark's future in a world characterized by increasing international competition.[92] As a follow-up to this, after the shock of the financial crisis had subsided, the government issued the *Strategi for uddannelse i entreprenørskab* in 2009, which was intended to ensure Denmark's future competitiveness in a globalized market economy.[93] The mediocre position of Denmark in several analyses of entrepreneurship is highlighted as a background for the preparation of the strategy: "Analyses show, however, that Denmark is still far behind the leading countries when it comes [to] entrepreneurship education."[94] The document does not specify which analyses are referred to, but the reference to their existence strengthens the argument of the chapter that the pressure established by the transnational organizations and then by the domestic debate influenced and accelerated the dissemination of the concept.

Thus, the strategy was part of Denmark's transition into a competition state and an ambition of making Denmark one of the countries with the most entrepreneurs, which, according to the strategy, would entail that: "Everywhere in society we must be innovative and transform ideas and knowledge into value."[95] Hence, entrepreneurship was no longer about creating value in the market economy, as with Schumpeter, but should apply *everywhere* in society, which very aptly reflects the marketization that is central to the neoliberal complex of ideas. The strategy emphasized that

---

92 Kristensen et al., "Globalisering og livslang læring," 367.
93 Ministeriet for Videnskab, Teknologi og Udvikling et al., *Strategi for Uddannelse i Entreprenørskab*, 5.
94 Ministeriet for Videnskab, Teknologi og Udvikling et al., *Strategi for Uddannelse i Entreprenørskab*, 7.
95 Ministeriet for Videnskab, Teknologi og Udvikling et al., *Strategi for Uddannelse i Entreprenørskab*, 5.

the education system should facilitate this societal change by encouraging students to become entrepreneurial: "Entrepreneurship education plays a role in two areas: First, it must stimulate the desire to become entrepreneurial. […] Secondly, the ability of pupils and students to become more entrepreneurial must be strengthened."[96] Entrepreneurship was used in several places in the strategy as an adjective in the form of the word entrepreneurial, which illustrates the broad definition, where entrepreneurship is described as a way of being, based on several abilities.[97] Hence, the use of the term in the strategy is in line with Schultz's argument that entrepreneurship is the ability to improve one's own human capital, but is also an extension of this, as entrepreneurship is no longer a single ability, but rather a way of being comprised of several abilities. With this, the government's understanding is almost like McClelland's definition of entrepreneurship as a behavioural trait, thus entrepreneurship was now a way of being.

According to the policy document, the creation of value was the overarching characteristic of the entrepreneurial way of being: "Education in entrepreneurship enables the individual to create value by starting new activities or improving existing activities, by thinking independently, dealing with uncertainty, identifying and exploiting opportunities and by setting ambitious goals and achieving them."[98] The description of entrepreneurship outlines that to be entrepreneurial involves a constant individual focus on innovation or optimization, including self-optimization. Here we see how the dissemination of entrepreneurship in the education system follows the logics of the competition state, as the entrepreneurial citizens must act on the basis of a rational calculation of where value can be created. This entails a constant optimization of all human activities, where it was the political expectation that the effect of the entrepreneurial way of being would optimize the competitiveness of all of Denmark.

Thus, according to the government, the task of the education system was to "develop pupils" and students' abilities to act entrepreneurially."[99]

---

96 Ministeriet for Videnskab, Teknologi og Udvikling et al., *Strategi for Uddannelse i Entreprenørskab*, 8.
97 Ministeriet for Videnskab, Teknologi og Udvikling et al., *Strategi for Uddannelse i Entreprenørskab*, 5, 8.
98 Ministeriet for Videnskab, Teknologi og Udvikling et al., *Strategi for Uddannelse i Entreprenørskab*, 8.
99 Ministeriet for Videnskab, Teknologi og Udvikling et al., *Strategi for Uddannelse i Entreprenørskab*, 8.

To realize this vision, a number of concrete initiatives were introduced at each educational level, which, among other things, meant that forms of examination that could measure entrepreneurial competencies were developed.[100] The government itself emphasized that entrepreneurship had in 2009 become a governing concept for the education system.[101] The introduction of measuring the students' entrepreneurial skills demonstrates that the concept had become a crucial buzzword in Danish education policy by 2009, but it also indicates that the implementation of entrepreneurship was part of promoting and disseminating a specific citizen ideal – the entrepreneur.

The adoption and dissemination of the concept of entrepreneurship became a politically viable way to launch a competition-inspired understanding of the state's role and not least to evoke the entrepreneur as a pedagogical citizen ideal, thereby encouraging citizens to be entrepreneurial and perform value-creating actions. The policy documents' definitions of entrepreneurship no longer align with Schumpeter's time-limited innovative action, but outlines a citizen ideal which states that the individual must be "an entrepreneur for one's own human capital" as the authors of *Pædagogikkens Idéhistorie* put it.[102] Entrepreneurship, a vague concept without a fixed definition, is an ideal way of disseminating and implementing a citizen ideal.[103] By rewarding students who manage to optimize their own entrepreneurial abilities, the Danish education system reinforces that entrepreneurship, as Dardot and Laval have emphazised, takes the form of self-government.[104] That entrepreneurship is linked to increased freedom in the government's publication, *Et samfund med plads til det frie initiativ*, thus appears as a paradox, as the spread of entrepreneurship implicitly implies the spread of a certain rational reaction pattern, which the entrepreneur captures and symbolizes as a citizen ideal.

In other words, this signifies a marketization of the education system, which should not be understood exclusively as a consequence of interna-

---

100 Ministeriet for Videnskab, Teknologi og Udvikling et al., *Strategi for Uddannelse i Entreprenørskab*, 12-13.
101 Ministeriet for Videnskab, Teknologi og Udvikling et al., *Strategi for Uddannelse i Entreprenørskab*, 5.
102 Kristensen et al., "Globalisering og livslang læring," 388.
103 Hoppe, "The Entrepreneurship Concept," 103.
104 Dardot and Laval, *The New Way of the World*, 111.

tional events, but also as a political choice to promote and legitimize the competition state through the citizen ideal of the entrepreneur. During the 2000s, entrepreneurship in the education system was proclaimed by Danish politicians to be the means to ensure strong competitiveness and future growth. This entails that the "the opportunistic personality" identified in *Konkurrencestaten* as the ideal of the competition state more precisely and with empirical evidence must be described as the entrepreneurial person.[105] This is a pedagogical citizen ideal that largely follows the understanding of entrepreneurship promoted by transnational organizations and has then been moderated to the Danish competition state through the implementation of entrepreneurship in the Danish education system. The empirical study of the concept of entrepreneurship has thus substantiated and nuanced the story of the Danish competition state by illuminating how the entrepreneur as a particular citizen ideal was disseminated, communicated and implemented as entrepreneurship became a governing pedagogical concept for the Danish education system.

Concluding Remarks

This chapter has shown how the entrepreneur has become an ideal of societal behaviour in the Danish welfare state through the implementation of entrepreneurship in the Danish education system in relation to Denmark's transition to a competition state. The chapter has empirically shown that the concept of entrepreneurship came to Denmark in the late 1980s and has argued that the concept found its way into Denmark through academia, as well as by the transnational organizations of the OECD, the World Bank and the EU Commission. These transnational organizations played a crucial role in promoting a specific understanding of entrepreneurship as a growth-creating ability, which could and should be learnt by all citizens as a pedagogical citizen ideal. In continuation of this, the chapter has argued that the criticism from the transnational organizations and the Danish think tanks and consulting companies levelled against Denmark's lack of entrepreneurship in the education system contributed to the con-

---

[105] Pedersen, *Konkurrencestaten*, 188.

cept becoming a governing buzzword in the VK-government's education policy in the mid-2000s.

The chapter has argued that the dissemination of the concept during the 2000s should be understood as a result of the VK-government's political response to globalization, where the implementation of entrepreneurship within the education system was articulated as the means of achieving the government's overall goal of future growth. The entry of the concept of entrepreneurship into the Danish education system is thus based on a significant conceptual shift, where the concept has lost the narrow economic significance Schumpeter assigned to it while it is still understood as the generator of economic growth. The government's definition of entrepreneurship as a way of being supports the argument that entrepreneurship was disseminated and implemented in the Danish education system because the concept captures a pedagogical citizen ideal, which is compatible with the competition state: the entrepreneur enhances value creation and implies a constant optimization of one's own abilities.

The Unemployed

From Guilting to Shaming the Jobless in the Welfare State

Jon Helt Haarder and Mathies Græsborg Aarhus

In recent years, a consensus has been established in Denmark on issues concerning unemployment and labour market politics. Parties from across the political spectrum have cut benefits for the long-term unemployed, reduced the amount of years one can receive unemployment insurance, removed basic citizen rights for the long-term unemployed, such as the right to family reunification and increased the "activation work" done by job centres.[1] We can look to recent years' cultural and mass media representations of the unemployed to notice a changing public perception of the unemployed as well as the cultural legitimacy for such policy changes. From the political Right's moral critique of the "underclass" – including "Poor Carina" who according to them was not poor enough[2] – to the Social

---

1 "Activation" is a word used to designate policies and practices meant to stimulate and motivate the unemployed to become more active jobseekers – often put into practice by state institutions or consultants.
2 The unemployed, single mother "Poor Carina" became a figure of public discussion in 2011 when her private budget was discussed in a live TV-debate and used by Liberal Alliance's labour market spokesman Joachim B. Olsen as an example to argue that unemployment benefits were too high.

Democrats' Employment Minister and his recent claim that unemployed academics should take jobs in supermarkets, the consensus seems to be that the unemployed should feel ashamed. Moral outrage in fact seems to arise when the unemployed do not feel sufficiently ashamed – as in the case of Lazy Robert who, of course, was an outrageous character because of his lack of shame or his shamelessness.[3]

These changes in attitude towards the unemployed should not surprise us when comparing them to recent changes in the institutions and "ethos" of the welfare state. Recently, sociologist Magnus Paulsen Hansen has argued convincingly that morality is key to understanding the "active turn" in the welfare state's approach to governing the unemployed, which, to him, involves "new understandings […] of what a socially just society entails and requires from the individual member and from the collective".[4] Similarly, in Ove Kaj Pedersen's now-classic definition of "the competition state", the changing Danish state has been designed to circumvent the individual failure of unemployment or welfare dependency as it "seeks to make the individual responsible for his/her own life, sees the community as tied to work, freedom as the freedom to realize the individual's own needs."[5]

In this article, we argue that morality is not enough to understand the changing welfare state's approach to the unemployed but needs to be supplemented with an eye for the *feelings* we associate with the experience of unemployment. This article then argues that, whereas the unemployed were earlier governed through the feeling of guilt and the notion of a violation of an implied social contract, unemployment is increasingly tied to the feeling of shame and of the whole self as a failing entity. By analyzing Danish literary representations of the unemployed and their encounter with the unemployment office – Bent Vinn Nielsen's *Work-Shy* (1978) and Lau Aaen's *Benefits Land* (2012)[6] – we show that the transition from guilt to shame is, in part, due to the fact that shame has been appropriated by central unemployment institutions of the welfare state as an affective gov-

---

[3] "Lazy Robert" appeared in a TV-debate in 2012 and claimed that he preferred to be on unemployment benefits rather than working low-paying jobs.
[4] Magnus Paulsen Hansen, *The Moral Economy of Activation: Ideas, Politics and Policies* (Bristol: Policy Press, 2019), 14.
[5] Ove Kaj Pedersen, *Konkurrencestaten* (København: Hans Reitzels Forlag, 2011), 12.
[6] Bent Vinn Nielsen, *Arbejdssky* (København: Gyldendal, 1978); Lau Aaen, *Dagpengeland* (København: Gyldendal, 2012).

ernmental strategy. We elaborate on the consequences of this turn in the welfare state's relationship to its unemployed population by reading two contemporary coming-of-age narratives – Karina Pedersen's *Far out* (Langt ude, 2016) and Morten Pape's *The Plan* (Planen, 2015).[7] In both texts, the ugly feelings with which the figure of the unemployed is now associated play a decisive role for children growing up with chronically unemployed parents. In a curious elaboration, shame and disgust directed at an unemployed parent help the child organize the complicated feelings involved in breaking away from a negligent primary caregiver.

Before moving on to our argument about the changing feelings that accompany the figure of the unemployed, a quick detour around the relationship of social class and culture in Denmark is necessary. Because of its robust welfare state, Denmark is sometimes claimed to have transcended class formations and class power, but even though the welfare state historically lessened some forms of economic inequality, it did not dismantle social hierarchies as such.[8] Rather, it is more accurate to say that the welfare state changed the parameters around which the struggle for power is played out, or reshuffled class power slightly, as it gave certain groups access to power which they would not otherwise have in more economically unequal societies. Class power nonetheless persists. The welfare state's reshuffling of class power, though still very much subject to economic capital, leaves important space for other forms of capital, such as cultural capital in Bourdieu's sense.[9] Recently, Danish sociologists, such as Aydin Soei, have pointed out that cultural capital remains one of the main barriers to class mobility in contemporary Denmark.[10] Today, class

---

7   Karina Pedersen, *Helt ude i hampen. Mails fra underklassen* (København: Gyldendal, 2016); Morten Pape, *Planen* (København: Gyldendal, 2015).
8   As Rune Lykkeberg has pointed out: "This welfare state does not oppose social class distinctions, but reproduces existing class distinctions and privileges a cultural upper class. It dismantles actual poverty, delivers social guarantees and ensures a general prosperity, but economic inequality is reproduced and cultural inequality is institutionalized." Rune Lykkeberg, *Kampen Om Sandhederne* (København: Gyldendal, 2008), 11.
9   Class domination by way of culture has thus often remained "hidden", as many important recent Danish class studies also point out. Stine Thidemann Faber, et al., *Det skjulte klassesamfund* (Aarhus: Aarhus Universitetsforlag, 2012); Gitte Sommer Harrits, *Hvad betyder klasse? En rekonstruktion af klassebegrebet med henblik på en analyze af politisk deltagelse i Danmark* (Aarhus: Politica, 2005).
10   Soei goes on to show that, today, cultural capital increasingly works to exclude descendants of immigrants, rather than the traditional working class or petite bourgeois, as was the case earlier. Aydin Soei, *Vrede unge mænd: optøjer og kampen for anerkendelse i et nyt Danmark* (København: Tidernes skifter, 2011).

distinctions are especially transferred via the educational system where the lower classes are not allotted the necessary language to negotiate and switch between scripts and codes and therefore find themselves alienated or excluded. This in some sense is parallel to other European welfare states, such as France where, as Didier Eribon has pointed out, higher education serves as a mechanism to exclude and silence the working class.[11]

Hierarchies built on cultural capital, thus, still play an important role in the welfare state even though the values and tastes around which cultural capital is formulated have adapted to our brave new world. As we shall see later, new norms regarding entrepreneurship and marketability seem to be becoming the central currency in the cultural hierarchy of the welfare state. This of course also creates new losers who fail to live up to these norms because they do not possess the necessary cultural (and affective) resources. Today, those who are uncultured are no longer those who do not possess the correct tastes but, rather, those who fail to display a repertoire of marketable affective dispositions and competencies. The losers are the ones who fail to sell themselves.

On one of the lowest steps of the welfare state's social and cultural hierarchy, we find the social group known as "the unemployed" or those excluded from paid labour. Whereas the welfare state's universal basic services such as free healthcare, the right to housing and unemployment relief abates the material suffering and physical vulnerability of the unemployed, it does not fundamentally change the societal worth afforded the unemployed.[12] In fact, in many ways, the welfare state bolsters the productivist agenda and "work ethic" as its rights and services in large parts depend on one's "readiness to work".[13]

---

11   Didier Eribon, *Returning to Reims* (London: Allen Lane, 2018).
12   Of course, the degree to which the welfare state demands that the citizen is available for the job market depends on the national context. See Gøsta Esping-Andersen, *The three worlds of welfare capitalism* (New Jersey: Princeton University Press, 1990).
13   "The welfare state is not a philanthropic agent but contains a productivist dualism. It seeks, on the one hand, to attenuate the life risks of wage earners, but on the other hand, to ensure that those able to work actually do so." Oliver Nachtwey, *Germany's Hidden Crisis: Social Decline in the Heart of Europe*. Translated by David Fernbach and Loren Balhorn (London: Verso, 2018), 12.

Even though unemployment has historically been associated with inferiority or low social worth, the feeling of *shame* was not always integrated into the welfare state's way of governing the unemployed. The fact that an earlier variant of the welfare state was not as such out to shame its unemployed population becomes clear when reading literature or fictional representation of the unemployed from the 1960s and 1970s – or the "golden age" of the welfare state[14].

Guilt and Disgust in the Golden age

In author Bent Vinn Nielsen's unemployment novel *Arbejdssky* (*Work-Shy*) (1978), the unemployed protagonist Lenny, though deeply entangled in the unemployment institutions of the welfare state, is characteristically *unashamed*. Consider for instance the following reportage from his weekly visits to the unemployment office.[15]

> On Tuesdays, I went to the unemployment office along with everyone else. I haven't had a very good relationship to Tuesdays since then. What is a Tuesday anyway? Cold? Hot? Warm? Lukewarm? A Tuesday is none of the above, Tuesdays are: Mugsy! Mugsy is worse than hot, warm, lukewarm and also worse than cold. Mugsy air is poison for the lungs, while one has to admit that cold air can be kind of refreshing.
>
> In an unemployment office the air is clammy. In the waiting room: Mugsy! In the hallways: mugsy! In the small, narrow offices where the "negotiations" (more like "interrogations") take place: Mugsy! If an abstract thing like "mood" can be described using concrete terms, a description of the mood of an unemployment office would be impossible without using *clammy*.[16]

---

14   Esping-Andersen, "After the golden age?"
15   In the Danish version: "socialkontor", which is a broader concept administering not only the unemployment office but also other public benefits and services. In this translation, we have chosen the English "unemployment office", as this comes close to what Nielsen is referring to. *in Danish "klam" which also means disgusting.
16   "Om tirsdagen gik jeg, som alle på tirsdage, på socialkontoret. Jeg har derfor heller ikke siden haft et særligt godt forhold til tirsdage. Hvad er nemlig en tirsdag? Kold? Varm? Lun? Lunken? En tirsdag er ingen af delene, tirsdage er: klamme! Klam er værre end varm, lun, lunken og også værre end kold. Klam luft er gift for lungerne mens man må indrømme at kold luft kan være forfriskende. På et socialkontor er luften klam. I venteværelset: klam! På gangene: klam! I de små snævre kontorer

In the above quote, the protagonist expresses his almost physical repulsion with the welfare state's foremost institution for supporting its unemployed. "Clammy" is the overall mood of the unemployment office that in meteorological terms is compared to damp and unpleasant weather. Highmore and Flatley have both highlighted, that as a concept for affective dispositions, a "mood" can be understood as similar to weather, in that it is inevitable (you cannot not have weather, just like you are always in some mood, one mood or another), all-pervasive ("about everything in general")[17] and preconditions the feelings we have ("the way the world presents itself to us").[18] In this way, a mood can be described as a kind of overall affective temperament through which we meet the world and which determines the emotions we associate with certain situations, places or institutions.

In Lenny's eyes, the mood in the unemployment office is clammy, which determines the feelings he is able to have as unemployed. To Lenny, collecting unemployment benefits feels like being monitored and in his own words "interrogated" by the watchful bureaucrats of the welfare state. Overall, in fact, the feeling of disgust is perhaps the most dominant feeling in the book, as it seems to taint the protagonist's relationship to the people outside of the unemployment office as well, including Lenny's relationship to his fellow unemployed roommate Alex: "[the unemployment officer] suddenly reminded me of Alex: the same dismissed attitude and the same stupid look which insisted on a dignity that was unthinkable in both Alex" case and in hers and therefore appeared detestable and ridiculous."[19] In this way, an employee at the unemployment office is compared and likened to Alex – even though they in a sense are opposites, on either side of the fence of unemployment – because of the all-pervasive disgust with the social world which the protagonist inhabits.

---

hvor "forhandlingerne" (snarere: afhøringerne!) finder sted: klam. Hvis en så abstrakt størrelse som "stemning" kan beskrives med konkrete egenskaber ville en karakteristik af stemningen på et socialkontor som *klam* overhovedet ikke kunne omgås." Nielsen, *Work-Shy*, 60.

17 Jonathan Flatley, "Reading for Mood," *Representations* 140, no. 1 (November 2017): 137–58.
18 Ben Highmore, *Cultural Feelings: Mood, Mediation and Cultural Politics* (London and New York: Routledge, 2017).
19 "Hun mindede mig pludselig om Alex: samme afskedigede holdning og samme dumme blik som insisterede på en værdighed som ikke var tænkelig i forbindelse med hverken Alex eller hende og derfor forekom afskyvækkende og latterlig." Nielsen, *Work-Shy*, 211.

As opposed to guilt or shame, disgust is in essence a distance-taking feeling – regardless of whether this taking distance is to something else or to parts of oneself, as in "self-disgust". As already George Orwell pointed out in the 1930s, disgust leads the self to create distance between itself and the disgusted other.[20] However, disgust is not exclusively a way for people to create distance to others but can also be directed against *parts* of the self. In Martha Nussbaum's words, disgust: "functions to distance us from something that we actually are […] an inherently self-deceptive emotion, whose function, for better or worse, is above all to conceal from us, on a daily basis, facts about ourselves that are difficult to face".[21] This kind of "self-disgust" also has particularly classed dimensions, as it often comes out in stories of class mobility – which we will also see later in this article in our reading of two contemporary Danish novels about growing up in deprived housing areas. As mentioned, we want to emphasize that this form of self-disgust – though clearly related to shame – is different from shame, because it does not envelop the whole self but rather parts or aspects of the self that the disgusted agent wants to distance himself/herself from.

In fact, as already mentioned, shame is conspicuously missing from Bent Vinn Nielsen's novel *Work-Shy* where the unemployed protagonist Lenny, apart from disgust, mostly feels more antagonistic and outwardly tuned emotions such as anger, defiance and frustration. Rather than turning his blame inward, as a shameful person would, Lenny's blame is particularly outward directed – often against more or less everything and everyone in the world. For much of the story, Lenny's anger and class hatred (of both the upper classes, the welfare state's unemployment system and his own

---

20 In this way, Orwell could claim that the "real secret" behind the English class system was that the bourgeoisie thought that "the lower classes smell" (Orwell) – meaning that disgust within the British class system was designed to create an almost insurmountable emotional distance between classes. If the lower classes were thought of as disgusting, there was no way for the bourgeoisie to approach them and any kind of significant solidarity between the classes was off the table. A further problem with this kind of "secret", which the bourgeoisie share amongst themselves, is that the lower classes, which are said to "smell", have no way of rebutting this claim but are left passive and dominated by the bourgeoisie. George Orwell, *The road to Wigan pier* (London: Penguin, 2001).
21 Nussbaum goes on to distinguish disgust from shame, which she claims is "more subtle: for it goads us onward with regard to many different types of goal and ideals, some of them valuable. In that sense, it is not inherently self-deceptive, nor does it always express a desire to be a sort of being one is not." In other words, Nussbaum prefers shame to disgust because she thinks it is more moral. Martha C. Nussbaum, *Hiding from Humanity: Disgust, Shame and the Law* (New Jersey: Princeton University Press, 2006).

unemployed peers) appears more or less unexplained as he plays the part of an unlikeable and resentful anti-hero.

In retrospect, the Lenny character is symptomatic of historical changes around class and unemployment, as these played out in Danish society at the time. First of all, Lenny can be interpreted as a character who because of his upbringing in "peripheral Denmark" coupled with his political association with the Left finds himself in a position in-between two different or incompatible cultures in the postwar Danish class society. Thus, Lenny is alienated from the dominant cultural elite, while on the other hand being equally alienated from his own local class belonging – which at this time with the election of Fremskridtspartiet (the Progress Party) and Mogens Glistrup was turning towards a kind of early right wing populism.[22] Lenny is left in a "no-mans land" in a position between the dominant cultural class and the peripheral working class as he shares important characteristics with both groups.

Secondly, when reading *Work-Shy* today, it is clear that it illustrates a welfare state governmental system that was rapidly becoming anachronistic and losing legitimacy.[23] In the novel, we see a welfare system where the administration and governing of the unemployed is run as a rigid, almost explicitly disciplining, system that treats the unemployed with a sense of distrust, suspicion and blame. In the novel, these discourses and their institutionalization in the unemployment office, however, do not create servile or governable unemployed people – as they were undoubtedly designed to – but rather rebellion, anger and disaffection.

Thus, in Bent Vinn Nielsen's novel, the unemployment system which treats its clientele with a sense of suspicion, distrust and moral blame seems to fail in important ways – at least in the case of Lenny who does not internalize the blame imposed on him by the unemployment system. On the contrary, in this case, the disciplining strategy of the unemployment office and its administrators makes the unemployed individual spiteful,

---

22   The 1973 Danish election (aka Jordskredsvalget) was in many ways a reaction of the resentful classes who felt left behind by the cultural upheavals and struggles over cultural power of the 1960s. Lykkeberg, *Kampen om sandhederne*.
23   See also one of the most important Danish political books of the times, *Oprør Fra Midten*, where the three authors – Niels I. Meyer, Kristen Helveg Petersen and Villy Sørensen – at this time suggested the dismantling of what they regarded as the welfare state's suspicious approach to its unemployed population by instead implementing a form of Universal Basic Income. Niels I. Meyer, Kristen Helveg Petersen and Villy Sørensen, *Oprør fra midten* (København: Gyldendal, 1978).

angry and resentful. In a central scene, for instance, Lenny comes to an outright confrontation with an unemployment officer who accuses him of being voluntarily unemployed because of his own "work-shyness":

> She had figured me out, she said, which she should have done a long time ago, she said, since there was absolutely nothing special about my case. I was exactly like hundreds of other "people like me": work-shy! I did not *want* to work, I *preferred* the dole.
>
> She looked at me sharply. – Am I right? she asked. That is the case, isn't it? […]
>
> No, I answered her, that's not the case.
>
> No? Perhaps you *want* a job? She smiled condescendingly.
>
> What was I supposed to answer? I was supposed to answer *yes*.
>
> Yes, I answered, I want a job.
>
> She seemed frisky and excited. But she did not believe me.
>
> Oh really. But I do not believe you. You prefer the dole, don't you. But that is no longer going to fly. You will learn.
>
> (Then let me learn, you fat bitch!)
>
> […] [Lenny rejects her offer of an underpaid job for which he is over-qualified]
>
> Who do you even think you are? she asked slowly and solemnly while an expression of deep disgust took over her blood red and fat face. I preferred not to answer that question.[24]

---

24 "Hun havde gennemskuet mig, hvilket hun, sagde hun, burde have gjort for længst, idet der (sagde hun) absolut ikke var noget specielt ("eller sådan") ved mit "tilfælde". Jeg var, som hundrede af andre tilsvarende personer af "min slags": arbejdssky! Jeg *ville* ikke arbejde, jeg *ville hellere* have socialhjælp!
Hun så skarpt på mig. – Ikke sandt, spurgte hun: det er sådan det forholder sig, ikke? […]
- Nej, svarede jeg hende, sådan forholder det sig aldeles ikke!
- Ikke det? De vil måske ligefrem *gerne* have arbejde? Hun smilede hånligt.
Hvad skulle jeg svare? Jeg skulle svare *ja*!
- Ja svarede jeg, det vil jeg gerne.
Hun struttede af lystenhed. Men hun troede mig ikke.
- Ser man *det*! Det tror jeg nu ikke De vil. De vil hellere have socialhjælp, vil De. Men den går ikke længere. De skal blive klogere!
(Så lad mig blive klogere, din fede so!)
[…]
Hvem tror De egentlig De er? spurgte hun langsomt og indtrængende mens et udtryk af dyb væmmelse bredte sig over hendes blodrøde og flæskede ansigt. Jeg foretrak ikke at svare hende på det spørgsmål." Nielsen, *Work-Shy*, 208.

In this scene, the female unemployment officer attacks Lenny for being unemployed, but she does so mainly by appealing to his failure on a moral level. The unemployment officer appeals to his sense of guilt on account of him not living up to his responsibility to the welfare state or the social contract based on the imperative for citizens to work. This seems to be the overall governmental strategy of the unemployment system depicted by Bent Vinn Nielsen in *Work-Shy*: attempting to make the unemployed feel guilty for being idle or a burden to society. At this time, the welfare state's unemployment system appealed to the guilt felt by the unemployed, rather than shame, because its institutions aroused a sense of moral failure rather than social failure. Conversely, rather than feeling guilty or submissive, Lenny feels a range of more antagonist feelings which sometimes direct themselves at the unemployment system and other times at class enemies.

Shame and Unemployment Today

As opposed to the welfare state system we see portrayed in *Work-Shy*, today's welfare state, we argue, is changing its approach to its unemployed population. Unemployment is decreasingly associated with to guilt and increasingly with a form of shame for failing to live up to the often neoliberal ideals for the "fashioning of the self".[25]

The novel *Dagpengeland* (Benefits land) (2012) shows this new fashioning of the unemployed in action as it is a satire on the ideology taking over the contemporary welfare state's unemployment institutions. According to the author Lau Aaen, the novel is a "true story about activation" where we follow the newly graduated political science major Lau and his experiences with the job search courses at the "secondary actor" Integro.[26] Integro is portrayed as a farcical consultant firm whose self-proclaimed goal is to "combine the workself and the private self" and to "build complete human beings from the bottom up". Integro thus tries to involve the whole self of the applicants in the job seeking process, which in Integro's case results in several new-age inspired motivational speeches and meaningless job courses, like "telephoning in theory", "handshaking in praxis" and the

---

25 Ulrich Bröckling, *The Entrepreneurial Self: Fabricating a New Type of Subject* (London: SAGE, 2015).
26 "Secondary actors" are private consultant firms hired by the state to do the activation work that was traditionally done by the unemployment offices.

"JOBsun" (illustrating personal skills around a self-drawn sun). These activities are not only absurd, but at times also humiliating to the job applicants whose real qualifications and skills are ignored in the failed attempt to create new "positive" and outgoing personalities for them.

Benefits Land is thus a parody of an unemployment system that has established unemployment as hard physical and emotional work, where the unemployed are forced to accumulate various pseudo-skills while their real and useful qualifications are ignored. At the same time, the novel criticizes and exposes an unemployment system that puts qualified workers through a demeaning, meaningless and self-fulfilling process that only emphasizes the harmful psychological injuries of unemployment. Rather than helping the unemployed cope with the negative emotions they share, Integro's courses seem to be designed to maintain or even produce these negative and tragic moods. Consider, for instance, the following monologue from the job consultant Britta about the disadvantages of being unemployed:

> What does the family say? What do the friends say? Many people regard it as a personal defeat, a personal tragedy. Like a death in the family. Many people do not even dare talk about it or tell others that they are unemployed. Not even the family or their closest friends. To be unemployed is taboo. It is associated with shame.[27]

Why would a job application course like Integro's feel the need to reiterate the negative feelings some unemployed people feel? Is the point of this lengthy passage not to produce rather than alleviate shame? Of course, these courses do not create jobs and are therefore not viable answers to the political and social problem of unemployment. Rather, they work as ideological platforms that maintain certain notions of unemployment as tragic and shameful.

---

27 "Hvad siger familien? Hvad siger vennerne? For mange er der tale om et personligt nederlag, en personlig tragedie. Som et dødsfald i familien. Mange tør slet ikke tale om det eller fortælle det til andre. Ikke engang familien eller de allernærmeste venner. At være ledig er et tabu. Det er forbundet med skam." Aaen, *Benefits Land* (Dagpengeland), 42.

Similar to the unemployment system portrayed in *Benefits Land*, a newly published study points out that a neoliberal governmentality forms the basis for the social work performed in today's Danish unemployment institutions.[28] Especially amongst young people, the unemployed increasingly associate their joblessness with a personal shortcoming based on a failure to "cultivate a repertoire of positive feelings and affects by working on motivations, passion and enthusiasm which are identified as key currencies in the contemporary Danish labour market."[29] The welfare state's jobcentres and the so-called "secondary actors" attempt to manufacture unemployed agents that know how to invest their whole being, including their feelings and affects, in the search for a job. However, this investment of the "whole self" in the jobseeking process simultaneously implies feelings of personal defeat when the investment turns out to be unsuccessful. For those who are unsuccessful in getting a job, this implies a more intensive shame, because one's unemployment is associated with the failure of one's innermost relationship to the self.

What we are talking about here is close to what sociologists of emotion, such as Arlie Hochschild, call "feeling rules" or "the side of ideology that deals with emotion and feeling".[30] In line with this, we can say that the feeling rules for the unemployed have changed; from a set of submissive and grateful feelings to a set of "positive" and enthusiastic feelings. Another way of putting this is by stating that while the unemployed used to be blamed for lacking skills or qualifications – and thus were bestowed with feelings of guilt that could be alleviated through education or upskilling – the unemployed are now increasingly accursed with a more personal *shame for being a failing self.*

Once described as "the most social of the basic emotions", shame can be seen as a feeling with explicit bearings on class and social formations.[31]

---

28 Sabina Pultz, *It's not you, it's me, governing the unemployed self in the Danish welfare state* (Ph.D. thesis, University of Copenhagen, 2017).
29 Pultz, *It's not you*, 4.
30 Arlie Russell Hochschild, "Emotion Work, Feeling Rules and Social Structure," *American Journal of Sociology* 85, no. 3 (November 1979): 551-575.
31 Thomas J. Scheff, "Shame and the Social Bond: A Sociological Theory," *Sociological Theory* 18, no. 1 (March 2000): 84-99. See also Nussbaum, *Hiding from Humanity*; Glen Pettigrove and Nigel Parsons, "Shame: A Case Study of Collective Emotion," *Social Theory and Practice; Tallahassee*, 38, no. 3 (July 2012): 504-30.

People turn away in shame when they feel a lack of recognition from a community or in the eyes of society. The metaphor of the "eye" here is not coincidental as shame is often associated with the visual sense, because, as Helen Lynd points out, experiences of shame centre on unwilling "exposure": "They are experiences of exposure, exposure of peculiarly sensitive, intimate, vulnerable aspects of the self".[32] In a classic distinction, many shame theorists separate shame from guilt because shame engulfs all of the self rather than just parts of it.[33] Guilt is caused by a transgression of moral obligations and can therefore be exorcized from the self through rituals of remorse or self-punishment. As we saw earlier, this in large parts was the strategy of the unemployment officer in Bent Vinn Nielsen's *Work-Shy* who attempted to guilt Lenny for being morally corrupt and not living up to his responsibility to the "common good". As opposed to guilt, however, shame is inseparable from the self because shame concerns the identity of the self and its place in a social order. Rather than our actions, it is our position vis-à-vis a social rank that we are ashamed of. Shame can thus be called an affective indicator that highlights how the subject does not live up to social expectations.

Nevertheless, shame is a very multifaceted political emotion that can have very different social and political functions depending on how it is used and by whom.[34] On the one hand, shame marginalizes and alienates; on the other hand, it helps open our eyes to injustices afflicted against our own selves. In relation to unemployment and social class, shame is not simply destructive or disciplinary – even though we should maintain an eye for these sides of shame – but also politically productive and motivating. In the following section, we elaborate on the relations between shame and guilt in connection with unemployment, but we change the focus from the unemployed to their children.

---

32 Helen Lynd, *On Shame and the Search for Identity* (New York: Science Editions, 1961).
33 Nussbaum, *Hiding from Humanity*; Rita Felski, "Nothing to Declare: Identity, Shame and the Lower Middle Class," *PMLA* 115, no. 1 (2000): 33–45; Agnes Heller, "Five Approaches to the Phenomenon of Shame," *Social Research* 70, no. 4 (2003): 1015-1030.
34 Mathies Græsborg Aarhus, "Skammen og dens brødre: Arbejdsløshed, maskulinitet og klasseskam," *K&K – Kultur og Klasse* 46 (2018): 179-198; Carsten Stage, *Tænkepause: Skam* (Aarhus: Aarhus Universitetsforlag, 2019).

The Figure of the Unemployed Parent

Questions concerning guilt, shame, disgust and anger have a particular pertinence in coming-of-age narratives, not least the ones concerning a childhood with problematic parents. For obvious reasons, children growing up with parental neglect or outright abuse must distance themselves from their grown-ups in a much more dramatic and absolute manner than children from more caring backgrounds. This is a complicated task, always bordering on the impossible, given that children in both biological, psychological and sociological senses are made by their parents. Thus, the agonistic feelings necessary for the creation of that vital distance will to some extent also be directed towards the child itself.

One way of handling this complexity is adding class distance to the mix: I am not my unemployed parent. In a number of Danish literary texts dealing with growing up with highly problematic parents in deprived housing areas, we find the distinctly contemporary shaming of unemployment applied as a kind of self-directed survival and identity formation strategy. Moving away from a deprived housing area and taking on the psychology and sociology of the class-traveller – in this case by becoming a writer – is a way of dissociating oneself from the characteristics and values associated with the unemployed and destructive parent.

Karina Pedersen's *Helt ude i Hampen. Mails fra underklassen* (Far Out. Letters from the Underclass) from 2016 is an epistolary text, ambiguous in terms of genre. According to the publisher, Gyldendal, Pedersen refused to call it a novel despite being advised to do so.[35] Once the book was out, Pedersen found herself in the middle of a storm of criticism since it turned out that some or much of the scornful picture she had painted of lazy and irresponsible underclass people living on the dole in the blocks of Korskærparken on the outskirts of Fredericia, a town in south-east Jutland, was based on exaggeration, if not outright untruth. Had she accepted to label and market the book as a novel such discrepancy with empirical facts would have mattered less.

The book consists of allegedly authentic emails from Karina Pedersen to a childhood friend. The emails relate horrible childhood memories of

---

[35] See Jon Helt Haarder, Peter Simonsen and Camilla Schwartz, "Hvem kan tale for prekariatet – og hvorfra? *In the Ghetto* med Kristian Bang Foss, Morten Pape, Yahya Hassan, Karina Pedersen og prinsesserne fra blokken," *Edda* 105 (03/2018).

neglect and endless present-day telephone conversations with the mother; most of these concern her mother's interactions with two criminal, stupid and utterly unreliable sons. The main concern of the book is to conflate this picture of an extremely negligent mother with "the underclass"– as she consistently calls the inhabitants of Korskærparken – in general:

> Once I read about a woman, who had been found a man who convicted of child abuse. For that reason, he was not permitted to be among minors. She had two children living at home and went right back and asked them to move out. God forbid that the underclass should take care of its own children, not least when their own needs are so important:-).[36]

Refusal to work and reliance on social security is a decisive feature of the behaviour of both the mother and "the underclass". In the beginning of the book, Karina tells her friend a story about a family from Sri Lanka living in her block: "They were actually rather nice, but their question: "so, where do you work?" was considered highly offensive."[37] The crux of her mother's career is when she manages to change her status from receiver of social security to disability pensioner. From that moment on, she never stops complaining about the laziness of the other inhabitants.

There are two strikingly symptomatic features of the book. One is the similarity between the hated mother and the letter writer: They both blame the welfare system for the misery of long-term unemployment. The mother complains that "the system" does not pay her enough, the daughter that the system pays out too much. However, once the mother has become a pensioner, her ranting attacks on her unemployed neighbours are very much aligned with Karina Pedersen's general critique of the welfare state for being much too soft on the irresponsible and work-shy unemployed. The second feature is the fact that we hear so very little about the letter writer's own present-day life. As much as she hates her mother and resents

---

[36] "Jeg læst engang om en kvinde, der fandt en mand, som var dømt for misbrug af børn og derfor ikke måtte befinde sig blandt mindreårige, og da kvinden havde to hjemmeboende børn, gik hun hjem og bad børnene flytte. Gud forbyde, at underklassen skulle tage sig af sine børn, specielt når deres egne behov nu er så vigtige:-)." Pedersen, *Far Out* (Langt ude), 8.

[37] "De var nu ellers meget søde, men deres spørgsmål "Hvor arbejder du så henne?", blev anset for at være dybt krænkende." Pedersen, *Far Out* (Langt ude), 12.

the phone calls from her, these phone calls and her mother's life seem to be the main content of her own life.

Halfway through in the book we do get a glimpse of the letter writer in her own kitchen, having put down the phone after yet another lengthy conversation with her mother, the umpteenth unwanted update on her mother's problems with the sublimely unsympathetic and untalented brothers: "Sitting in my nice, clean kitchen listening to my mum's language, it seems as if the calls come from another world. And, in a way, they do. I am simple dumb founded by the huge difference me and my mum."[38]

The claim that a "big difference" exixts is as much a performative as a constative, i.e. these statements and the emails in general are meant to create the social distance between her and her mother that is stated as an established fact.

The attitude towards unemployed people in *Helt ude i hampen* (Far out) is a good example of the completed transition from guilting to shaming of the unemployed. To Pedersen, unemployment is the hallmark of an alleged "underclass" whose problems are of their own making – and beyond repair. Such crude neoliberalism, not least the construction and shaming of an inherently work-shy "underclass", is of course worth discussing on a general political and sociological level and since Pedersen was using real people from her own family and neighbourhood as evidence for her views, the empirical truth of her claims in the book and media appearances very much deserved the critical scrutiny to which they were subjected.

Read more like a novel, however, the text brings out psychological aspects of shaming on an individual level, which can in turn be interpreted as an allegory of the shaming of the unemployed on a societal level. The narrator's petrification of the destructive mother as a specimen of an irresponsible "underclass" is her way of creating an all-important distance and difference between herself and a mother whose neglect almost destroyed her as a child and whose present-day influence is a continuous threat. The text testifies to the necessity of these operations, but also to the dangers of them: The present-day life of the protagonist is a haunted house, the

---

[38] "Når jeg sidder her i mit pæne køkken og lytter til min mors sprog, så virker det, som om opkaldene kommer fra en anden verden, hvilket de jo på en måde også gør. Jeg er simpelthen målløs over, hvor stor forskel der er på min mor og mig." Pedersen, *Far Out* (Far out), 51.

repressed similarity of mother and daughter returns in a variety of forms, as we have shown above. It is reasonable to suggest, on a societal level, that a house built on the idea of unemployment as a shameful defect of individual character that can be mended by the kind of courses described in *Benefit Land* will be haunted by problems that are not solved, only displaced.

"Underclass par Excellence"

Early on, Karina ridicules her mother's way of walking: "I wonder if it is caused by her perennial fear of shitting her pants – a fear that often comes true – and most of all it is perhaps the result of decades of abuse of alcohol and medicine."[39] The introduction to this description of a worn-out and maltreated body states that "my mother is underclass par excellence". In Morten Pape's *Planen* (The Plan), an autofictional coming-of-age novel from 2015 taking place from the early 1990s onwards, the bodies of the protagonist's parents function in the same way, not least that of his fat and unemployed father. "The precarious body works as a marker of class", as one commentator on Pape's novel has it.[40]

Just like Karl Ove Knausgård's *Min kamp* (2009-11, translated as *My Struggle*), both Pedersen's and Pape's books are novels of symbolic patricide. The narrator of the latter is keenly aware of this; the realist narrative about a childhood spent in Urbanplanen, the deprived housing area in Copenhagen referred to in the title, is surrounded by and interspersed with italicized passages recounting a dream or vision wherein Morten's flabby and unhealthy father falls and hurts his head on an icy football ground while playing football with his son: "*He was dying. For fuck's sake. Right in front of my eyes – and it was my fault.*"[41] Where the emotional complexity of breaking with a negligent parent of the precariat and the ensuing attempt at class travel is a stowaway in Pedersen's epistolary "novel", it is a very visible part of in Pape's *Planen*.

---

39 "Jeg tænker på, om det skyldes hendes evige frygt for at skide i bukserne – en frygt der ofte bliver realiseret – og måske mest af alt er et resultat af årtiers misbrug af alkohol og medicin." Pedersen, *Far Out* (Langt ud), 7.
40 Niclas Freisleben Lund, "De fremtidsløse tager ordet. Klasse, precariat og velfærdskritik i dansk samtidsprosa," *Passage* 76 (2016): 27-39.
41 "*Nu døde han. Kraftedeme. Lige foran mine øjne – og det var min skyld.*" Pape, *The Plan* (Planen), 8.

One way of describing the long and detailed narrative of Morten's coming of age would be to point to a change in feelings. As a young child, Morten is highly anxious both at home and at school: He fears a divorce between his parents and he is the victim of relentless bullying by school mates, not least the tough and dominant ones from immigrant homes. This is related to a larger atmosphere of anxiousness; the whole area seems to become more violent and desolate as the 1990s turn into the 2000s.

To young Morten, a divorce between his parents would mean that they become like all the other families in Urbanplanen – at least the ones with Danish surnames as he explains, indicating the rather different family structures among the inhabitants of this ethnically highly heterogenous area. Once his worst nightmare has become real, his mother asks him what it is he fears: "I am afraid that no one will care for each other", he replies: "That's the way things have gone in all the other families."[42] His mother reassures him that his father is basically a good man, he will never become indifferent towards his son. When he does exactly that, neglects even the minimal obligations of a weekend father – while losing his jobs and eating compulsively – Morten's feelings of anxiousness gradually give way to anger and disgust, the feelings that seem to have shaped the grown-up narrator's story about the father-son relationship.

As we accounted for earlier in this article, disgust – unlike shame or guilt – is essentially a distance-creating feeling as it creates a distinct difference between the subject and the object of the feeling.[43] *Planen* (The Plan) and its representation of Morten's unemployed father is a good example. The disgust Morten feels towards his father culminates in a nightmarish passage well into the narrative where the by now divorced father has failed to provide beds so that his three visiting children have to sleep in the same bed. From that bed, the sleepless Morten watches his father fart, pick his nose and masturbate in front of the tv. Morten is horrified but keeps watching: "It turns me on to watch something that hurts my eyes and my mind."[44] The fat father comes in and sleeps in the same bed as the children. The next

---

42 "Jeg frygter at alle bare bliver ligeglade med hinanden. Sådan er det gået med de andres familie." Pape, *The Plan* (Planen).
43 See also the postscript to Ngai where she highlights this point as opposed to both desire and the ugly feelings she deals with in the book. Sianne Ngai, *Ugly feelings. Vol. 6.* (Cambridge, MA: Harvard University Press, 2005).
44 Pape, *The Plan* (Planen), 123.

morning, Morten must pee down a toilet soiled with faeces and his father's white semen.

In the finishing passage of the book, the son sees his father on the street. By now, Morten is a young man on his way out of the ghetto. He is majoring in film studies, but here he is also at work as a writer of a novel. In that capacity, he skilfully stages this farewell scene using the windows of the kebab joint as a picture frame, a frame from which his father then disappears. The scene is about the distance between someone at work – namely as a writer – and his unemployed parent. Morten's father seems more abject and disgusting than ever; he is not only obese and dirty, but also disabled and malfunctioning. His body is very much a class marker and signifies a complete loss of contact with the job market: The sweat-stained clothes cannot conceal the whale-like belly, his hearing aid is covered in yellow-brown grease, one leg is wrapped in a huge bandage. Morten does not go out to meet this sorry creature and, he claims, is frightened by his own cynicism.

It would seem that this cynicism is, in fact, reassuring rather than frightening. Morten's cynicism is the successful outcome of the emotional distance-taking he – like Karina must perform – out of hard necessity. The *sociological* distance between the disgusting and unemployed father and the middle-class writer at work seems to stabilize the *psychological* complexity of the necessary parricide. Contemporary notions of the shamefulness of chronical unemployment is applied as a way of dealing with a weak and deceptive father and enables the early stages of a class journey. While this is understandable in narratives about children from deprived homes, it is obviously not tenable that the welfare system takes up the same position vis-à-vis the unemployed.

This chapter then, has shown some of the psychological consequences of recent years' shaming of unemployment, including the class distinctions this seems to stir up. The violent feelings of class dis-identification that both Morten Pape and Karina Pedersen feel, such as physical repulsion, disgust and anger directed at their parents, would not have been possible without recent years' increasing shaming of unemployment and the exposure of the self that this entails. Not that these characters feel the class system more acutely than earlier, as we saw in the comparison with unemployment in the golden age of the welfare state, rather they feel it *differently*.

Editors

Citizen Categories in the Danish Welfare State: From the Founding Epoch to the Neoliberal Era

Jesper Vestermark Køber, PhD in history and Postdoc at the Saxo Institute, University of Copenhagen. He is an expert on democracy in postwar Denmark and Europe. He has published articles on a variety of themes, including concepts of local democracy, the works of Theodor Geiger, Danish library history and Danish postwar democracy. As editor for Selskabet for Arbejderhistorie he has edited several books, including *Arbejderbevægelsens Demokrati* (2019) with Rasmus Knold Andersen.

Niklas Olsen, Dr. phil in history and Professor at the Saxo Institute, University of Copenhagen. Among his many publications are the two monographs *The Sovereign Consumer: A New Intellectual History of Neoliberalism* (Palgrave Macmillan, 2018) and *History in the Plural: An Introduction to Reinhart Koselleck* (Berghahn Books, 2012). Moreover, he has edited more than ten volumes in English and Danish, including *Histories of Knowledge in Postwar Scandinavia* (Routledge, 2020) with Johan Östling and David Larsson and Heidenblad and *Critical Theories of Crisis in Europe: From Weimar to the Euro* (Rowan and Littlefield, 2016) with Poul Fritz Kjær.

Heidi Vad Jønsson, PhD in contemporary political history and Associate Professor at the Institute of History and Danish Centre for Welfare Studies, University of Southern Denmark. Her publications on welfare state history include the monographs *Fra lige muligheder til ret og pligt: Socialdemokratiets integrationspolitik* (University Press of Southern Denmark, 2018), *Indvandring i velfærdsstaten* (Aarhus University press, 2018), book chapters (*Dansk Velfærdshistorie vol. IV-VI*) and edited books (*Migrations and Welfare States: Policies, discourses and institutions*, 2013). Moreover, she is editor of *Scandinavian Journal of History* and former editor of the Danish journal *Arbejderhistorie*.